HIGHL

CARIBBEAN

1990/1991 Edition

By the staff of Berlitz Guides

How to use our guide

- An **introduction** by James G. Godsman, President, Cruise Lines International Association, gives you the feel of the Caribbean.

- **The Caribbean in a Nutshell** section on pages 7–20 provides an encapsulated briefing on the major vacation destinations in the Bahamas, Bermuda, the Caribbean, and Panama.

- An in-depth description of **43 Caribbean ports** starts on page 21, with introduction, history, sightseeing, shopping, eating out and practical information sections for each one.

- Finally there is a comprehensive **index** at the back of the book on pages 365–368.

Printed in England by Cradley Print Ltd.

3rd Printing
1990/1991 Edition

Revised 1990

Contents

Introduction 6

The Caribbean in a Nutshell 7

Ports of Call

Antigua		21
Aruba	Oranjestad	29
Bahamas	Freeport	37
	Nassau	45
Barbados	Bridgetown	53
Barbuda		61
Bermuda	Hamilton/	
	St. George's Town	69
Bonaire	Kralendijk	77
Colombia	Cartagena	85
	San Andrés Island	93
Curaçao	Willemstad	97
Dominica		105
Dominican Republic	Puerto Plata	113
	Santo Domingo	121
Grand Cayman		129
Grenada		137
Grenadines		145
Guadeloupe	Pointe-à-Pitre	153
Haiti	Cap Haïtien	161
	Port-au-Prince	169
Iles des Saintes		177
Jamaica	Montego Bay	185
	Ocho Rios	193
	Port Antonio	201
Martinique	Fort-de-France	209
Mexico	Chichén Itzá/Tulúm	217
	Cozumel/Playa del	
	Carmen/Cancún	221
Montserrat		229

Ports of Call (cont.)

Panama	Panama Canal	23
	Sas Blas Islands	24
Puerto Rico	San Juan	24

St. Barthélemy		26
St. Kitts-Nevis		27
St. Lucia		28
St. Vincent		28
Sint-Maarten (St. Martin)		29

Tobago		30
Trinidad	Port-of-Spain	31

Venezuela	La Guaira/Caracas	32
	Isla de Margarita	32
Virgin Islands (U.K.)	Tortola	33
Virgin Islands (U.S.)	St. Croix	34
	St. Thomas/St. John	34

Index 36

Maps

The Caribbean pp. 10–11, Antigua p. 25, Nassau pp. 48–49, Barbad
p. 55, Cartagena p. 89, Dominican Republic p. 115, Santo Doming
Old Town p. 125, Grand Cayman p. 133, Grenada p. 142, Haiti p. 16
Jamaica pp. 186–187, Panama Canal p. 237, Old San Juan p. 252, Sain
Barthélemy p. 271, St. Lucia p. 285, St. Vincent and the Grenadin
p. 293, Sint-Maarten (St. Martin) p. 302, Tobago p. 307, Port of Spa
p. 314, British Virgin Islands p. 337, St. Croix p. 345, St. Thomas p. 35

*Found an error or an omission in this Berlitz Guide? Or a change
new feature we should know about? Our editor would be happy
hear from you, and a postcard would do. Be sure to include your nam
and address, since in appreciation for a useful suggestion, we'd li
to send you a free travel guide.*

*Although we make every effort to ensure the accuracy of all th
information in this book, changes occur incessantly. We cannot there
fore take responsibility for facts, prices, addresses and circumstanc
in general that are constantly subject to alteration.*

5

Layout: Doris Haldemann

Cartography: Falk-Verlag, Hamburg
Map pp. 10–11: Photolitho Ducommun SA, Ecublens, Switzerland.

Photos: Cover Photo by courtesy of Carnival Cruise Lines. Kurt Ammann pp. 249, 250, 254, 255, 257, 260, 261, 263, 333, 338, 339, 341, 346, 349, 350, 353, 358, 361, 362; Antigua and Barbuda Tourist Office pp. 21, 26; Aruba Tourist Bureau p. 32; Bavaria (Manfred Eckebrecht) p. 233; Bildarchiv Kh. Schuster p. 86; Bonaire Tourist Information Office pp. 77, 78, 81, 83; Caribbean Tourism Association Europe p. 277; Jürg Donatsch pp. 53, 58, 69, 73, 113, 117, 119, 121, 122, 126, 127, 129, 131, 134, 137, 141, 161, 167, 169, 173, 185, 191, 193, 196, 201, 204, 205, 206, 281, 286, 289, 294, 305, 308, 313, 317; Robert Harding p. 229; KEY-color/ZEFA pp. 29, 85, 273, 278, 321, 325; Len Sirman Press p. 105; Mexican Government Tourism Office pp. 217, 221, 225; Netherlands National Tourist Office pp. 97, 101; Office National du Tourisme Colombien p. 93; Panama Government Bureau pp. 241, 244, 246; PRISMA/James Davis p. 145; PRISMA/Schuster GmbH p. 148; RAPHO/G. de Steinheil p. 329; Spectrum Colour Library p. 109; Venezuelan Tourist Board p. 322; Daniel Vittet pp. 37, 41, 45, 51, 61, 65, 153, 158, 177, 180, 182, 209, 212, 214, 265, 268, 269, 270, 297, 301.

Introduction

Never in the history of cruise vacations has there been a more consistently popular destination for cruise ships and their passengers than the Caribbean—and for so many good reasons.

What better way to experience all the Caribbean has to offer, including those dazzling beach days and enchanting evenings, than from your very own floating resort centre—a cruise ship. With all the comforts of home and more, your cruise ship, designed specifically for warm-weather cruising, will gently convey you from island to island as you experience the romance, the majesty and the relaxation of life at sea.

The Caribbean Basin covers a huge area, dotted with thousands of islands, large and small, inhabited and uninhabited. For convenience the area is often divided up into segments—Eastern, Central, Western and Lower Caribbean.

Besides their breathtaking beauty, the tranquil isles of the Caribbean offer diverse cultures and traditions, varied cuisines, scenic splendours and glorious beaches. You'll be caught up by the very atmosphere in the Caribbean. The people exude a *joie de vivre,* in the way they walk and in their music, yet they live life at a leisurely pace, sparing time to enjoy the pleasures that this very special place on earth brings. The Caribbean is all you imagined and much, much more.

The sea, of course, is ever present, and the beaches of the Caribbean rank among the best in the world. The climate is balmy, with temperatures that don't generally vary more than a few degrees all year round. When it does rain, it is most welcome in the islands—but then, as the islanders will tell you, it isn't really rain, merely "liquid sunshine" and it never lasts long.

Whether you want to dive to a coral reef, snorkel amongst the multicoloured marine life, fish for the "big one", participate in any number of watersports, play the dazzling casinos, swim, or just laze on one of the beautiful white-sand beaches, the Caribbean has it all, and your cruise ship will be there with you.

James G. Godsman
President
Cruise Lines International Association

The Caribbean in a Nutshell

Contents

Antigua	Iles des Saintes
Aruba	Jamaica
Bahamas	Martinique
Barbados	Mexico
Barbuda	Montserrat
Bermuda	Panama
Bonaire	Puerto Rico
Colombia	St. Barthélemy
Curaçao	St. Kitts-Nevis
Dominica	St. Lucia
Dominican Republic	St. Vincent
Grand Cayman	Sint-Maarten/St. Martin
Grenada	Trinidad and Tobago
Grenadines	Venezuela
Guadeloupe	Virgin Islands (U.K.)
Haiti	Virgin Islands (U.S.)

Antigua

There's a beach for every day of the year on this charming 108-square-mile island. Antigua was once the headquarters of the British naval hero Lord Nelson. Today you can visit the Admiral's House and delightfully restored Nelson's Dockyard. On the island you'll find a good range of accommodation, as well as duty-free shopping, a museum, and even a casino. Antigua is a popular centre for sailing, especially during April when Antigua Sailing Week draws participants and spectators alike to the Caribbean's most prestigious yachting event. The nightlife becomes especially stimulating during the period, with everyone heading to the local bars to take in the screening of the races.

Barbuda, about 25 miles to the north, makes a great side-trip for scuba-divers interested in exploring old wrecks.

Aruba

This enchanting Dutch island offers a real postcard setting of pure white-sand beaches and Dutch gabled houses. There are also monolithic rock formations, strange *dividivi* trees and yellow-blossomed kibrahchas. You can see South America from the top of Hooiberg Mountain, explore coral reefs alive with rare, tropical fish, picnic on the spectacular snow-white sands of Palm Beach, swim in the warm blue waters or enjoy the top-notch windsurfing.

Oranjestad is the tiny capital and main port, with tempting duty-free international shops and an open marketplace. Tourist accommodations range from small hotels, villas and apartments to luxury resorts, all new and very modern. Dutch and Indonesian cuisine is the general rule, and nightlife includes action at the casinos and Las Vegas-style revues.

Bahamas

With year-round warmth and sunshine, the Bahamas are a haven for swimming, sunning, scuba-diving and golf, with over a dozen excellent courses. Although not strictly in the Caribbean, the islands are a scant 50 miles from the Florida coast, and within easy cruising distance of all east coast ports. About 600 of the 700 islands that make up the Bahamas are uninhabited, the main population being clustered around Nassau (seat of government) and Freeport.

Nassau, on New Providence Island, has long been a favourite stop for cruise ships venturing into the Caribbean, offering duty-free shopping and great swimming. Here you can see the Changing of the Guard, colonial mansions, 18th-century forts and the straw market, or ride in a horse-drawn surrey.

In **Freeport**, on Grand Bahama Island, some head for the huge casino, while others laze in the sun or shop at the extensive International Bazaar.

Some of the outlying Family Islands have long been frequented by those in the know; others are just beginning to develop their tourism potential. The Abaco archipelago has some of the best diving and snorkelling sites in these Islands. San Salvador, where Columbus landed, is also appreciated by scuba divers. Yachtsmen haunt the Exumas, and anglers congregate at Bimini. Some cruise lines have purchased or leased their own Family Island for their passengers to enjoy a whole day of swimming, sun and fun.

Barbados

Barbados is as British as teatime. And tropical beauty is everywhere on this fertile sugar cane island on the eastern perimeter of the Caribbean. Luxurious hotels, excellent nightlife, glorious beaches and a

ull array of sports (cricket is followed passionately), watersports
and sights are there to be enjoyed. View the rugged east coast from
st. John's Church, 820 feet above sea level and a photographer's
cream, or head for the numerous palm-fringed beaches on the calm
Caribbean coast.

Bridgetown, the capital, offers colourful markets and a thriving
commercial centre. If you like to eat out, there are some wonderful
old-world dining spots here.

Barbuda

Barbuda is everyone's vision of an unspoiled island, with not much to
see in the way of standard tourist sights—a Martello tower and ruined
18th-century manor house—but rich in natural assets. The wild fowl,
pigs and deer and the bird sanctuary attract hunters and nature-
watchers, and adventurous types like to explore the uncharted network
of caves or the underwater wrecks in the reefs. On the other hand, the
just plain lazy enjoy the pristine sandy beaches that are virtually
deserted. This paradise has kept developers at arm's length, and only a
few hotels exist for a minimum number of lucky guests. Fifteen minutes
away by shuttle airplane is sister-island Antigua, which boasts a long
tradition of catering to tourists.

Bermuda

This little gem of an island (actually several chain-linked islands, and
Britain's oldest colony) is just 20 square miles in size. Not quite in the
Caribbean, it sits atop a submerged mountain in the Atlantic 600 miles
due east of Savannah, Georgia, warmed by the waters of the Gulf
Stream.

Anyone who visits Bermuda falls in love with its beautiful scenery
and charming people. The houses of pastel colours with sparkling
white roofs are a delight to the eye. **Hamilton,** the capital, boasts one
of the finest sheltered harbours in the world. Cruise ships dock on
Front Street, where stores offer high-quality products. Policemen
wear Bermuda shorts and direct traffic from the "Birdcage".

Quaint **St. George's Town,** the island's original capital, has loads of
charm, and you can be photographed in the old stocks and pillory
at King's Square.

The beaches along the South Shore are among the world's finest,
with pink coral sand and crystal-clear blue waters.

At Ireland Island, just off the northern tip of the main island, the

Royal Naval Dockyard is now the centre of a lively restored complex of museums, shops, craft expositions and regimental band animation—a aimed at amusing the tourist.

Bonaire

One of the Netherlands Antilles, this charming Dutch island is noted for excellent swimming, scuba-diving (those knowledgeable about diving rank it in the top 10 spots in the world)—and flamingoes. It is quiet in comparison to its sister islands, Aruba and Curaçao, so if you are not off bird-watching or viewing the underwater life, just lie back and relax.

The capital is **Kralendijk,** where you'll find a tiny harbour in storybook setting, and only 1,200 inhabitants.

The off-shore island of Little Bonaire is a favourite with snorkellers and scuba-divers; beneath the crystal-clear waters, a startling world of marine life can be enjoyed.

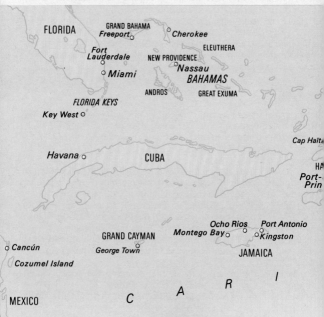

Colombia

Sporadic violence associated with the drug trade—fortunately confined mostly to the interior and away from the vacation spots—is momentarily eclipsing the charms of this fascinating country, famous worldwide for its emerald mines. The formidable San Felipe de Barajas, built almost four centuries ago to protect the treasures of the Spanish Main, guards the approach to the historic walled city of **Cartagena.** The city blends old-world culture and history with modern attractions and conveniences. A spectacular view awaits those who visit the restored 17th-century La Popa Monastery, some 492 feet above the city. Where dungeons once lined the base of the wall, flashy boutiques are now in evidence.

San Andrés Island, which belongs to Colombia although off the Nicaraguan coast, is sometimes visited by cruise ships. There you will find lovely beaches and good duty-free shopping.

Curaçao

Curaçao is the largest of the five islands of the Netherlands Antilles, and the most Dutch in atmosphere. In **Willemstad,** the capital, little canals and pastel-coloured gabled houses create a picture-postcard setting that justifies comparison with Amsterdam. Stroll across the lowest floating bridge in the world, Queen Emma Pontoon; ride the free ferry to the shopping district; call in at the casino, always open to accommodate cruise passengers; or visit the festive floating market.

Although this is a busy port visited by rafts of businessmen, nature lovers will find plenty to occupy themselves at the 4,500 acres of wildlife at Christoffelberg Park—with a hikers' trail—and the charted snorkelers' route of the Curaçao Underwater Park. Enjoy some fine Indonesian cuisine after your exertion, and top it off with the island's orange-flavoured Curaçao liqueur (the distillery is open to the public).

Dominica

Dominica can lay claim to being one of the most ruggedly beautiful of the Caribbean islands—with a heart of lush, mountainous rainforest—as well as one of the least developed. Lodging is mainly in little inns and guesthouses, and don't even bother to look for any nightlife or duty-free shopping. This haven for hiking and exploring boasts some interesting physical phenomena, such as an emerald grotto, multiple cascades, a boiling lake and sulphur springs. You can occupy yourself energetically with a challenging trek into the Morne Trois Pitons National Park, or just idly browse through the colourful Saturday market or the Botanical Gardens of the capital **Roseau.** In the coral reefs off the beaches—mainly black sand—there is good scuba diving, with numerous wrecks to explore.

The island is the last home of the Carib Indians. The once-warlike tribe engage today in their reservation in peaceful basket-weaving and canoe-making.

Dominican Republic

Developing tourism is high on the list of priorities of the Republic. The new resort complexes of Casa de Campo and **Puerto Plata,** on the Amber Coast, offer high class hotels and resort surroundings. The capital is **Santo Domingo,** where relics of 16th-century Spain include the oldest house still standing in the western hemisphere. There's a Spanish flavour to everything, including the food. The remains of Christopher Columbus reputedly lie in a huge mausoleum in the capital. Not far from Puerto Plata (home of the famous Brugal rum distillery, which you can tour) is the delightful bathing area of Sosúa Beach.

Grand Cayman

Grand Cayman is the largest of the three Cayman Islands, known locally as the Alligator Islands, due no doubt to the once-plentiful reptiles. The islands have become famous for the ring of coral which has brought more than 300 ships to grief, and also as a tax-free mecca for international finance. The 100-foot-deep visibility of the waters is the joy of divers, who are catered to by over 20 diving operations. Non-divers can explore, too, but in a submarine.

George Town is the tiny capital and main port, with duty-free shopping. There's not much to do except relax, swim or soak up the sun on Seven Mile Beach—a thin ribbon of talcum-soft white sand leading into a sparkling blue sea. Delightful as a haven from the hectic life. Expensive, too.

Lodging is largely in the form of condominiums, although there are a few luxury resorts and some hotels with the diver especially in mind.

Grenada

There's a lot more to the sweetly scented Isle of Spice than just nutmeg. There are long stretches of sandy beach (try Grand Anse but beware of the hawkers), fine sailing waters, a volcano, small hotels and tasty (spicy) local food. Grenada is the smallest independent nation in the western hemisphere, but that doesn't alter the charm and chivalry of the local people. The capital, **St. George's,** is set around a picturesque half-moon harbour.

Grenadines

The Grenadines number about a hundred or so idyllic isles—the northernmost under the jurisdiction of the island of St. Vincent, and the others watched over by Grenada. These tiny islands, among the least-developed spots in the Caribbean, offer superb sailing. They demonstrate natural beauty at its awesome best, varying from islets of rich, lush vegetation to rocky and uninhabited places protected by sheer breathtaking cliffs. Some of them, like Mustique, Palm Island and Petit

St. Vincent, have gained reputations as luxurious hideaways. Even by Caribbean standards, the Grenadines are the ultimate escape spot, with solitude and tranquility their watchwords. Some of the highlights:

Tobago Cays' excellent snorkelling in the coral reefs; Canouan's inviting lagoons; Bequia's Old Fort and quaint whaling village of Paget Farm, soon to receive an airstrip nearby; the friendly hospitality of Carriacou, acclaimed by yachtsmen who really wake up the island during August Regatta time; the sandy beaches and turquoise waters of Mustique.

Guadeloupe

This butterfly-shaped island (largest in the French West Indies) features a semi-active volcano, towering crystal waterfalls, nude sunbathing, good beaches and exciting nightlife. A thick, tropical rainforest covers much of the island, and the vegetation is green and lush. The capital, **Pointe-à-Pitre** is typically French, and features a tempting selection of Parisian imports at duty-free prices. Great place for French perfumes.

The islanders are charming and very friendly—more so than on Martinique. There's a splendid range of accommodation to choose from, all with excellent beaches.

Just across the bay lies the tiny cluster of eight islands called Iles des Saintes. Occasionally a cruise ship will call at Terre-de-Haut where you can enjoy some superb snorkelling and good beaches in quiet solitude.

Haiti

This land of voodoo, black magic and primitive art is the world's first Black republic. Also one of the world's most densely populated countries, Haiti occupies one-third of the island of Hispaniola, while the Dominican Republic occupies the other two-thirds. Haiti is a fascinating and controversial country—best described as a cultural experience you'll never forget.

Cap Haïtien is the oldest city in Haiti and point of departure for tours to the fantastic Citadelle Laferrière and the eerie Sans Souci Palace, called the eighth Wonder of the World.

Port-au-Prince is the main cruise port. You can haggle for bargains all day at the famous Iron Market. Visit Habitation Leclerc, once the mansion of Napoleon's sister, Pauline Bonaparte. A view of the whole city can be had from 3,500-foot Boutillier.

Îles des Saintes

Totally unspoiled and serenely beautiful, Les Saintes, just off the coast of Guadeloupe, are French spiced with Caribbean flavour. The harbour of the main island, Terre-de-Haut, is ringed with red-roofed houses nestling in the hills—a lookalike for a Mediterranean port. Here and on the other two inhabited islands (of eight total) the pace of life is lazy—until the music and dancing start up in the evening. The usual Caribbean activities are available to help the tourist unwind—boating, snorkelling, skin-diving and swimming. Pick your beach carefully, though; most are safe, protected sandy shores, but at others swimming can be dangerous.

The life of the villagers revolves around fishing, and their long, bright boats, lobster traps and ubiquitous netting make great backdrops for the cameraman. Don a straw *salako* hat and blend in with the islanders.

Jamaica

A mountainous island with four peaks of over 6,000 feet, Jamaica has just about everything: tropical vegetation, refreshing waterfalls, excellent beaches, elegant resorts, good sports facilities and a rich cultural tradition. Once beset by internal turmoil that discouraged tourism, Jamaica has seen a remarkable recovery under a new government, and is popular again.

Montego Bay is the largest of the cruise ports on the northern coast. It used to be the playground of the rich, but the glamour has long gone. Visit Rose Hall, a famous restored plantation house. The beaches are good and hotels are getting back into shape, although problems still exist.

Ocho Rios is the most beautiful resort area in Jamaica and favoured by the international jet-set. Here you'll find sophisticated nightlife, coral reefs, plantations, tropical gardens and a spectacular strip of golden beach.

Thanks to the gentle rainshowers drifting over from the Blue Mountains, **Port Antonio,** a centre for the banana trade, is one of the greenest places on the island. Visitors shouldn't miss the Blue Lagoon, reputed bottomless, or Nonsuch Caves.

Martinique

This isle of flowers, northernmost of the French West Indies chain, is decked with bougainvillea, wild orchids and hibiscus. Sugar cane, bananas, pineapples and coconuts are the bounty of the land.

The capital is **Fort-de-France,** where you can shop for exciting Parisian imports, especially perfume. You can tour to St. Pierre, destroyed completely in1902 by Mt. Pelée, a 4,500-foot volcano. Or you can take a local ferry to the topless beaches at Les Trois Ilets, across the bay.

Mexico

Mexico extends a warm-hearted welcome to cruise passengers. From the port of **Cancún,** it's a three-hour drive to Chichén Itzá, the last great city of the mysterious Mayan civilization. The ancient city of Tulúm is located on the coast, a short drive from Cancún. Tulúm became an important link in the network of Mayan maritime towns and is one of the most ancient cities in Mexico.

The visibility of **Cozumel's** crystal clear waters—200 to 300 feet—is thought to be the best in the world. Nearby Palancar Reef is a magnet for snorkelling and scuba enthusiasts, while Playa del Carmen boasts one of the most magnificent beaches in the Caribbean. The town of San Miguel is noted for its cafés and shady terraces.

Montserrat

If you should wonder why this miniscule island has shamrock-shaped passport stamps and a trefoil adorning Government House, and how it has come to designate St. Patrick's Day a public holiday, thank the Irish Catholics who were among the island's first inhabitants. The green theme carries on in the scenery of this virgin forest-cloaked, essentially undeveloped "Emerald Isle". There are only a few small hotels and guest houses, but alternatively it's possible to rent homes or apartments. The somewhat dangerous currents prevent the diving from being first-class, but in compensation, the hiking trails up to the island's volcano and bubbling sulphur springs offer rewarding encounters with raw nature.

Panama

Balboa is the modern Pacific port city where the Panama Canal Commission has its headquarters. It is populated by immigrants from all over the world. Bargains galore can be found in the duty-free shops.

Just two miles away is **Panama City,** with its Golden Altar recalling the beauty of Old Panama. The city is now run-down and petty crime has given it a bad name. The ousting of strongman Noriega in December, 1989, gives the country new faith in the future.

At the Caribbean entrance to the canal on the island of Manzanillo ie **Cristóbal** and **Colón**, divided by the Panama Railway Line. Cristóbal is a typical port city, while Colón is notorious for its low nightlife, yet popular for shopping in some areas. Food in Panama tends to be on the spicy side.

You'll step back a thousand years when you visit the thatched huts of the primitive Cuna Indians (creators of the famed colourful "molas") on the **San Blas Islands.** The beaches are lovely, and the gentle waters are protected by giant barrier reefs. The fishing here is good.

The Panama Canal, with massive locks surrounded by lush green jungle, is indeed an engineering marvel; if you are lucky enough to cruise through it, it will be an experience you'll never forget.

Puerto Rico

An island of great contrasts, Puerto Rico can be as brassy as the crowded Condado strip or as gracious and rich in history as the restored Spanish section of Old San Juan. Penetrate the El Yunque rainforest, sample charming *parador* inns Out on the Island, or just live the leisurely life at Luquillo Beach.

San Juan is both the Caribbean's most modern capital and the oldest city under the U.S. flag. Scale the ramparts of El Morro castle, follow the winding, narrow streets or laze on one of the superb Condado hotel beaches.

St. Barthélemy

Located in the French West Indies and known affectionately as "St. Barts", this peaceful yet chic little island has only 3,000 inhabitants. Whether you head for one of the 22 lovely, unspoiled beaches, sip a cocktail while overlooking the blue Caribbean, or just stroll about this little piece of France, you'll enjoy the serenity and charm of the island and its people.

St. Kitts-Nevis

Relatively "undiscovered", the sister islands of St. Kitts and Nevis have an enchanting appeal. Brimstone Hill Fortress at Sandy Point on St. Kitts dates back to 1694; from the top there's a great view of St. Eustatius. Sugar cane abounds, caressed by the gentle trade winds. For sunning and beaching, there's Frigate Bay, where the island's finest hotel—the Royal St. Kitts—is located. **Basseterre** is the charming sleepy capital, with shades of Victorian England in the town centre aptly named Pall Mall Square.

Just two miles from St. Kitts is the 35-square-mile island of Nevis, birthplace of Alexander Hamilton and site of the famous Fig Tree Church, where Admiral Horatio Nelson married young Fanny Nisbet. You'll find long, unspoiled beaches and off-shore coral reefs, where fishing is a delight. There are some 200-year-old thermal baths, and in the centre of the island are three mist-shrouded mountain peaks.

St. Lucia

A beautiful volcanic island covered with rugged green jungle and banana groves, undulating fields and dazzling beaches, the island of St. Lucia claims to have the world's only drive-in volcano. For utter peace, Marigot Bay (used in the film Dr. Doolittle) is hard to beat, and boasts one of the prettiest yacht anchorages in the Caribbean. Bustling **Castries** is the capital and the main harbour for cruise ships. Try the delicious home-made passion-fruit ice-cream in town.

St. Vincent

Named, the "Breadfruit Island", St. Vincent is fringed with shiny black beaches and crowned with lush, terraced hills, including an active volcano. The capital is **Kingstown**, which boasts Botanical Gardens said to be the oldest in the western hemisphere, and British-built Fort Charlotte, where you can enjoy a panoramic view back over the capital. North-west up the coast, just before Layol Bay, look for 1,400-year-old Indian petroglyphs. The Falls of Baleine, at the northern tip of the leeward coast, have become a popular day trip from Kingstown and idyllic picnic site. They're accessible only by boat.

Sint-Maarten/St. Martin

Half Dutch, half French (since 1648), this island with a split personality has no border formalities and is a relaxed, friendly place, long popular with cruise visitors for its excellent duty-free shopping, a sedate casino and 36 beaches. The larger French section has plenty of small villages and local markets. **Philipsburg** is the capital and main port on the Dutch side.

Saba and St. Eustatius are the two other islands that make up the three Dutch Windward Islands.

Trinidad and Tobago

Trinidad offers excitement and the finest calypso steel band music in the Caribbean. And its carnival is nothing short of spectacular. **Port-of-Spain** is the capital, and if you like sports, there's always a game of cricket going on somewhere nearby. Visit the Angostura Bitters factory, the Botanical Gardens, and take in the wonderful vista from atop Fort George, 1,000 feet above the capital.

Sleepy little **Tobago** offers good beaches, sun and a leisurely way of life. The weather is often better than on nearby big sister Trinidad. There's a colourful market at **Scarborough.**

Venezuela

A vast country occupying the north-easternmost portion of South America, Venezuela is a land rich in minerals and oil, yet the majority of its people are poor.

Caracas, the capital city set in a valley 3,000 feet above sea level, has 3 million inhabitants. Everywhere you'll find buildings and monuments dedicated to Simón Bolívar, the liberator of Venezuela. Also famous are the traffic jams at all hours.

To get to Caracas, you'll drive on the Super-Highway from **La Guaira,** the port for cruise ships, some 16 miles away. It is a fascinating ride—the rugged countryside dotted with clusters of tiny dwellings stacked against the hillsides. There's little to do in La Guaira, it being a typical port city, except perhaps taste the excellent seafood at Timotes or Avila. You may want to visit the resort area of Macuto, a short distance to the south, where there's a good beach.

If you're an island fancier, you may prefer the beaches of **Isla de Margarita,** north-east of La Guaira, which are regularly besieged by sun-and-sea seekers from the mainland. Don't worry—there should be enough palm-fringed sandy shore to go around for all. The interior landscape is amazingly diverse, varying from mysterious mangrove lagoons and lush, humid valleys planted in bananas and pineapples to semi-arid scrub and cactus country. Margarita's climate is temperate, with cooling breezes blowing in continuously off the ocean. The local pearls in all shades are much sought after, as well as the tantalizing imported goods of this free-port.

Virgin Islands (U.K.)

Unpretentious and completely unspoiled, the British Virgin Islands are ideal for escapists. You can seek out your own private beach, charter a yacht for a few hours or sample the excellent seafood.

Tortola is the best known of the British Virgin Islands, and Road Town is its capital—the biggest yacht charter haven in the Caribbean. Remnants of sugar mills and plantations abound, as do white-sand beaches kissed by aquamarine Caribbean waters.

Virgin Gorda is noted for The Baths—huge, sea-worn rock formations jutting out from the sea. Forms and shapes mingle with the beautiful clear waters and abundant marine life.

Other islands nearby include Treasure Island (made famous by Robert Louis Stevenson), Peter Island, Cooper Island and Jost Van Dyke, plus many more that are completely uninhabited.

Virgin Islands (U.S.)

Much favoured by pirates in days of yore, the Virgin Islands continue to be popular with modern-day sailors, underwater buffs and land-lubbers alike. They're noted for sunny skies, steady trade winds and wonderful white beaches.

St. Thomas is the most frequented cruise destination in the Caribbean, and where once Blackbeard's booty filled the cavernous warehouses along Charlotte Amalie's Main Street, duty-free stores are chock-a-block with goods from all over the world—truly a shopper's paradise. Try the superb view of renowned Magens Bay from Bluebeard's Castle or Drake's Seat, or visit the underwater observatory at Coral World.

St. Croix, the largest of the Virgins, has retained even more of a Danish influence, while little **St. John,** a short ferry ride from St. Thomas, offers an underwater snorkel trail at Trunk Bay, 60 per cent of the island being a National Park. You'll find lots of pelicans and sandpipers here, too.

Caribbean Tourism Association
U.S.A.: 20 East 46th Street, New York, N.Y. 10017;
tel. (212) 682-0435

ANTIGUA

Lesser Antilles

Introduction

Set between the Atlantic and the Caribbean, the former British naval bastion of Antigua resembles a giant amoeba on the map—or maybe it's an inkblot. Whatever you think it looks like, don't call it anything other than An-*tee*-ga.

The inkblot outline is what gives Antigua its special attraction—scores of bays and inlets, set with so many beaches that you can stay there a year and never visit the same beach twice. There are 365 of them and they are reckoned to be among the finest in the world.

Antigua's coastline was prized in the 18th century for strategic reasons, and this is why the 108-square-mile (276-sq.-km.) island was much sought after by French, Spanish and British in their battle for supremacy in the Caribbean. You could hide and defend a whole fleet in landlocked English Harbour. Today the only fleets are those of yachts. Sailing Week, held towards the end of April every year, sees some of the world's leading yachtsmen descend on the island, and English Harbour has become the base for blue-water cruising.

This is a dry island, lacking the humidity of some other Caribbean resorts, which makes it particularly popular among sun-seekers. The heat is mitigated by the trade winds, and when it does rain, the whole island assumes a lush green livery almost overnight.

It is not the place for those who want things done by yesterday. The pace of life is easy—Antigua's 80,000 people take their time. That is why cricket is popular—it's more than the national sport, it's almost the national religion.

Take the time to get to know the Antiguans; you may have to overcome an initial shyness, but you will be rewarded with typical Caribbean warmth and friendliness.

A Brief History

15th and 16th centuries	Columbus sights the island, inhabited by Arawak Indians, on his second voyage in 1493 and names it after the church of Santa Maria la Antigua in Seville. The Spaniards visit Antigua in 1520, but there is no permanent European settlement until a century later

17th century	English planters from St. Kitts colonize Antigua in 1632 despite harassment from the warlike Caribs. The island is coveted by the French and Spanish, but apart from a brief and bloodless French occupation in 1666, it remains British until independence. Antigua becomes the seat of government of the "Leeward Caribbee Islands".
18th century	American independence robs Antigua and other islands of their markets and the plantation economy declines. English Harbour becomes the main British naval base in the Caribbean, serving Hood, Rodney and Nelson in their forays against other European powers in the area. Rodney sets out from here to defeat the French fleet in 1782 and to regain Britain's West Indies possessions. The dockyard is named after Nelson who is stationed here in the 1780s as commander-in-chief of the Leeward Islands squadron.
19th century	After the Napoleonic Wars the island's strategic importance declines and Nelson's Dockyard is eventually abandoned in 1889. The island suffers drought and soil depletion. A major earthquake in 1843 hastens the ruin of the sugar plantations. Antigua becomes part of a federated Leeward Islands Colony in 1871 and retains the seat of government.
20th century	Antigua becomes one of the West Indies Associated States of Britain in 1967 with a new constitution and self-government. Agriculture is revived and, with the awareness of the island's tourist potential, Nelson's Dockyard is restored. Antigua attains full independence in 1981.

Sightseeing

St. John's, Antigua's capital, is a neatly laid out town and easy to explore on foot. If you are lucky enough to arrive here early on a Friday or Saturday, you will see it come alive at the **Public Market.** This colourful and bustling market is the focal point of the city life, where housewives bargain noisily with farmers over fruit and vegetables, while fishing boats land their catch at the nearby pier.

St. John's is the starting point for an island tour, but

The Kingdom of Redonda

Antigua has two remote dependencies, Barbuda and Redonda, an uninhabited, one-square-mile rock, which has its own king.

The kingdom was founded in 1865 by Matthew Dowdy Shiel, a descendant of Irish kings, who sailed past the island. Later, he landed on the island and crowned his infant son, Matthew Phipps, King Felipe I. The title passed to the British poet John Gawsworth, who, as King Juan I, created a number of dukes and duchesses from among his literary friends. The latest king is John M. Wynne-Tyson of Sussex—also known as King Juan II. His subjects consist of a few goats.

Barbuda, lying about 30 miles (48 km.) north of Antigua, is 62 square miles (160 sq. km.) of low-lying scrub fringed by a magnificent beach.

An unspoilt tropical hideaway, Barbuda caters for those who like the desert-island atmosphere.

and hurricane-proof structure was built of pitch pine encased in stone. It has yet to be put to the test. The figures of St. John the Baptist and St. John the Divine at the **South Gate** are said to have been captured from one of Napoleon's ships.

Another point of interest is the 18th-century **Court House,** the former seat of justice and parliament, which now houses the **National Museum and National Archives.** It contains portraits supposedly painted by Sir Joshua Reynolds.

To the north-west, overlooking the harbour, are the ruins of old **Fort James,** which once guarded St. John's in pirate days. Built in 1703, vestiges of the ramparts still stand and its cannons point out to sea.

From the St. John's airport it's a mere 15-minute flight to Antigua's sister island Barbuda, the quintessential unspoilt island paradise.

before you go it's worth visiting **St. John's Cathedral,** one of the most impressive Anglican churches in the Caribbean. It was originally constructed in 1683 and has been rebuilt twice since. After the earthquake of 1843 destroyed the last cathedral, a quake-

English Harbour

It's a 30-mile (48-km.) round trip to one of the most interesting historical sites of the Caribbean—Nelson's Dockyard at English Harbour.

On your way there, you'll drive through tiny villages set in Antigua's dry, central plain

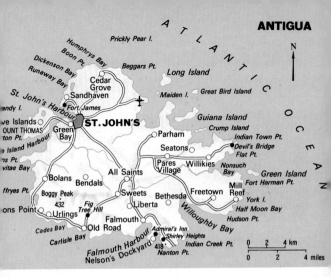

Liberta village was, as the name suggests, founded by freed slaves in 1834.

Nelson's Dockyard was developed in the mid-18th century to shelter English warships protecting the West Indies possessions. It saw its heyday during the War of American Independence and the wars against the French.

Admiral Horatio Nelson made it his base in the 1780s and gave it his name, but when ships became too big to negotiate the landlocked harbour, the dockyard went into decline and was abandoned in 1889. By 1951 it was described as "a scene of appalling deso-

lation". Restored during the fifties, it now looks much as it did in Nelson's day.

The best restored building is the **Admiral's House**, furnished in the style of the period and used as a nautical museum. It contains relics of the days of Nelson and mementoes of the Admiral himself. Other restored buildings now cater for English Harbour's modern role as a yachting centre.

An excellent vantage point from which to sip a rum punch and reflect over the great sea battles of the past is the elegant **Admiral's Inn** with its romantic atmosphere.

During his tour of duty, Nelson made friends with one of his captains, Prince William Henry, Duke of Clarence, who later became William IV of England, the "Sailor King". Biscuit-coloured **Clarence House,** built by English masons for the Duke, stands on a small hill which commands a fine view of the dockyard.

Overlooking English Harbour on **Shirley Heights** are the ruins of the garrison buildings and fortifications that protected the naval base. The view from here is stupendous—inland you can see most of Antigua, and out to sea on a clear day you can make out the neighbouring French island of Guadeloupe.

Take the scenic way back to St. John's via **Fig Tree Drive** —"fig" is the Antiguan name for banana—through the forests, banana groves and hills of the island. The road continues past west-coast fishing villages and the island's highest point, 1,360-foot (414-m.) **Boggy Peak.**

And, in the evening, as you watch the sun set over the Caribbean, you will be entertained by soul music, calypso, reggae or limbo. Antigua's steel bands are famous throughout the West Indies.

Eating Out

Restaurants in Antigua offer specialities from around the world, including Italy, France and Viet Nam. However, the islanders have added their own spicy culinary touch and they make good use of the abundance of tropical fruit and vegetables.

Black pudding is an adapted European dish and the familiar blood sausage has a highly spiced variant here.

Favourite island dishes are pepperpot, *coo-coo* (cornmeal dumplings) and *souse*, which is boiled pig's head and trotters served with lime juice, sliced cucumber and pepper.

Doucanah is a sweet potato dumpling flavoured with coconut and raisins, traditionally boiled in banana leaves. It's served with codfish, anchovies and eggplant.

There is a wide variety of seafood as well as fresh game and reef fish. The crayfish are excellent—most of them are caught at the nearby island of Barbuda.

Rum makes the Caribbean go round, and the particular island speciality is called Cavalier and is renowned for its flavour. A little of it goes a long way in punches, daiquiris and *piña coladas*.

Shopping

The shops in St. John's are well stocked with imported tax-free items, especially **English goods** including cashmere, china, jewellery and crystal. Not everything is a bargain, however, and you should compare prices with those at home.

Two new areas to shop are at Redcliffe Quay and Heritage Quay, the new cruise ship dock in the centre of St. John's.

Sea island cotton is the most popular local product—it's grown on the island. There is a wide selection of **straw goods,** such as bags, hats, slippers and mats made of sisal, palm fronds, palmetto or banana leaves.

Local crafts include tortoiseshell **jewellery, batik** and **dolls.** **Pottery** is an Antiguan cottage industry and the red-clay products are much sought after. The islanders make clay charcoal pots for grilling fish and meat.

A **warri board** makes an unusual souvenir—if you can get someone to teach you how to play the game. It's an Antiguan equivalent of backgammon, and some say it is as challenging as chess.

Practical Information

Banks: Generally open from 8 a.m. to 1 p.m., Monday to Friday and on Friday also from 3 p.m. to 5 p.m.

Currency: The official currency is the East Caribbean dollar (EC$). Major credit cards are accepted in tourist hotels and shops, as are U.S. dollars.

Shops: Open from 8 a.m. to 2 p.m. Monday to Thursday and 8 a.m. to noon and from 2 to 4 p.m. on Friday. A few shops close Thursdays.

Telephoning Home. Antigua (area code 809) is linked to the U.S. network.

Transport: Taxis are marked with a letter H on a green numberplate. There are standard rates for standard trips—inquire in advance. The bus is cheap but the schedules are strictly informal.

Water: The tap water is safe to drink.

ORANJESTAD

Aruba

Introduction

There are many reasons for visiting the pretty little island of Aruba: water sports galore, shopping bargains from all over the world, attractive scenery, friendly people—and some of the most beautiful white sand beaches in the Caribbean.

This isle, once overshadowed by its better-known neighbour, Curaçao, has its own special pleasures, just waiting to be discovered. First visit Oranjestad, the capital, with its colourful floating market and pastel gabled houses. Then head out into the countryside, or *cunucu,* as it's called in Papiamento. (This is the language of Aruba, a *mélange* of Dutch, Spanish and English with a smattering of Carib Indian dialect.) A typical tour will take you through desert terrain, past colourful plantation houses enclosed by cactus fences, to secluded bays shaded by *divi divi* trees, sway-ing in the trade winds. Then you'll head back to town for a delicious meal of Aruban specialities, perhaps, or a bountiful Indonesian *rijsttafel.* Afterwards you might want to try your luck in one of the casinos, or catch the floor show at a hotel nightclub.

The western and southern shores of Aruba are scalloped by the island's best white sand beaches, great for swimming and sunning. Snorkelling and scuba fans appreciate Aruba's warm, clear waters teeming with vivid tropical fish. There are spectacular coral formations and even a few sunken vessels to be seen. You may want to try out a typically Aruban pastime: dune-sliding.

The Arubans are genuinely glad to meet tourists. They're proud of their island, its history and legends (sometimes a little difficult to separate) and want to show it off. So when an Aruban says *"Bon bini"* ("welcome" in Papiamento), you can be sure he means it.

A Brief History

15th–16th centuries	Alonso de Ojeda discovers Aruba in 1499, claiming it for Spain. He may have given the island its name from the Spanish phrase "Oro uba" (gold was there), but the name may also have come from the language of the

indigenous Carib Indian population. The Spanish make almost no effort to exploit Aruba.

17th–18th centuries

The Dutch take over Aruba with little opposition from the Spanish in 1634. Peter Stuyvesant (who later becomes famous in North America) is appointed governor of Aruba and the other Dutch West Indian islands from 1643 to 1647, but spends most of these years on Curaçao and St. Maarten.

19th–20th centuries

The British occupy Aruba in 1805, finally returning it to the Dutch in 1816. Gold is discovered on the island in 1824, and more than 1,350,000 kilos (3,000,000 lbs.) of it are taken from the mines until around 1915, when declining yields force them to close.

In 1929, a large oil refinery opens on the island, bringing renewed prosperity. Aruba and five other Dutch-speaking islands form the autonomous federation of the Netherlands Antilles in 1954. Aruba secedes from the federation in 1986. Today, oil refining remains big business on Aruba, but the tourist industry is quickly catching up.

Sightseeing

Start your tour of Aruba in **Oranjestad** the island's lovely old Dutch-gabled capital, situated on the south-western coast. Walk along the wharf to the **old schooner harbour.** A lively open-air market takes place here every morning, as merchant-sailors sell fresh fish, fruit and vegetables directly off their boats to passers-by. In the centre of all the hubbub, you'll spot an exotically decorated Indonesian houseboat, the *Bali,* which has been converted into a restaurant, with an adjoining spot on the wharf for cocktails. Here you might try Aruba's very own liqueur, *cucui.* Made from the leaves of the aloe plant, this red, licorice-flavoured liqueur dates back to the times of the Arawak Indians.

Wilhelminastraat is a showcase for the 18th-century houses of old Oranjestad—tall, narrow-gabled buildings with red-tiled roofs, painted in cool pastel shades, as well as intense yellows and royal blues. This architectural style can be seen throughout the Netherlands Antilles.

Fort Zoutman/Willem III

Tower now houses a historical museum and hosts the weekly Bonbini festival in its courtyard. You can enjoy local crafts, food and music.

Now head for the main shopping area, around **Nassaustraat.** An enormous number of shops lie close at hand. Since Aruba levies a low duty on imported goods, you can find some real bargains here. The luxury articles for sale come from Asia as well as Europe.

Around the Island

On an island 32 kilometres (20 miles) long by 10 kilometres (6 miles) wide, nothing is very far away. A well-maintained coastal road circles the island and a network of secondary roads covers the interior.

West Coast

Begin sightseeing with a leisurely drive up the west coast, passing the fine white sands of Eagle Beach and Palm Beach. **Eagle Beach** is free and public.

with palm-thatched shelters for picnicking. Many of Aruba's luxury hotels line **Palm Beach,** and **De Olde Molen,** a windmill built in Holland in 1804, was shipped across the Atlantic and reconstructed here in 1960. The mill now serves as a restaurant. There's plenty of atmosphere—and a marvellous panorama from the terrace. At the north-western tip of Aruba, take a walk around **California Dunes,** the windy and barren site of an old lighthouse.

Now head back to Oranjestad, but this time take the road that leads inland to Noord and **St. Ann's Church,** where you can see a lovely hand-carved oak altar, the work of a 19th-century Dutch artisan.

From Noord, the road travels on through the cunucu, dotted with brightly coloured houses, patches of cacti, enormous boulders and *divi divi* trees permanently bent by the ever-present trade winds.

Points Inland

Some of Aruba's most popular tourist sights lie inland from Oranjestad, within easy reach of the capital. You'll want to have a look at the unusual **rock gardens** of Casibari and Ayo. Huge boulders weighing thousands of tons are scattered near and far, as if thrown about by some crazed giant. Several of the boulders display ritual Indian carvings, centuries old, made by the Caribs or Arawaks.

Another favourite outing is the trip up **Hooiberg** (Haystack Mountain). Though not Aruba's tallest peak, Hooiberg features a long flight of steps that takes you 165 metres (541 ft.) to the top—a breathtaking look-out. If visibility is good, you'll see Venezuela, a mere 24 kilometres (15 miles) away.

The ghost town of **Balashi** was the centre of a profitable gold mining area in the 19th century. You can visit the abandoned mine and the ruins of a gold-smeltery. Continue on to **Frenchmen's Pass** in the Aruba uplands, the haunt of the huge green parakeet, a species found only in this part of the Caribbean.

Not far from the town of Santa Cruz lie the **caves** of Canashito. Here you'll see some mysterious hieroglyphs dating from the 12th to 15th centuries, made either by Carib or Arawak Indians.

North-east of Santa Cruz, **Miralamar** nestles between Aruba's two highest peaks, Aritok and Jamanota, both around 180 metres (600 ft.).

The road rises to give some excellent views. Various caves in the area around Arikok are decorated with Indian drawings.

North Coast

You can explore an abandoned gold mine in the north coast ghost town of **Bushiribana.** Long before gold-rush days, Bushiribana was a pirate's stronghold, and you'll spot the ruins of a pirate's castle that may date from the 16th century.

The coast road travels east to **Andicouri,** where over the centuries the pounding surf has carved a natural bridge out of the coral rock. An old coconut plantation on the inlet makes a particularly scenic spot for a picnic.

East again at **Dos Playa** and **Boca Prins,** you'll have a once-in-a-lifetime chance to try the unusual Aruban sport of dune-sliding. It's not at all difficult if you wear tennis shoes. And the view from the dunes is fantastic.

South Coast

San Nicolaas, on the southeast coast, is the island's second largest city. This modern community was built for the workers of Aruba's giant Lago Oil Refinery.

Eating Out

Island restaurants serve a selection of Aruban dishes, redolent of coconut and Caribbean spices. But there are also a number of fine Indonesian eating houses, giving you a chance to sample this excellent cuisine without a trip to the Pacific! You'll find Chinese, American and European-style establishments, too.

Aruban Specialities

Sopito makes a good starter. This tasty fish and coconut soup is flavoured with salt pork and assorted spices. Hearty island hors-d'œuvres include *funchi* (maize or cornmeal patties), *ayacas* (plantain or banana leaves stuffed with a maize meal and savoury meat filling), and *calas* (mashed beans fried in batter).

If you're really hungry, try one of these delicious but filling main courses: *keshi yena,* Edam cheese stuffed with meat, chicken or fish and raisins, then baked, and *capucijners,* a combination of meat, bacon, onions and pickles. Aruba's best known dish is *stoba,* a highly seasoned lamb or goat stew, often served with banana fritters.

Indonesian Specialities

Don't miss the chance to sample authentic Indonesian *rijsttafel,* an array of 20 to 30 different dishes served with rice. Among them: *ikan asem manis* (sweet-sour fish), *babi ketjap* (pork cooked in sweet soy sauce), *semur sapi* (beef stew with tomatoes) and so on. You'll get wildly hot *sambal* on the side—lime juice and chilli peppers with a paste of roasted shrimp or fish.

Nasi goreng is a sampling of dishes from the *rijsttafel,* called *bami goreng* if noodles are substituted for the rice. *Saté* is also popular: beef, chicken, mutton or prawns are marinated in sugared spices, skewered and cooked over charcoal, accompanied by a peanut sauce.

Drinks

All the famous Dutch beers are available, as well as Amstel, brewed on nearby Curaçao. Aruba's neighbour is also the home of the famed curaçao orange liqueur, distilled from a secret recipe. Dutch brandy is milder than its French counterpart, cognac.

You'll find a full range of imported French wines. Ask for a carafe of the house wine, always cheaper and often quite good.

Shopping

Throughout its history, Oranjestad has been a bustling centre of Caribbean trade. Today, shops in the area around Nassaustraat offer goods from all over the world. Oranjestad is a low duty port, so you may find considerable bargains, compared to prices in your home country.

Here are just a few of the items available:

Clothing. The latest in designer fashions from Italy and France, African *dashikis,* men's and women's sports clothes, swimwear, Madeira embroidery.

Foodstuffs. Spirits and liqueurs (especially curaçao), Indonesian spices.

Jewellery. Look out for Danish silver and pewter ornaments, Indonesian ivory bracelets and necklaces, delicate Indian gold and silver earrings, fine Caribbean jewellery.

Porcelain, pottery and crystal. Dutch Delftware, Royal Copenhagen porcelain, Hummel figurines, English bone china, Swedish crystal.

Watches. A wide range of Swiss and Japanese makes, divers' watches.

Practical Information

Banks and currency exchange. Open 8 a.m. to noon and 1.30 p.m. to 4 p.m., Monday to Friday.

Clothing. Aruba has warm, rarely hot weather year-round, with temperatures most often between 24° and 29° C (75° and 85° F). Chances are you won't need a raincoat in the near-desert climate. Women should bring a scarf or two to protect their hair, as the trade winds can be fierce.

Credit cards and traveller's cheques. Major credit cards are widely accepted by most hotels, better restaurants and shops. Traveller's cheques are also accepted, preferably those in U.S. dollars.

Currency. Aruban florin, at par with the Netherlands Antilles guilder. Prices are usually quoted in the local currency, but shops also accept U.S. dollars.

Shops. Generally open 8 a.m. to noon and 2 to 6 p.m., Monday to Saturday.

Telephoning Home. To call the U.S. direct from Oranjestad, dial 00 + 1 + U.S. area code + local number. To phone Oranjestad from the U.S., dial 011 + 2978 + local number. To call the U.K. direct from Oranjestad, dial 00 + 44 + area code + local number. To call Oranjestad from the U.K., dial 010 + 2978 + local number.

FREEPORT

Bahamas

Introduction

The Bahamas, 3,000-odd islands and cays strung out in the vast Atlantic, bask in breezy semi-tropical sunshine.

Starting as close as 50 miles to the Florida coast, the archipelago swoops south-east for some 600 miles almost to Haiti and eastern Cuba.

It is usually considered to consist of three elements: New Providence (capital Nassau), Grand Bahama (capital Freeport) and all the rest—referred to collectively as the Family Islands, as official nomenclature has it.

Its strategic location, along the major shipping routes between the Caribbean and North America, has been a crucial factor in the history of the islands. Ever since Christopher Columbus came ashore on the Bahamian out island of San Salvador in 1492, wreckers, pirates, rum runners and modern smugglers have been among those who found the reefs, cays and coves useful.

The great glory of these islands is the incredible sea they ornament. The water is so clear you hardly need a snorkel mask to enjoy the astonishing array of marine life at countless coral reefs. Divers can explore fish-filled holes and seek the wrecks of the many treasure ships which came to grief over centuries in the treacherous shoals of what the Spaniards called *baja mar* (shallow sea). From that came the anglicized name, Bahamas.

Sea, sun and sand are the perpetual lures for tourists. But the Bahamas has another major attraction. The nation is one of the world's leading tax havens, an offshore money centre with some 400 licensed financial institutions.

Nowadays on posters, brochures, television and T-shirts you find the slogan, "It's Better in the Bahamas". That's unquestionably true about the marine scene. But ask an islander why, and you may well get this reply: "Cuz we got no snow, no taxes and no ulcers."

A Brief History

| 15th and 16th centuries | Christopher Columbus lands at San Salvador on October 12, 1492. Disappointed in his search for gold and other riches, he sails out of the Bahamas towards neighbouring Cuba. |

The Spanish remove the Indian inhabitants of Lucaya to work in Spain, Haiti and Cuba.

7th century — A group of English Puritans from Bermuda establish the first permanent European settlement on Eleuthera in 1648, followed in 1666 by a second colony on New Providence island. King Charles II of England grants the Bahamas to six Lords Proprietors, who are powerless to suppress the piracy that rages in the archipelago.

8th century — The Bahamas become a crown colony in 1718. The first royal governor cleans out the pirates and calls an Assembly. Spain rules the islands for one year in 1782, but the Treaty of Versailles (1783) returns them to the British. Cotton plantations flourish but prosperity is short-lived. The weak soil is soon depleted and a plague destroys crops. Most planters leave the islands.

9th century — Slavery, never widespread, is officially abolished in the 1830s. The Confederate States are supplied from the Bahamas during the American Civil War.

0th century — During the first two decades of the century massive emigration takes place, mainly to the United States. During World War II American bases are established in the Bahamas and the Duke of Windsor becomes governor. Tourism increases steadily, especially after the Cuban revolution. The Bahamas achieve self-government and, in 1973, independence.

Sightseeing

Freeport

f Grand Bahama island is typical of the Bahamas, the surprising commercial and resort centre of Freeport/Lucaya certainly is not. Despite English place names and tours by red London double-deck bus, basic Bahamian local colour is in short supply here.

The atmosphere is more palpably American than anywhere else in the Commonwealth — not unexpectedly, since it was a Norfolk, Virginia financier, Wallace Groves, who conceived and set in motion the "Freeport miracle" in 1955. (Under the Hawksbill Creek agreement of that year, a deep-water harbour was decided upon along with the tax and duty-free port. Tourism began to boom when the first casino opened in 1964.) Most of the island's 32,000 residents live in this city—or at the West End settlement some 25 miles away. Smooth highways—neatly landscaped, clearly signposted and even at times divided—connect modern hotels with golf courses, marinas, a shopping and gambling complex.

Freeport's **International Bazaar,** an unusual mixture of architecture and offerings from various parts of the world, is the city's major sightseeing attraction, and worth wandering through even if you're not buying from any of the scores of shops. Built in 1967, it was, as you'll see, the work of a Hollywood set designer. Within the Bazaar's 10 acres is a Ministry of Tourism information centre. Close by are the huge **Bahama Princess Casino** with its strange Moorish façade, and the island's main straw market where ladies with broad smiles are used to posing for photographers. Major hotels and golf courses are also in the area.

The atmosphere is more authentically Bahamian at the native fruit and vegetable market, an all-weather cluster of family stalls in Churchill Square, and at the occasion fairs, parades and "jumpin' religious events.

Starting a few miles east of Freeport's central attraction the sprawling **Lucaya** resort area features beachfront and marina hotels, the island best golf courses and severa sightseeing possibilities.

"Please do not touch th plants—many are poisonous", says the entrance sig at the **Garden of the Grove** But that's the only jarring no in these thoroughly delightfu 11 acres of tropical flora, man made waterfalls and pond Lizards scamper as you stro among the 10,000 plants an trees.

From Bell Channel Bay wind conditions permitting what's billed as the world largest **glass-bottom boat** take tourists over coral garden and along Grand Bahama deep reef. Sharks, barracudas stingrays and other large crea tures are usually seen.

Undersea buffs might enjo the **Museum of Underwate Exploration** at the Underwa ter Explorers Society in th same inlet. Aside from variou items brought up by divers some early underwater gear including primitive-lookin cameras and masks, is on dis play.

Around the diving facilities in the area, you'll hear about the million or more dollars worth of Spanish pieces-of-eight found offshore from Lucaya in 1964. The shallow site, long since stripped of its gold, is nicknamed Treasure Reef. To the north, on East-Settlers Way, the 100-acre **Rand Memorial Nature Centre** offers 90-minute guided walks with a naturalist through a protected Bahamian forest, a chance to photograph flamingoes and other uncommon birds.

Freeport sightseers retreat from the heat at Garden of the Groves.

Out on the Island

To the west of Freeport at the settlement of **Eight Mile Rock,** which is strung out along a good highway, guided tours stop at a Bahamian rarity, a perfume factory, formerly a Baptist church. You can watch oils from around the world being mixed and bottled as various fragrances. Mysteriously, a number of old cannonballs have been found in this area recently, though not even pirates were supposed to have lived on Grand Bahama until the 1840s.

Signs make good reading along the road, as you pass such places as **Sea Grape, Deadman's Reef** and **Bottle Bay.** Near **Holmes Rock** a small commercial nursery called **Hydro Flora Gardens** offers a tour and lecture on tropical plants grown without soil.

West End, sadly, isn't what it used to be. Searching the sleepy seaside village, you'll find only the scantiest traces of the bad old days of Prohibition when merchants and rum runners here made fortunes smuggling liquor into the United States. A few old-timers recall the bootlegging boom days when, for example, a boat owned by Al Capone was loaded with booze here. In the

"gin clear" water just offshore in front of the aged Star Hotel landmark and the so-called Old Factory, you'll see some concrete slabs of Prohibition era piers and bits of old iron rails used to roll contraband down to waiting boats. In this oldest Grand Bahama settlement there are six churches and over 20 bars or clubs, mostly small wooden affairs. West End's 5,000 inhabitants don't benefit as much as they'd like from a large, self-sustaining tourist hotel complex which dominates the area. From here you can go on deep-sea fishing and scuba diving excursions.

Tourists won't normally find it convenient to take the bus which goes most days between Freeport and the eastern end of the island. By taxi or rented car, it's a long drive on a road which deteriorates dramatically beyond the U.S. Air Force missile tracking installations around **High Rock.** From the road you'll see impressive radar dishes and antennae, but stern signs prohibit closer inspection. On this trip you parallel the majority of Grand Bahama's advertised 60 miles of beaches, mostly long windswept stretches frequented only by birds and crabs. Tiny **Pelican Point** is a

...idy, friendly roadside settle-ment where the centre of all things is the Baptist church.

McLean's Town, metropolis of the east end, has about 250 inhabitants who live in pastel wooden houses. Here, too, almost everyone attends every service at the Baptist church. This settlement is unusual in that the majority of the women go out fishing for a living, as do the menfolk. They bring in snapper, grouper, conch, porgy and crawfish. A bit shy at first, villagers are genuinely pleased to welcome strangers—in the fashion of Family Islanders around the Bahamas. They're particularly happy to tell you about the town's biggest event of the year, the Conch Cracking Contest held on Discovery Day, October 12, when huge crowds turn up to watch competitors from as far afield as Bimini crack, empty and clean up to 25 conches in less than three minutes.

At a fishing camp on nearby **Deep Water Cay,** you'll hear other sea sagas from the regulars. There's very good bonefishing in the shallows among the east end mangroves, and collecting seashells (shelling) can be superb along such beaches as **Crabbin Bay** and **John Davis.**

Eating Out

Local chefs specialize in some interesting seafood variations, many of which contain **conch** (pronounced conk). This chewy mollusc, beloved by Bahamians, is prepared in a multitude of ways: fried, stewed, in soup (conch chowder), in salad (with onions, celery, sweet and hot peppers and tomatoes). Grouper, a flaky white fish, is the most popular in the Bahamas. Crawfish and crab are grilled, steamed, creamed, minced, baked, stewed, devilled or stuffed. Turtle steaks, stews and soups can be delicious. Peas'n rice, a traditional accompaniment, is a national passion.

For dessert try fresh fruit, tart key lime pie or guava duff, a kind of pie served with rum sauce.

Rum figures in a whole gamut of **tropical drinks:** *piña colada* (rum, coconut cream and pineapple juice), Yellow Bird (light rum, coffee, banana liqueur and fruit juices) and Skinny Minnie (rum, Cointreau, coconut liqueur, Galliano, cream and grenadine to name but a few). Leading American soft drinks are sold everywhere. For a refreshing change, try canned sea grape soda.

Shopping

Though not duty-free, the Bahamas offers a range of European and Commonwealth goods at prices far lower than in the United States. Local craftsmen who have resisted mass-production to satisfy surging tourist demand produce some distinctive souvenirs.

The best buys include:

Coconut-shell jewellery and **artefacts** are said to be nearly indestructible.

Printed fabrics, particularly batiks from Andros, are handwaxed and dyed with colourful island designs.

Rum is a runaway favourite, Eleuthera pineapple rum above all, and the coconut variety.

Shells and **jewellery** made from conch shell, whelk shell, coral, sharks' teeth, etc.

Straw goods take in everything from sunhats and carryalls to straw aeroplanes complete with pilot or straw model of Nassau surreys.

Imported goods often sell for competitive prices: china, cutlery, fabrics, glass, leather, perfumes, silver, watches, cameras and alcohol.

Practical Information

Banks keep hours from 9.30 a.m. to 3 p.m. Monday through Thursday, to 5 p.m. on Friday, closed weekends and holidays.

Clothing: pack casual, lightweight resort wear. People tend to dress up at night. A jacket or sweater can come in handy both for arctic airconditioning and cool evening breezes.

Currency: The Bahamian dollar is pegged to American currency and divided into 100 cents. Coins: 1, 5, 10, 25 and 50 cents, and $1 and $5. Banknotes: 50 cents and $1, 5, 10, 20, 50 and 100.

Restaurants serve lunch from noon to 2.30 p.m.; dinner from 7 p.m. to 10 p.m. or later.

Shops open 9 a.m. to 5 p.m. daily, except Sundays and either Thursday, Friday or Saturday afternoon.

NASSAU

Bahamas

Introduction

Strewn over a vast expanse of the Atlantic ocean, the Bahamas bask in breezy, semi-tropical sunshine. Out of about 700 islands, over 100 are at least minimally inhabited though only some two dozen have vacation facilities. The other 2,400 smaller cays (pronounced "keys") of the Commonwealth of the Bahamas are blissfully deserted.

The great glory of these islands is the incredible sea they ornament. The water is so clear you hardly need a snorkel mask to enjoy the astonishing array of marine life at countless coral reefs.

Yachts glide gingerly into cluttered marinas; barefoot children cruise resort beaches hawking shell necklaces t rows of oiled sunbathers camera-clicking holidaymak ers bob and sway in over worked glass-bottom boats honeymooners hold hand (and their breath) as the ca sino roulette wheels spin o and on.

Tourism is overwhelmingl the nation's biggest busines providing two-thirds of a local jobs. Nassau has bee designed for holiday pleasure and is jam-packed much o the time with visitors deter minedly pursuing it.

And while there's plenty o goodwill about being helpfu to tourists, there is rarel any great hurry about gettin things done. "We have thre speeds," you may hear a Baha mian explain, "slow, stop and reverse."

A Brief History

15th & 16th centuries	Christopher Columbus lands at San Salvador on Octo ber 12, 1492. Disappointed in his search for gold an other riches, he sails out of the Bahamas toward neighbouring Cuba.
	The Spanish remove the Indian inhabitants o Lucaya to work in Spain, Haiti and Cuba.
17th century	A group of English Puritans from Bermuda establish the first permanent European settlement on Eleuther in 1648, followed in 1666 by a second colony on Nev Providence island. King Charles II of England grant the Bahamas to six Lords Proprietors, who are power less to suppress the piracy that rages in the archipelago

The Spanish attack Nassau, but the pirates are undeterred. Blackbeard, Henry Morgan and others operate out of Nassau.

18th century The Bahamas become a crown colony in 1718. The first royal governor cleans out the pirates and calls an Assembly. Spain rules the islands for one year in 1782, but the Treaty of Versailles (1783) returns them to the British. Cotton plantations flourish but prosperity is short-lived. The weak soil is soon depleted and a plague destroys crops. Most planters leave the islands. Nassau becomes a free port in 1787.

19th century Slavery, never widespread, is officially abolished in the 1830s. The Confederate States are supplied from the Bahamas during the American Civil War. The sponge industry (later destroyed by fungus) is introduced.

20th century During the first two decades of the century massive emigration takes place, mainly to the United States. During Prohibition, Nassau booms as a centre for bootlegging. The city's first gambling casino opens in 1920, and an air service links Nassau to Miami nine years later. During World War II American bases are established in the Bahamas and the Duke of Windsor becomes governor. Tourism increases steadily, especially after the Cuban revolution. The Bahamas achieve self-government and, in 1973, independence.

Sightseeing

Nassau

With its hotel glitter and restaurant sophistication, its day-time traffic jams and night-time naughtiness, Nassau is certainly not typical of the Bahamas. But it is a magnet.

Bay Street is the commercial centre of the city, but the traditional tourist hub is the **Straw Market** at Market Plaza. Amiable sales ladies here have been creating straw items since childhood.

The picture-postcard **Public Buildings** dating from 1812 and a bleached marble statue of a young, seated Queen Victoria in this area recall the British colonial era.

The oldest and most interesting building is the **Public Library** of 1797, between

Shirley Street and the Court House. The seashell collection in the entry has some rarities, but the really interesting things are upstairs where you can inspect fine old prints, maps and portraits, a carved stone Arawak ceremonial stool and other artefacts.

Taking a brief stroll you'll find at least half a dozen other venerable buildings to admire, mostly from the outside. Up Parliament Street opposite the new Post Office is **Jacaranda**, a 140-year-old private residence.

A white statue of a dashing Columbus commands steep steps up to pink **Government House** (closed to the public residence of governors an governor-generals for nearl two centuries.

Christ Church Cathedra (Anglican) in George Street, pleasantly airy building with dark timbered roof, was con structed in 1841, while th three-storey **Deanery** in Cum berland Street dates fron about 1710 and may be th oldest residence in the Baha mas.

Slaves hacked the **Queen' Staircase** in Elizabeth Avenu from the black rock cliff as passageway for troops garri soned above at Fort Fincastle Ascending, you'll reach Nas

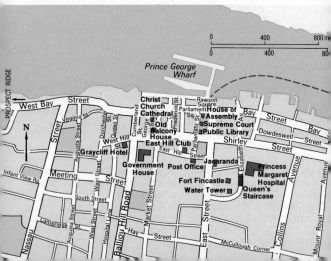

sau's water tower which offers a stunning **panorama** of New Providence and the harbour.

West of Nassau there's no missing the grey stone ramparts of **Fort Charlotte,** named after the consort of George III. Tourists are escorted into the dungeon which never held prisoners but today houses a mockup of a torture chamber complete with stretching rack. Beneath Fort Charlotte, the **Nassau Botanical Gardens** display a variety of carefully kept tropical flowers and plants.

At the **Coral World** marine observatory, you'll see some of the incredible underwater life of the Bahamas. It's said

to be the biggest man-made coral reef in the world.

Appropriately perched on a hillock overlooking the eastern approach to Nassau harbour is **Blackbeard's Tower,** popularly supposed to be a lookout built by the 17th-century pirate chief.

The tower is along a short path off Eastern Road, which meanders back toward town past scores of lovely residences.

One of the best beaches is past Northwest Point at **Old Fort Bay.** This gentle arc of soft sand is backed by dense tropical foliage in which stand the remains of an old fort.

Small, isolated and charm-

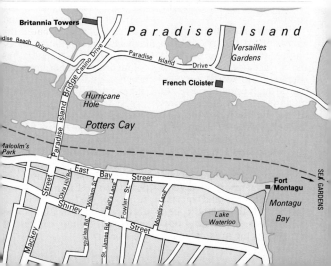

ingly unspoiled, **Adelaide Village** on Southwest Bay dates back to 1832 when it was settled by slaves freed from ships stopped by the Royal Navy. A prominent sign announces the next "Be Healed Revival Meeting." Friendly villagers are pleased to chat for as long as a visitor wishes.

Grand Bahama

If Grand Bahama island is typical of the Bahamas, the surprising commercial and resort centre of **Freeport/Lucaya** certainly is not. The atmosphere is palpably American: smooth highways connect modern hotels with golf courses, marinas, a shopping and gambling complex.

Freeport's **International Bazaar,** stocked with goods from various parts of the world, is the city's major sightseeing attraction, and worth wandering through even if you're not buying from any of the scores of shops. Close by are the huge **Bahama Princess Casino,** with its strange Moorish façade, and the island's main straw market.

East of Freeport, the sprawling **Lucaya** resort area features beachfront and marina hotels and the island's best golf courses. Sightseeing possibilities in the area include a tropical garden and glass-bottomed boat rides.

The Family Islands

The smaller islands in the Bahamas are referred to collectively as the Family Islands.

The **Abaco** archipelago boasts some of the best diving and snorkelling sites in the Bahamas, while **Eleuthera** has outstanding tourist facilities. Remote **Cat Island** offers wide open beaches, deep creeks and scenic hills. **San Salvador,** site of Columbus's landing, is a favourite of scuba divers. Columbus claimed **Long Island** was the most beautiful he had ever seen. Sharing the coastline with rugged cliffs are scores of dazzling white sand beaches. Yachtsmen haunt the **Exumas,** a 100-mile string of isles and cays. Nobody has counted all the pristine beaches and coves. **Andros** claims the world's second-largest fringing reef, a scuba and snorkel wonderland. The 30 cays in the **Berry Islands** amount to a total of a dozen square miles (about 30 square kilometres). There are some chic resort facilities and superb sport fishing in the Tongue of the Ocean. Anglers also congregate at **Bimini,** the self-styled fishing capital of the world.

Eating Out

Local chefs specialize in some interesting seafood variations, many of which contain **conch** (pronounced conk). This chewy mollusc, beloved by Bahamians, is prepared in a multitude of ways: fried, stewed, in soup (conch chowder), in salad (with onions, celery, sweet and hot peppers and tomatoes). Grouper, a flaky white fish, is the most popular in the Bahamas.

Crawfish and crab are grilled, steamed, creamed, minced, baked, stewed, devilled or stuffed. Turtle steaks, stews and soups can be delicious. Peas'n rice, a traditional accompaniment, is a national passion.

For dessert try fresh fruit, tart key lime pie or guava duff, a kind of pie with rum sauce.

Rum figures in a whole gamut of **tropical drinks:** *piña colada* (rum, coconut cream and pineapple juice), Yellow

Bird (light rum, coffee, banana liqueur and fruit juices) and Skinny Minnie (rum, Cointreau, coconut liqueur, Galliano, cream and grenadine to name but a few. Leading American soft drinks are sold everywhere. For a refreshing change, try canned sea grape soda.

Shopping

Though not duty-free, Nassau offers a range of European and Commonwealth goods at prices far lower than in the United States. Local craftsmen who have resisted mass-production to satisfy surging tourist demand produce some distinctive souvenirs:

Coconut-shell jewellery and **artefacts** are said to be nearly indestructible.

Printed fabrics, particularly batiks from Andros, are hand waxed and dyed with colourful island designs.

Rum is a firm favourite especially Eleuthera pineapple rum and the coconut variety.

Shells and **jewellery** made from conch shell, whelk shell, sharks' teeth, etc.

Straw goods take in everything from sunhats and carryalls to straw airplanes complete with pilot or straw models of Nassau surreys.

Imported goods are on sale at attractive prices: china, cutlery, fabrics, glass, leather, perfumes, silver, watches, cameras and alcohol.

Practical Information

Banks keep hours from 9.30 a.m. to 3 p.m. Monday through Thursday, to 5 p.m. on Friday, closed weekends and holidays.

Currency: The Bahamian dollar is pegged to American currency and divided into 100 cents. Coins: 1, 5, 10, 25 and 50 cents, and $1 and 5. Banknotes: 50 cents and $1, 5, 10, 20, 50 and 100.

Telephoning Home. Nassau (area code 809) is linked to the U.S. network. For U.K. visitors to ring home, dial 011 + 44 + area code + local number. To call Nassau from the U.K., dial 010 + 500 809 + local number.

BRIDGETOWN

Barbados

Introduction

Pretty Barbados is the most easterly of the Caribbean islands, a coral and limestone-capped isle lying in the path of cooling trade winds. Though just 21 miles by 14 miles, its shores are lavished with almost 60 miles of shimmering white spunsugar beaches. The dramatic, wind-swept east coast is washed by Atlantic waves and dotted with huge boulders—a photographer's dream—while the tranquil Caribbean beaches of the west coast, edged with palms, are perfect for swimming, snorkelling and sunbathing.

Pear-shaped, cosy Barbados throngs with 253,000 inhabitants—though you're rarely aware of crowds, except on a shopping day in Bridgetown, the capital. Bridgetown was founded in 1628 and is today a bustling centre of commerce and sea-going activity. The town probably takes its name from an old Indian bridge said to have spanned the River Constitution. The colourful port, with its venerable coral stone mansions, cool green savannahs and lively open-air markets is what one imagines an authentic West Indian capital to be.

Though almost sedate in some respects and as British as teatime, Bridgetown and Barbados extend a welcome as sunny as the climate. You'll find the Bajans (as the Barbadians like to call themselves) warm, genuinely helpful people.

A Brief History

16th century	Barbados is discovered by Portuguese explorer Pedro a Campos in 1536. He names it *los Barbudos* ("the bearded ones") after the island's hoary-looking banyan trees, whose hanging roots resemble beards. But Portugal is not particularly interested in Barbados and establishes no permanent outposts there.
17th and 18th centuries	The *Olive Blossom,* an English vessel, claims Barbados for Great Britain in 1625. Englishmen from the ship *William and John* found Barbados' first settlement, Jamestown (later renamed Holetown), in 1627. Large tobacco, cotton and sugar cane plantations are set up. Thousands of slaves are introduced to work the fields.

19th century   Both black and white Barbadians enter the new century with optimism as Great Britain ends the slave trade in 1806 and abolishes slavery completely in 1833. But the island passes through hard times, periodic massive destruction from hurricanes and a decline in the value of sugar, the principal cash crop, whose price plummets more than 50% in 50 years.

20th century   Great Britain takes steps to improve the economies of its West Indian dependencies, inaugurating an agricultural revolution on Barbados that brings new prosperity. The island begins to diversify its economy, adding sectors such as light industry and tourism. Barbados achieves full independence within the British Commonwealth and joins the United Nations in 1966.

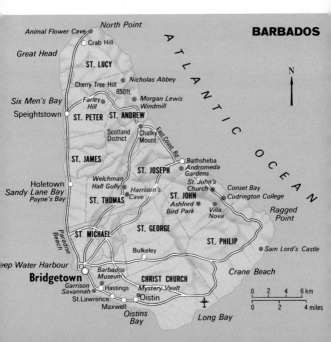

Sightseeing

Lying west of Bridgetown, picturesque Deep Water Harbour is somewhat outside the centre of town. It has its own tourist office, and in the vicinity the interesting **Pelican Crafts Village.**

East along the wharf takes you to the Careenage—a shallow inlet where boats were "careened" (beached) for repair. Fishing boats and pleasure yachts bob cheerfully in the harbour, alongside replicas of the pirate ships that once roamed the Caribbean.

The first sight in Bridgetown has Nelson connections: **Trafalgar Square,** a bustling plaza at the centre of city activity. In the square you'll see a dignified bronze monument to the famous admiral, erected in 1813. Although London's famous memorial may be bigger, Brigdetown's was first— by quite some years!

Nearby is **Broad Street,** a colourful, bustling thoroughfare with old colonial buildings.

Just north of the square, you'll notice the quaint neo-Gothic Parliament Buildings, that have housed the Barbados legislature ever since a fire in 1860 destroyed most of the neighbourhood. Little roads leading to Swan Street contain nice examples of Barbados architecture, both old and new.

North-east, past the bus terminus, lies **Fairschild Market** with a tempting selection of tropical produce.

From here take O'Neal Bridge to Trafalgar Street and St. Michael's Row, the site of **St. Michael's Cathedral.** A typical Caribbean-style Anglican edifice, it was rebuilt in 1831 after a hurricane destroyed the original.

Up the road from St. Michael's you come to Queen's Park, an elegant residence that once housed the British Commanding General.

To the east lies the **Belleville** district, a residential area full of pretty Victorian houses and **Government House,** home of the Governor General, a mansion dating from the early 18th century.

The **Garrison Savannah,** former British military headquarters, lies on the southern outskirts of town. The old military prison now houses the **Barbados Museum.** Scattered about the grassy courtyard are sugar moulds, penny-farthing bicycles and ships' anchors. Gallery exhibits highlight local lore, seashells, fish and aspects of the life and culture of the Arawaks, first inhabitants of the Caribbean. There is a special display of prints relating to the islands, as well as fine English furniture.

St. Ann's Fort close by dates from the early years of the 18th century. The fortification, with its conspicuous clock tower, has become a local landmark.

Atlantic Sights

The rugged Atlantic coast offers some spectacular panoramas. Admire the windswept and dramatic view from **Crane Beach,** where the sea can be quite rough.

Somewhat farther to the north-east is **Sam Lord's Castle,** a hotel and prime tourist attraction. Visit the old plantation house, beautifully decorated with furniture of Barbados mahogany made locally in the Regency style. Much of the china and many of the portraits on show are spoils taken from ships wrecked on the rocks off-shore by the legendary Sam Lord, who is said to have hung lanterns from the cliffs to lure the ships onto the shallow reef.

Continue north along the east coast to Conset Bay and the St. John's area. **Villa Nova,** a dignified old plantation Great House, is still privately owned. Beautiful furnishings enhance the light and airy house.

St. John's Church, perched 825 feet above sea level, offers lovely views of the St. John's area. The present structure dates back to 1836, and the cemetery, older still, contains the mossy grave of Ferdinando Paleologus, a possible descendant of the Byzantine emperors.

Now follow the coast road north to picturesque **Bathsheba,** where small pastel houses cling gallantly to chalky cliffs.

Be sure to visit nearby **Andromeda Gardens,** a must on any east coast tour. This botanical garden contains dozens of varieties of flowers and trees. Among them is the shaggy banyan tree that inspired the name "Barbados".

From Bathsheba the coast road becomes narrow and dangerous in places, but you'll enjoy the view, especially from **The Potteries,** a village of ceramic craftsmen.

In the area is another botanical showplace: the **Flower Forest** at Richmond Plantation. Some splendid views of the sea and Scotland district compete with the horticultural attractions—from ginger lilies to cabbage palms.

The Platinum Coast

The west coast takes its name from the brilliant white of its sandy beaches. Many luxury hotels and big private mansions are situated along this "Millionaire's Row".

In Holetown, a monument commemorates the first landing of a British ship on Barbados, the *Olive Blossom,* in 1625. The Anglican **St. James's Church** was founded in 1660 and rebuilt in 1874.

Drive inland a short distance from Holetown t **Welchman Hall Gully.** Th vast tropical forest, now run ning wild, was originally spice plantation.

Return to the coast an travel north again to **Speight town** (pronounced "spite" once the sugar capital of th north-west area. The town wa known as "Little Bristol" since the Speight family mad most of their trade with th English port. Speightstow has remained typically Wes

ndian, with small, pastel wooden houses and shops, old churches and an easygoing populace greeting one another in the streets. Just north at Six Men's Bay, old cannon are ranged about the silvery shore, another picturesque reminder of the past, and bright fishing boats bob in the surf.

Continue north to North Point and **Animal Flower Cave,** where a willing guide will lead you down steep steps to a cavern carved out by the sea. You'll see the animal flower itself—an exquisite, tentacled sea anemone. High waves occasionally close the caves, so check before going.

Farley Hill, once a venerable plantation house, lies a short distance away over a road with many turns. Many royal visitors were entertained here, including King George V, and the house was the setting for the film *Island in the Sun.* A fire damaged the building and the government finally took over the property.

Nicholas Abbey, another plantation house in the area, delights visitors with its Persian arches and well-kept gardens. A short distance east stands the **Morgan Lewis Windmill,** a well-restored reminder of the days when sugar-making was introduced

by Dutch settlers from Brazil.

Not far from the old windmill is **Harrison's Cave,** a cool cavern whose stalagmites and stalactites are still in constant, slow formation. The cave's highlights are a large chamber known as the Great Hall and a 40-foot-high waterfall cascading into an underground lake.

Eating Out

Soup
Callaloo is popular throughout the Caribbean, a blend of dasheen leaves, okra, onions, garlic, chicken stock, salt-pork or beef, coconut milk, crab meat and hot pepper.

Fish and Seafood
You'll be tempted by crab backs, crab shells stuffed with a spicy crab-meat filling. Shrimps are wonderful, whether deep-fried, served in a cream sauce, or grilled. So is spiny lobster.

Be sure to try flying fish, a speciality of Barbados: it's lightly fried and served with lime wedges and tartar sauce or cut into fingers and deep fried.

Red snapper, scallops, swordfish and kingfish are prepared in every imaginable way, from sautéed or fried to poached or baked.

Meat Specialities

The outstanding meat dish of Barbados is pepperpot, a succulent stew of pork and beef.

Try *sancoche;* it's a "soup" of pork and pig's tail, beef, cassava, yams, potatoes, peppers, perhaps coconut milk.

Desserts and Drinks

The wealth of fresh fruit provides a host of refreshing desserts. Mangoes, passion-fruit, soursop, grapefruit, pawpaws and pineapple are just a few of the possibilities.

Try some *mauby* at a street stand, a popular beverage with heavy lacings of cinnamon, clove and other spices.

Rum is the obvious drink all over the Caribbean.

Shopping

The main shopping street in Bridgetown is Broad Street.

Duty-free buys include transistor radios, cameras and Swiss watches, as well as a selection of china, glass and crystal. You'll also find tobacco, cigarettes, perfume and spirits, with Barbados rum a best-seller.

Other items of interest: *Clothing* (women's), particularly sportswear and beachwear. Also colourful overblouses, sarongs, caftans, sundresses. *Handicraft items,* such as reed or straw mats, sisal bags, seashell and coral jewellery, ceramics, batik and woodcarvings.

Practical Information

Banks and currency exchange: Open 8 a.m. to 3 p.m. Monday to Thursday, and to 5 or 5.30 p.m. Friday afternoon.

Currency: Barbados dollar = 100 cents. Coins: 1, 2, 5, 10, 25 cents; 1 dollar. Notes: 5, 10, 20, 50, 100 dollars.

Shops: Generally open 8 a.m. to 4 or 5 p.m. Monday to Friday, 8 a.m. to noon on Saturday.

Telephoning Home. Bridgetown (area code 809) is linked to the U.S. network.

BARBUDA
ANTIGUA

Lesser Antilles

Introduction

In these days when ever-growing numbers of tourists are flocking to the sunny Caribbean, and hotels are sprouting like bumper crops, Barbuda is that rarest of jewels—an island paradise that has turned its back on development to preserve its inherent assets: pristine sandy beaches, usually deserted, unsurpassed scenery, a natural habitat for deer, wild fowl and wild pigs and, above all, peace and quiet in abundance.

Once known as Dulcina, Barbuda lies in the eastern Caribbean, in the southern end of the Leeward Islands chain. Its composition is coral, and reefs surrounding the island have been the bane of navigators over the centuries, as the numerous sunken wrecks of ships attest. Today they are the joy of divers revelling in the plentiful, brilliantly coloured fish. A wooded wilderness of 625 square miles (1,620 sq. km.), the island is basically flat but rises to about 200 feet (60 m.) in the Highlands section on the island's eastern side. Barbuda counts a scant 1,200 inhabitants, descendants of slaves, most of them living in the island's only village of Codrington. The lo-

cal industries include the production of sea island cotton, salt and charcoal, as well as lobster trapping and cattle and horse raising.

The island is united with Antigua and minute Redonda as an independent nation within the British Commonwealth, known collectively as Antigua and Barbuda. Barbuda's association with Antigua goes back to the 17th century, to the days when Barbuda was the private fief of the English Codrington family who used it to raise provisions for their sugar plantations on Antigua and to run a sordid slave breeding colony.

The ties between the two islands have not always been the most amicable, as Barbudans have sometimes felt like poor neglected cousins of the Antiguans. The traditional independent turn of mind of Barbudans manifests itself today in the way the two islands have chosen to approach the question of tourism. Antigua has opened its arms wide to this means of economic advancement, while Barbuda is intent on keeping things more or less in the idyllic state they have always been. Barbudans look upon their land as communally owned, and local custom dictates that property can nly be leased and not sold to on-Barbudans, and then only by unanimous consent of all he inhabitants. This has effectively served to discourage eaer developers from outside he island. Today, with a few xceptions, the island is essentially devoid of any major esort developments.

But visitors staying at Baruda's couple of hotels like it xactly that way. They come o enjoy the miles and miles of uperb beaches (better than Antigua's, say the Barbudans roudly), to hunt deer or wild igs, to shoot duck and other vild fowl or to go deep-sea fishing. They glory in the snorkelling and scuba-diving around the reefs, explore the more than 70 underwater shipwrecks, go caving, horseback riding, bird watching, or just idle the time away in beachcombing. This is the quintessential island paradise; if you want a lot of action, you go elsewhere—Antigua is just 15 minutes away by regularly scheduled daily air shuttle. But Barbuda's visitors overwhelmingly choose to stay put—standard Caribbean resorts can be found any day but unspoiled places like Barbuda are rare indeed.

A Brief History

Prehistory	Barbuda is first inhabited by Carib Indians.
16th–17th centuries	Although the Spanish are thought to have discovered the island in the 16th century, the first attempt at settlement by a European was made in 1628 by an Englishman, but failed because of the hostile Indians.
17th–18th centuries	In 1680 the British lease Barbuda to the English Codrington brothers, Christopher and John, who established the island's first sugar plantation 11 years earlier. However, the plantation system is not compatible with Barbuda's infertile soil and poor rainfall. The Codringtons use Barbuda instead to grow supplies and raise animals for their Antigua sugar estates. They also breed slaves, who are known for their physical fitness and tall stature.
19th century	The British abolish slavery on Antigua in 1834 but neglect to do so on Barbuda. The Barbuda slaves riot, as the Codringtons refuse them land to cultivate and at the same time cease to pay for their upkeep. The British

are forced to intervene, and to raise money they lease Barbuda to private business entrepreneurs, whose ventures fail. The government then attempts to attach Barbuda to other territories in the Caribbean, and the island passes from one to another for almost three decades. Finally in 1860 Barbuda is made a dependency of Antigua.

20th century · In 1903 Barbuda is declared a Crown Estate, but by 1980 the island feels so neglected economically that it threatens to secede. The negotiations that follow result in 1981 in an independent state, within the Commonwealth, comprised of Barbuda, Antigua and Redonda. Despite some misgivings on the part of Barbudans, talk of secession is forgotten as the Antigua-based government gradually assures Barbuda of more equitable economic treatment. The new republic joins the United Nations and the Organization of East Caribbean States.

Sightseeing

An unspoiled island making few concessions to tourism, Barbuda nonetheless offers many diversions to keep the visitor happily occupied. Just about everything is within a few miles from **Codrington**, the island's only village, situated at the edge of a lagoon.

The notorious Codrington family built **Highland House** around 1750 on the northwest shoulder of the elevated Highlands region. Today it lies in ruins, almost entirely overgrown. Floors, lower walls and a large cistern remain.

The island's **Martello Tower**, popularly known as River Fort, may have been built by the Spanish before the English occupied the island. It towers over the south coast, a massive structure with thick walls that look like they could resist any attack, although nowhere in the island's history is there any indication that the tower had to defend the island from anyone. Nonetheless, it was probably a useful landmark to guide friendly vessels approaching from the south.

As the island is composed of coral limestone, it abounds in caves and sink holes. The largest, and probably the most interesting to explore, is **Darby Sink Cave**, located due north of Highland House. The sink hole measures about 300 feet (90 m.) in diameter and 80 feet (25 m.) deep, and the descent to the bottom is not difficult. The region's cave network is virtually unexplored, and therefore there are no maps to follow. Fans of speleology and potholing can discover for themselves whether the rumours of underground lakes, sightless freshwater crustaceans and prehistoric rock carvings have any substance to them.

While the beaches are spectacular everywhere on the island, and those on the south and west coasts run for several miles, the smaller ones on the east coast between **Hog Point** and **Rubbish Bay** have a special feature. Swept by the Atlantic, these beaches receive flotsam originating in Western Europe, West Africa and all of the North Atlantic. Beachcombers will have a ball.

Nature lovers will want to take a boat across the lagoon from Codrington to visit the **frigate bird sanctuary**. The frigate bird is a large seabird, mainly black with a long forked tail. When the males court, they inflate their throat pouch so that it appears like a bright red balloon. The bird gets its name from the frigate ship of a pirate, as its behavior is equally unsporting: it steals

fish from other seabirds in midair.

The Barbudans have inaugurated a yearly cultural festival called **Caribana**. You may be lucky to have your visit coincide with this celebration of drama and music.

Excursion to Antigua

A mere 15 minutes by air shuttle brings you to Antigua, Barbuda's sister island and seat of its government.

Antigua was much sought

The Kingdom of Redonda

Barbuda is united with Antigua and Redonda in a three-in-one nation. Of the three parts, Redonda is the most curious—an uninhabited, one-square-mile rock, which has its own king.

The kingdom was founded in 1865 by Matthew Dowdy Shiel, a descendant of Irish kings, who sailed past the island. Later, he landed on the island and crowned his infant son, Matthew Phipps, King Felipe I. The title passed to the British poet John Gawsworth, who, as King Juan I, created a number of dukes and duchesses from among his literary friends. The latest king is John M. Wynne-Tyson of Sussex—King Juan II. His subjects consist of a few goats.

---

after by the French, Spanish and British in their battle for supremacy in the Caribbean. You could hide and defend a whole fleet in land-locked English Harbour. Today the only fleets are those of yachts, and English Harbour has become the base for blue-water cruising.

St. John's is a neatly laid-out town and easy to explore on foot. If you are lucky enough to arrive here early on a Friday or Saturday, you will see it come alive at the **Public Market**. This colourful and bustling market is the focal point of the city life, where housewives bargain noisily with farmers over fruit and vegetables, while fishing boats land their catch at the nearby pier. It's worth visiting **St. John's Cathedral**, one of the most impressive Anglican churches in the Caribbean. It was originally constructed in 1683 and has been rebuilt twice since. The figures of St. John the Baptist and St. John the Divine at the south gate are said to have been captured from one of Napoleon's ships.

Another point of interest is the 18th-century **Court House**, now housing the **National Museum** and **National Archives.** The edifice contains portraits supposedly painted by Sir Joshua Reynolds. To the north-west, overlooking the harbour, are the ruins of old **Fort James**, which once guarded St. John's in pirate days. Built in 1703, vestiges of the ramparts still stand and its cannons point out to sea.

It's a 30-mile (48-km.) round-trip to one of the most interesting historical sites of all the Caribbean—**Nelson's Dockyard** at **English Harbour**. The dockyard was developed in the mid-18th century to shelter English warships protecting the West Indies possessions. It saw its heyday during the War of American Independence and the wars against the French. Restored during the fifties, it now looks much as it did in Nelson's day. The best restored building is the **Admiral's House**, furnished in the style of the period and used as a nautical museum. An excellent vantage point from which to sip a rum punch and reflect over the great sea battles of the past is the elegant **Admiral's Inn** with its romantic atmosphere.

Biscuit-coloured **Clarence House**, built for Prince William Henry, Duke of Clarence, later William IV of England, stands on a small hill which commands a fine view of the dockyard. Overlooking English Harbour on **Shirley Heights** are the ruins of the garrison buildings and fortifications that protected the naval base. The view from here is stupendous—inland you can see most of Antigua, and out to sea you can make out the island of Guadeloupe.

Eating Out

This sparsely populated island has very little in the way of restaurants, but you'll find one on the waterfront near Codrington. In addition, the few hotels on the island welcome tourists in their dining rooms, even if they are not staying at the hotel.

Seafood is readily available, the star of the island being the **lobster** that is trapped locally. **Red snapper** and **curried conch** are also highly recommended. In season be sure to order **venison**, which comes from the island's own game reserve.

Favourite island dishes with a spicy touch are pepperpot, a succulent stew of pork and beef which reputedly originated with the South American Indians, seasoned rice, *coo-coo* (cornmeal dumplings) and *souse,* which is boiled pig's head and trotters served with lime juice, sliced cucumber and pepper.

Doucanah is a sweet potato dumpling flavoured with coconut and raisins, traditionally boiled in banana leaves. It's served with codfish, anchovies and eggplant.

Fresh vegetables and fruits are plentiful, including tropical favourites such as **mango** and **papaya**.

Rum makes the Caribbean go round. A little of it goes a long way in punches, daiquiris and *piña coladas*.

Shopping

Codrington boasts a Handicrafts Centre, so this is the spot to purchase **straw goods** such as bags, hats, slipper and mats made of sisal, palm fronds, palmetto or banana leaves. **Woven and knitted fabrics** are worked from the locally grown sea-island cotton and are among the best buys here.

Colourful Barbuda **postage stamps**—collectors' items—are available from the Post Office in Codrington.

Practical Information

Bank. First Bank of Barbuda. Open 8 a.m. to 1 p.m. Monday to Friday, and 3 to 5 p.m. Friday.

Climate. Generally dry and pleasant with little year-round temperature variation. Temperatures range in winter from the low 70s F (20s C) to low 80s F (27° C and above); in summer, five degrees F (3 C) warmer. The island is always cooled by trade winds.

Currency. The official currency is the East Caribbean dollar (EC$). Major credit cards are accepted in tourist hotels, as are U.S. and Canadian dollars.

Post Office. Open 8 a.m. to noon and 1 to 4 p.m. Monday to Friday.

Telephoning Home. Barbuda (area code 809) is linked to the U.S. network.

Transport. Barbuda is accessible via daily flights from Antigua.

BERMUDA
HAMILTON, ST. GEORGE'S TOWN

Introduction

From Acacia to Zygophylla-
ceae, the flowers, shrubs and
trees of beautiful Bermuda
come in more than a thousand
varieties. Bougainvillea, hibiscus, oleander and morning
glory bloom in profusion
along the narrow island roads,
and local gardeners carefully
tend bird-of-paradise flowers,
frangipani and orchids. With
its soothing climate, pink
beaches and cozy air of prosperity, you'd think this very
British mid-Atlantic colony
could want for nothing. But
Bermuda has no skyscrapers,
no parking meters, no neon
signs. No pollution or slums.
It doesn't even have income
tax!

With an area of only about
20 square miles (52 sq. km.)
—slightly smaller than Man-
hattan Island or the Channel island of Guernsey—Bermuda makes a significant
mark on the world not only as
a coveted holiday destination.
It's also a centre of high finance, with gross domestic
product per capita one of the
richest in the world. Tax ad-
vantages and flawless satellite communications have in-
duced a distinguished stream
of corporations to set up offices on the island, contribut-
ing to the colony's impressive
invisible exports.

Bermuda is not a single
island but a long, curving archipelago of more than 100.
The seven principal islands
are linked by causeways
and bridges (including what's
claimed to be the world's
smallest drawbridge), giving
the impression of one lush
body of land attended by
throngs of picturesque islets
and reefs.

Those reefs, considered the
most northerly coral outcrops
in the world, account for the
unease with which early sailors approached Bermuda. The
first inhabitants, in 1609, were
castaways, and hundreds of
wrecks followed—to the delight of modern treasure-
hunters.

Like their forebears, who
were sailors, fishermen, priva-
teers and, frankly, pirates,
the Bermudians are hardy and
self-reliant. They respect the
old traditions, the ceremonial
occasions, the courtesies. Hel-
meted "bobbies" in Bermuda
shorts direct the traffic, which
keeps to the left as in the
mother country. The judges
wear white wigs. And the
name of the national game is
cricket.

A Brief History

16th century	Bermuda appears on an Italian map in 1511. An eyewitness report of the uninhabited island comes from Henry May, an Englishman shipwrecked in 1593, on his return to Europe.
17th century	*Sea Venture*, carrying English colonists to Virginia, goes aground near Bermuda in 1609, reputedly inspiring Shakespeare to write *The Tempest*. The first colonists specifically destined for Bermuda arrive in 1612. In 1684 the Bermuda Company loses its charter and the island becomes a British colony enjoying a degree of self-government.
18th century	London forbids Bermuda to trade with rebellious colonies of America, but 100 kegs of gunpowder reach the insurgents from the magazine in St. George's in 1775. Bermuda's future capital, Hamilton, is founded in 1793, eclipsing the historic town of St. George's.
19th century	With the loss of its American colonies, Britain turns Bermuda into the "Gibraltar of the West" from which Royal Navy ships strike U.S. targets in the War of 1812. Convicts from Britain join slaves from Africa in a mammoth project to build Britain's naval base and dockyard on Ireland Island. Slavery is abolished in 1834 but the prison ships remain until 1863. In the American Civil War, Bermuda plays an important role as supply base for Confederate forces.
20th century	German submarines in the two world wars threaten Bermuda's lifelines. After World War II, British military forces pull out of Bermuda, tourism booms, island self-government is strengthened, and "exempt companies" flock to Bermuda to take advantage of offshore financial advantages—and the climate.

Sightseeing

Bermuda's capital, **Hamilton,** sets the scale for the rest of the island. It's a unique historic town fronting a colourful harbour. Most of the buildings are low-lying wood and limestone houses, often adorned with decorative arcades or balconies, and tidy cottages with roofs "exactly the white of the icing on the cake," as a frequent Bermuda visitor, Mark Twain, described them. The furrowed roofs serve a special purpose here, channelling rainwater into underground tanks. Bermuda needs all the water the sky provides, for there are no rivers or lakes.

At the intersection of Queen and Front streets stands what is probably Bermuda's most photographed landmark, although it merits only limited aesthetic or historical interest. This is the **Birdcage,** a shaded platform for the policeman supervising the traffic.

Front Street, dividing the town from the harbourfront, has the air of an exotic trading port. And well it might: one strong reason for moving the colonial capital to Hamilton in 1815 was to keep a closer eye on all the smuggling. The 18th- and 19th-century buildings of Front Street, with their arcades, verandas and filigree, have survived many a drama.

Another important shopping street, **Queen Street,** contains historic buildings, exotic flora, and shops for tourists and locals. You can buy stamps for your postcards in the **Perot Post Office,** a nicely restored white house with big black shutters. Here in 1848 Bermuda's Postmaster, William B. Perot, issued and signed the colony's first postage stamps, now considered exquisite rarities in the philatelic world.

Queen Street climbs as far inland as Church Street, a main east-west thoroughfare so named because of its many churches. The most spectacular building here is the modern **Hamilton City Hall,** opened in 1960, topped by a weathervane of the sailing ship *Sea Venture.*

The tallest tower on Hamilton's skyline belongs to the Anglican **Bermuda Cathedral.** The first church on this site was burnt down in 1884 by an arsonist so broadminded in his grudges that he also set fire to the Catholic church and some non-denominational buildings as well.

St. George's Town

Older and smaller than Hamilton, **St. George's Town,** Bermuda's original capital, makes for a delightful stroll.

On tiny **Ordnance Island,** an old wooden **sailing ship** has been recreated—a replica of *Deliverance,* built by survivors of the original wreck of the *Sea Venture.* The island's ucking stool, also a repli-a, simulates the punishment neted out 300 years ago to hronic gossips. The island's founder and owner of the *Sea Venture*, Sir George Somers, has been honoured by a bronze statue, erected to commemorate the island's 375th anniversary in 1984.

Across the bridge on the "mainland", **King's Square** provides another of those irresistible picture possibilities—tourists pose as "prisoners"

in the **stocks.** Among the historic buildings in the area: the restored 18th-century **Town Hall,** the **Old State House** (built in 1620), and **St. Peter's Church.** The oldest object in this church was an antique even when the early settlers brought it here: a stone font used before the era of Columbus. The **churchyard** alongside is well worth a browse; the tombstones tell of epidemics, shipwrecks, war and assassination.

The old Globe Hotel flourished during the American Civil War when St. George's was a boom town—an offshore supply base for the blockaded Confederate States. The building is now the **Confederate Museum,** run by the Bermuda National Trust, documenting Bermuda's role in the War Between the States, and the Confederacy's struggle in general.

Harrington Sound

When conditions are too rough beyond Bermuda's shores, it's usually clear sailing in **Harrington Sound,** an inland sea popular with boatmen. The southernmost end of the Sound is the site of **Devil's Hole,** Bermuda's oldest tourist attraction. For more than 150 years the owners of this collapsed cave have been showing off the curiosity—and charging admission since 1843. The deep natural pool contains a multitude of fish who've been hopelessly spoiled by the largesse of all the tourists.

On the north side of Flatts inlet, Bermuda's **Aquarium** is open 364 days a year (the fish take Christmas off). The show features creatures as lovable as parrotfish and angelfish, and villains like the enormous blue-eyed green moray eel.

Outside, the Aquarium run a zoo and an aviary. Watc the spontaneous races of th Galapagos tortoises; thes huge landlubber reptiles thriv in the Bermuda environmen The aviary's cockatoos an giant macaws say "hello" ar "sorry".

Among the sights at Ba ley's Bay, the **Bermuda M seum** (at the intersection North Shore Road and th charmingly named Fractio Street) concentrates on the li and times of notable Berm dians. The house is filled wit old Bermuda furniture, acce sories and handicrafts.

Nearby, a small **perfun factory** is set in a cheerf garden. If the real-life zephy of Bermuda weren't alread so fragrant, the sweet atm sphere of this cottage indust would be even more remar able. Among the scents bo tled here: passion flower, Ea ter lily, oleander, jasmine ar sweet pea.

The stretch of land betwee Harrington Sound and Cast Harbour is riddled with cave **Crystal Caves,** discovered 1907, makes the most of th stalagmites and dripping sta lactites. Down the road, **Le mington Caves** uses lighting e fects to dramatize the fantas underworld.

eland Island

he **Royal Naval Dockyard**—mbol of what was once the ibraltar of the West—is now e centre of some of the Is-nds' liveliest tourist attrac-ons. Restored historic build-gs, museums, an open mar-et, craftsmen at work, res-urants and shops, military igeants—all this and more fer plenty to do and see.

ating Out

ermuda's many restaurants n the gamut from candlelit *iute cuisine* to the most own-to-earth cafés. The ices, too, vary from daunt-g to moderate.

In mid-Atlantic, you'll xpect to find tasty local fish n the menu. Be sure to sk what's fresh today—Ber-iuda red snapper, rock-fish, ahoo, tuna steak, or lobster season. But much of ie seafood is habitually im-orted—for instance giant irimps, scallops, Dover sole nd crab.

A favourite Bermuda sea-ood dish, mussel pie, is a ightly curried thick clam ew in a pastry shell. Another land speciality, Bermuda hark, is cooked with onions, eppers, parsley, thyme and mustard greens.

Seafood provides some rousing local soups, as well: Bermuda fish chowder, a highly spiced thick broth usually served with a dash of sherry or rum; and conch chowder, based on imported mollusks.

For meat-eaters all the familiar cuts and recipes are on the menu: steaks and chops, baby lamb, veal *scallopine* and chicken *cacciatore*. On the side, look for mild Bermuda onions, pawpaw (papaya), plantain, christophine and similar exotica.

Drinks

A Rum Swizzle is a thoroughly Bermuda way of enhancing the appetite. It may contain two types of rum, lime juice, fruit brandy, a sweet syrup, and a dash of bitters —and plenty of crushed ice.

With dinner you can choose wine, beer (American or European), imported mineral water, fruit punch, or even pure Bermuda rainwater.

Shopping

The understated atmosphere adds to the pleasure of shopping in Bermuda. It's like London's Bond Street without

Value Added Tax. Incidentally, the price on the tag is definitive, as no taxes are levied and no haggling is involved.

Though goods from Britain and Europe are the biggest attractions for visiting shoppers, don't overlook the work of Bermuda's artisans. Among the offerings:

Cedar candlesticks, goblets, letter openers and stylized sailing boats.

Condiments. The local sherry pepper sauce, hot rum pepper sauce, etc., in travel packs.

Coral and **seashells,** collected for tourists too rushed to do their own beachcombing.

Fashion. Island themes or flowers figure in Bermuda-made scarves, skirts and hand bags.

Jewellery. Bermuda arti sans work with gold, silve precious stones, beads an minute sea shells.

Perfume. Island flower distilled into scent—or majo bargains in French perfume

Straw goods. Bags, hats an knick-knacks, hand-plaited.

Imported Goods

If you've done your home work on comparative pric ing you may find bargain in cameras and accessories china, crystal, fashions fo women, figurines, sweater and watches. Duty-free li quor, available only in five bottle packs, runs from Scot tish and American spirits t locally blended rum.

Practical Information

Banks and currency: Bermuda's banks are open from 9.30 a.m. to 3 p.m Monday through Friday, with an extra hour every Friday from 4.30 t 5.30 p.m. The Bermuda dollar is pegged to the U.S. dollar, and in fac greenbacks are accepted everywhere on the island. But be sure t convert all your Bermuda money before you leave.

Shopping: Shops and stores are generally open Monday throug Saturday from 9 or 9.15 a.m. to 5 or 5.30 p.m. Some stores reopen in th evening when cruise ships are in port.

KRALENDIJK

Bonaire, Netherlands Antilles

Introduction

Bonaire boasts some of the most beautiful fringing reefs in the Caribbean—and more flamingoes than people. The whole island, surrounded by crystal-clear waters, forms a natural sanctuary. Experts rate it one of the world's top spots for snorkelling and scuba-diving. Bird-watchers come to view the flocks of pink flamingoes feeding in the briny lagoons.

Lying 50 miles (80 km.) off the Venezuelan coast, Bonaire is the easternmost of the Netherlands Antilles trio known as the ABCs (the others are Aruba and Curaçao). The island curves round with its back to the trade winds, sheltering the tiny capital of Kralendijk in the central crook of its western curve. Across the natural harbour from Kralendijk (pronounced Kraalendike) lies the uninhabited rocky islet of Little Bonaire, a favourite picnic and diving spot.

The narrow island, 24 miles (40 km.) long, is the dryest in the Caribbean, strewn with cactus and prickly pear. The south is sandy and flat, running down to salt pans, while the north

Bonaire's slaves once called these simple dwellings home.

overed with rocky acacia-clad ills, culminating in 784-foot 39-m.) Mount Brandaris.

Because of the abundant oral growth and variety of sh, the Netherlands Antilles ational Parks Foundation has stablished a programme for eef protection. The waters ound the coast have been eclared a Marine Park. Spear shing is strictly forbidden. ollection of black coral or ther corals is allowed only or the Handicrafts Founda- on. Forty diving spots have een designated and mooring uoys placed to prevent anchor amage to the reefs.

Bonaire's chequered history successive Spanish and utch hands is reflected in the omposition of its 10,000 in- abitants of mixed Indian, Af- can and European descent. any have Spanish names and e Catholic by religion. But l are Dutch. The island forms 1 autonomous part of the Kingdom of the Netherlands. Dutch is the official language, though Spanish and English are also spoken and among themselves the people speak a dialect known as Papiamento.

North of Kralendijk, a stor- age depot has been built for transhipment of oil from Af- rica and the Middle East des- tined for the United States. To the south of the capital soar the giant antennae of a short wave broadcasting station. Other- wise the island's economy de- pends on the production of salt and the export of aloes for pharmaceuticals.

Recently, tourism has begun to take over, spurred by the div- ing fame of the reefs and the prolific bird life. Flamingo Air- port has been built near Kralen- dijk to receive the international flow of visitors. On an island so arid that only goats and birds seem to prosper, the advent of tourism comes as a welcome boon.

Brief History

efore 15th ntury	Bonaire is settled by Caiquetios Indians, an Arawak tribe from South America, who carve inscriptions in the island caves.
th and 16th nturies	A Spanish landing party from Amerigo Vespucci's expedition discovers the island in 1499. The Indians are deported to Hispaniola to work in the copper mines.

17th and 18th centuries	The Dutch succeed the Spanish in 1623 and start producing salt, using imported slaves. Spanish and English pirates call regularly at the island to requisition food.
19th century	The British take over and leave the island with 30 slaves to a U.S. planter. The Dutch return in 1815. With the abolition of slavery in 1863, the salt trade becomes uneconomic and is abandoned.
20th century	The salt trade is revived. Tourism expands and bring new sources of revenue.

Sightseeing

Kralendijk means "coral dike", and it is easy to see why: the beaches that sweep away to north and south are edged by coral reefs running out 100 yards (91 m.) into the blue-green sea. The town's population of 1,600 live in trim colour-washed houses set in neat gardens. Down by the harbour, the bustling **fish market** is housed in a miniature Greek temple. Nearby, **Fort Oranje** displays a 150-year-old cannon. The **Folklore Institute** is worth a visit to see artefacts from Bonaire homes and to learn something of the island's early history.

But you won't have come to Bonaire just to see Kralendijk. Those who want to go snorkelling or scuba-diving will head straight to Lac Bay or one of the diving spots along the reefs. Those interested in birding will take off for the salt pans in the south or the Washington Slagbaai National Park in the north. And those who want to see a bit of everything will take a day trip right round the island and a tour of the reefs in a glass-bottomed boat.

Heading north from Kralendijk along the coast road, stop from time to time to look down 100 feet (30 m.) through the translucent waters to the reef below, a paradise for skin divers who can spend whole days cruising through canyons of coral that swarm with multi-coloured tropical fish.

Civilization returns with a jolt as you pass the storage depot where supertankers unload oil for onward shipment to North America. But nature takes over again at **Goto Meer**, a blue salt lake, edged by brilliant roseate flamingoes feeding long-legged in the shallows. Occasionally great flights of the

...e underwater life round Bon-...re constantly fascinates.

...rds take off, unravelling like ...piece of pink knitting and cir-...ng round to land again and ...sume their feast of algae.

The lake lies on the edge of ...e **Washington Slagbaai Na-...nal Park,** a 13,500-acre (548-...) reserve with Mount Bran-...ris as its centre point. A ...otorable road runs through ...e park's rugged wilderness

where a rich variety of birds (130 species have been counted) can be observed, including parrots, parakeets and humming birds.

You may wonder at the name: "Washington" was the headquarters of a plantation known as "America" that once occupied the north of the island; Slagbaai is a Dutch word meaning "slough", referring to the flamingo lake and marsh.

South of the park, you come to the little village of **Rincón,**

What to Look For

In the Sea

Antlers of **elkhorn coral,** spreading above the sea at low tide.

Boulders of **brain coral,** etched with convoluted patterns.

Beaked **parrot fish** feeding on algae along the reefs and excreting coral as fine sand.

Transparent **squid,** trailing tentacles.

Blue-spotted **jewelfish,** speeding through Gorgonian gardens of sea fans.

Black **sea urchins,** with long spiny prickles, that can inflict a nasty wound on divers foolish enough not to wear sandals.

On Land

Flamingoes on the salt lakes, sieving water through their hooked beaks to feed on the brine shrimps and algae which give them their startling pink colour.

Green **iguanas,** up to 5 feet (1½ m.) long, sunning themselves on the boulders in the rocky hills.

Vivid green **parakeets,** with orange heads, emerging from nests dug deep inside termite mounds.

Hermit crabs, which have no shell of their own but squeeze into any vacant shell that fits.

Brilliant yellow **warblers** flitting through the mesquite trees.

Tiny blue-tailed emerald **humming birds,** hovering over aloe flowers to sip the nectar.

once the home of black slaves who worked in the salt pans. From here you can visit **Boca Onima** on the east coast to view shallow caves with rock carvings coloured in red, the work of the original Indian inhabitants and estimated to date back more than 500 years. Archaeologists have so far failed to decipher them.

From **Seroe Largu,** further south, you can look out over Kralendijk and Little Bonaire and westwards as far as Curaçao on a fine day.

A trip round the south of the island starts once again from

ralendijk. An arc of man-
roves curves round the lagoon
Lac Bay, where the fisher-
en harvest conch and leave
e shells piled up on the beach.
his is the ideal spot for a swim
, safe clear water—or a trip
, a glass-bottomed boat. Seas
ash in and out over a coral
ef into a bay, making it the
erfect nursery for fish and a
avourite diving spot.

From Lac Bay the road runs
outh to the **Flamingo Sanc-
uary** at Pekel Meer, where
ou'll find the largest colony
f flamingoes in the western
emisphere. In spring, the fla-
iingoes build their round mud
ests and raise their young on
he salt flats where the local salt
ompany has set aside 125 acres
50 ha.) as a reserve.

The **Willemstoren Light-
ouse,** built in 1837, rises on

the coast just before you reach
the main **salt pans** ringed by
pyramids of white salt. The salt
is deposited by the sea in a
series of ocean-washed ponds
and dried into crystals by sun
and wind.

Three tall stone **obelisks** on
the shore in the Dutch colours
of red, white and blue once
guided ships to their moorings
by the salt ponds. Along the
beach, the remains of 19th-
century slave huts have been
restored and rethatched. The
slaves worked here all week and
at weekends trekked 15 miles
(24 km.) across the island to
their homes in Rincón.

*Reactivation of the salt indus-
try has not disturbed the peace-
loving flamingoes.*

Eating Out

There's an international flavour to food on Bonaire, with a bias towards Dutch and Indonesian dishes. Fish is fresh-caught and excellent. The well-seasoned goat stew is tasty and more tender than you might imagine.

If you want to sample something really local, order the pickled conch. Or try conch stew, made from meat winkled out of the huge conch shells you see at Lac Bay.

Indonesian *rijsttafel*, Chinese dishes and barbecued beef and chicken are available in hotels. You can even get American-style steak and hot dogs.

The island is too barren to produce much in the way of tropical fruits, but there is wide variety of standard desserts, including ice-cream. And of course, Dutch cheese.

Shopping

Handicrafts to look for a coral jewellery, shell necklaces and bracelets, polished conshells, driftwood carvings an wrap-around skirts with locdesigns.

Other souvenirs include shirts and tea-towels decorated with the ubiquitous flaming motif, divers' watches and tortoise-shell trinkets.

Low duty makes for attractive prices for watches, perfumes, china, glass and cameras.

Practical Information

Climate. Average temperature is 82 °F (28 °C); water temperature 26 °C. Light rainfall only in October and November.

Clothing. Summer dress throughout the year with sweater or jacket for cool evenings. There is a constant sea breeze. If you're interested in the flamingoes and other birds, don't forget binoculars.

Currency. Netherlands Antilles florin (NAf), also called *guilder* divided into 100 cents. U.S. dollars are accepted.

Banks. Banking hours: 8.30 a.m. to midday, and 2 to 4 p.m. Monday to Friday.

CARTAGENA

Colombia

Introduction

The walled city of Cartagena, one of the oldest in the Americas, has seen four centuries of tumultuous history. The riches of the New World—fabulous shipments of emeralds and gold—passed through this Caribbean stronghold, founded for the glory of Spain by the conquistador Pedro de Heredia in 1533.

Right from the beginning, the French and English coveted the place. Robert Baal and Martin Côte, John Hawkins and Sir Francis Drake, Baron de Pointis and Sir Edward Vernon all tried their hand at taking it, with varying degrees of success. A sophisticated system of fortification was developed, but would-be usurpers were not deterred. Townsfolk relied on the Virgin of Candelaria for deliverance from plague and pirates, and indeed, the city's survival was little short of a miracle.

Today's Cartagena is a sprawling town of 500,000 inhabitants, a bustling maritime and industrial centre. And yet the past is still important here. Visitors to the Caribbean port find themselves transported back in history as they wander along the twisting,

treets of the old city with its mposing architecture. In co--peration with the National ourist Corporation, many uildings of the colonial era ave been restored and opened o the public. This has been a oon to the tourist industry, n increasingly important element in Cartagena's economic equation.

But Cartagena has more han monuments to offer. The egacy of Spain is as strong as the predilection for bullfights, *paella* and *sangría*. Local holidays are celebrated with gay abandon. People take to the streets, dancing to the sound of *maracas* and drums as befits the African heritage of much of the coastal population.

There's nothing like a fiesta to reveal the real Cartagena. Yet even on the most ordinary day, the city has a certain magic, an undeniable allure.

A Brief History

6th-18th centuries	Cartagena is founded by Pedro de Heredia in 1533. By the end of the century the city becomes Spain's principal South American port, the most important centre for the slave trade and seat of the Inquisition. Naturally such wealth and power invite acts of piracy, notably Francis Drake's 1586 incursion, and the Spanish are compelled to fortify the town. In 1697 and 1741 Cartagena is again besieged, first by the French and then the British, but manages to resist on the second occasion. Together with Panama and Venezuela, Colombia forms the Viceroyalty of New Granada.
19th century	In 1810 Colombia and Venezuela begin the fight for independence from Spain, a struggle led by the Venezuelan Simón Bolívar. Cartagena finally wins freedom from Spanish rule in 1821. The town's fortunes begin to decline towards the middle of the century, when it is supplanted by the port of Barranquilla.
20th century	In 1903 Panama (still united with Colombia) stages a successful bid for independence. Colombia quickly recovers from the loss and goes on to become one of the world's biggest producers of coffee and emeralds.

Sightseeing

Most of Cartagena's historic sights lie within the old walled city, one of the best preserved in all of Latin America. This warren of narrow, twisting streets comprises three distinct districts: El Centro, formerly the aristocratic neighbourhood, San Diego, once reserved for the clerical and mercantile classes, and Getsamaní, built in the 17th century with modest, one-storey artisans' houses or *casas bajas*.

Situated on a triangle of land that projects into the Caribbean Sea, the old city is also bordered by the Bahía de las Ánimas (an arm of the Bahía de Cartagena), lagoons and a lake. The surrounding wall extends for some seven miles, averaging about 40 feet high and 55 feet wide. Construction began in 1634 and continued for just over 100 years.

Beyond the confines of the old city stretch the residential districts of La Manga and La Popa, developed at the turn of the century, and thoroughly modern El Laguito, with its skyscrapers, luxury hotels, casinos, restaurants and beaches. But it is on old Cartagena and a few outlying sights that we focus our attention.

For nearly four centuries a monastery has stood atop l Popa hill, at 492 feet the hig est eminence in Cartagen There's no better vanta; point for views of the city ar bay. The monastery churc houses the image of the Virg of Candelaria, credited wi Cartagena's deliverance fro plague and pirates. Every yea on Candlemas Day (Februar 2) the virgin is venerated in spectacular candlelit proce sion that winds its way up th hill to the church.

Just outside the city wal lies the most impregnable ba tion of the Spanish Main: **Ca tillo de San Felipe de Baraja** The fort rises a lofty 135 fe above sea level on the summ of San Lázaro hill. The de fences were completed in 165 only to be reduced to ruins 4 years later by the French p rate Baron de Pointis. A pro gramme of strengthening an expansion was undertaken i the 1760's, once again er abling San Felipe to withstan marauders in pursuit of th treasure that passed throug Cartagena en route to Spair

You'll want to explor the massive battlements an maze of subterranean tunnel apartments and store rooms Regular "Sound and Light performances highlight th fort's historical associations

typified by the statue of the Spanish admiral Blas de Lezo at the entrance. In 1741 this one-eyed, one-armed, one-legged hero of Cartagena encouraged the citizenry to resist a debilitating siege of 56 days led by Sir Edward Vernon and troops 27,000 strong.

Puente Heredia leads from San Felipe across the Laguna de San Lázaro to the Getsemaní district of the old city with its distinctive architecture. It is unwise to wander about here, though, as the area has a high incidence of petty crime.

The **Convento de San Pedro Claver** marks the southern perimeter of El Centro. The monastery is dedicated to San Pedro Claver (1580–1654), a Jesuit known as the "slave of slaves", who devoted his life to the Africans brought in bondage to Cartagena.

A particularly impressive section of the **city wall** runs north and east alongside Paseo de la Muralla to Plaza de las Bóvedas—in full sweeping view of the harbour and bay. Cars are permitted to drive along the rampart, which reaches 60 feet at its widest point. In keeping with the changing times, the dungeons at the base of the wall have been converted from cheerless prison cells to flashy souvenir shops. Buyers beware.

A statue of Simón Bolívar graces the plaza that bears his name. To one side of the square stands the **Palacio de la Inquisición,** the Baroque edifice constructed in the early 1700's for the Holy Office. The magnificent carved stone portal, a masterful expression of the Baroque style, was completed in 1776.

Instruments of torture and other exhibits on display trace the cruel history of the Inquisition in Cartagena, where more than 700 so-called heretics died. The lavish living quarters of the Chief Inquisitor can also be seen. Space has been set aside for an interesting museum of pre-Colombian and colonial art and artefacts. The star exhibit is a receipt for a bribe of 10 million pesos signed by Sir Francis Drake, who threatened to burn Cartagena to the ground in 1586.

Another landmark holds down the north-eastern corner of Plaza de Bolívar: the 16th-century **cathedral.** Drake inflicted serious damage on the structure during negotiations for the infamous settlement of 1586, but repairs were completed by 1612. Severe without, richly ornamented within,

Cartagena's Renaissance cathedral (restored and altered early this century) boasts a gilded Baroque altar and pulpit of Carrara marble.

Colombia's National Tourist Corporation makes its headquarters in the **Casa del Marqués de Valdehoyos** (Calle de la Factoría), the restored residence of a flour merchant and slave trader. This superb example of colonial domestic architecture features hanging balconies and latticework windows, thick walls, high ceilings and attractive interior patios. Handicraft and souvenir shops have been installed on the premises.

Eating Out

The gastronomic pleasures of Cartagena may be as simple as a snack of fresh fried fish from a beachside food stall or as sumptuous as a leisurely meal in one of the fine restaurants of the old city or Bocagrande district.

Cazuela de frutas del mar, a kind of bouillabaisse, may include squid, clams, oysters —even barracuda. *Viuda de pescado* is fish stew. Colombians have a weakness for *paella,* especially when it contains generous amounts of jumbo shrimp and Caribbean crawfish.

Sobrebarriga, steak with onions and cumin, is served with *papas chorreadas,* potatoes boiled and covered with a sauce of shallots, tomatoes, cheese, coriander and cream. *Aguacate picante* combines avocados, onions, green peppers, bacon, tomato sauce and spices in a cooked dish that is served as a vegetable. *Choclo,* roasted ears of sweet corn, and *frijoles,* beans prepared in a variety of ways, accompany many meat specialities.

The Colombians eat *tortillas de maíz* (sweet corn pancakes) with cream and parsley. *Arepas,* sweet corn cutlets fried or baked, are also popular.

Typical sweets include coconut pie, *dulce de coco*—coconut pudding with raisins and cloves—and strawberries with sweetened whipped cream.

Be sure to sample the exotic array of fresh fruit juices. Cooling *sapicón,* a fruit drink, contains chunks of fresh fruit. Club Colombia beer is a favourite thirst quencher and the local rum is good. But nothing can compare with espresso coffee *(tinto),* Colombia's famed export.

Shopping

Cartagena's better shops are to be found in the El Centro district of the old city (in and near Plaza de Bolívar) and to the south in Bocagrande. Colombian emeralds can be purchased locally in a range of prices and qualities, together with a selection of gold jewellery and gold and silver trinkets. Pre-colombian and colonial antiques and reproductions are offered for sale, as are contemporary works of Latin American art. Cartagena excels in leather goods, as well as articles of crocodile, alligator and snakeskin. But handicrafts may make the most tempting buys of all: wool rugs, *blusas* and *ruanas* or ponchos, hammocks, articles of straw and native fibres.

Practical Information

Currency: Peso (symbolized $) = 100 centavos. Coins: 5, 10, 20, 25, 50 centavos; 1, 2, 5 pesos. Notes: 1, 2, 5, 10, 20, 50, 100, 500, 1,000, 2,000 pesos. For exchange purposes, it is advisable to use U.S. dollars, either in cash or traveller's cheques.

Crime and theft: Be on your guard against pickpockets and thieves. It is unwise to wear jewellery, nor should you carry valuables or large amounts of cash. The old city can be dangerous after dark; the Getsemaní district is considered unsafe in the daytime as well.

SAN ANDRES ISLAND

Colombia

Introduction

Pirates once found a secure hideaway on remote San Andrés and famed buccaneer Henry Morgan is said to have stashed away treasure worth millions in an underwater cave. Some may still dream of discovering chestfuls of gold doubloons and caskets of gems. But most visitors are content to enjoy the natural delights of this enchanting little coral island.

The main island of a small archipelago belonging to Colombia, San Andrés occupies a strategic position in the western Caribbean, 118 miles (190 km.) off the coast of Nicaragua. Warm blue seas, fine-grained white sandy beaches fringed by coconut palms, and a colourful underwater paradise are ideal for all water sports.

The 25,000 inhabitants are mainly black, Anabaptist by religion, many of them descendants of slaves brought over 300 years ago from Jamaica. They speak both English and Spanish—and among themselves a dialect all their own.

Only 8 miles (14 km.) long, the island depended mainly in the past on growing coconuts, sugar cane, cotton, oranges and copra. But tourism is overtaking these in importance. And since the declaration of a free trade zone in the 1950s, planeloads of shoppers regularly fly over from mainland Colombia on a spending spree.

The second island in the group, Providencia, smaller and more rugged than San Andrés lies some 50 miles (83 km.) to the north. Its isolation makes it an ideal holiday centre for those who want to get away from it all on lonely beaches or in remote valleys where waterfalls drop down sheer through tropical vegetation.

The narrow Aury channel separates Providencia from the third island, Santa Catalina, only a square kilometre in size, where the ruins of defence works built by Morgan's pirates are still visible. The archipelago is completed by 13 coral island reefs known as cays or keys, scattered round the three main islands.

A Brief History

16th century	Spanish explorers discover San Andrés on the eve of the feast of St Andrew in 1527 and name it in his honour.

17th century	English puritans fleeing persecution settle on the island in 1629 at about the same time as the *Mayflower* reaches the United States. Planters arrive with slaves from Jamaica to grow sugar cane. Buccaneers, led by privateer Henry Morgan, make the island a base for raids on Spanish colonies on the mainland, with the connivance of the English in Jamaica.
18th and 19th centuries	The islands are awarded to Spain in 1786 and become part of the new Republic of Colombia when it gains independence from Spain in 1821.
20th century	In the first half of the 20th century, the population declines through emigration. But from the 1950s regular air services end the archipelago's isolation and its declaration as a free trade zone swells the number of tourists.

Round the Island

The town of **San Andrés** fills the northernmost promontory of the island, between the bays of San Andrés and Sardinas and out to Paradise Point. International flights land at the airport only a few minutes walk from the town centre. From close by the air terminal the Avenue Colombia runs along the seafront into Avenue La Plaza, where clusters of small hotels and shops face the sea. Across Sardinas Bay lies the palm-fringed coral reef of **Johnny Cay,** a not-so-desert island, ideal for a picnic enlivened by strolling minstrels.

Don't miss the 20-minute boat ride to **Haynes Cay,** 5 miles (8 km.) from San Andrés town, where you can view the underwater marvels of reef life within the coral walls of a natural **Aquarium.** Snorkelling equipment can be hired on the spot.

A mini-range of hills runs down the length of the island. From **Loma Hill,** above San Andrés town, site of a Baptist church built in 1874, a magnificent view opens up over the oleander and orange trees to white beaches and the surf-edged blue sea breaking on the reefs below.

An asphalt road encircles the island of San Andrés along the coast; and you can see everything in a lazy afternoon. Stop at **Morgan's Cave** to look down into the underwater cavern where the famous pirate is said to have buried his treasure. Not a single doubloon or ingot has yet been recovered, but that doesn't stop divers from hoping.

Past **El Cove** on the west coast, where the waters are at their deepest, you reach the southernmost point of the island. Here you will find an extraordinary formation of little underground tunnels in the reef, ending in a single opening known as Hoyo Soplador or the **Blowhole,** where the wind forces the sea up in a jet of spray like a whale's spout.

Travelling up the eastern shore, you come to the peaceful picturesque fishing village of **San Luis.** Try some of the island's seafood dishes in one of the tiny restaurants.

Eating Out

Both San Andrés and Providencia specialize in seafood. Sample the delicious *Sopa de Cangrejo,* a soup of freshly caught crab; *rondón,* a stew prepared with coconut milk, fish, yuca (a local kind of potato) and bananas; and *dumpin* made of white flour and breadfruit. Desserts are prepared with local fruits.

Shopping

You can buy bargains from all over the world in the island's duty-free shops. This is the place to buy jewellery, particularly Colombian emeralds. You'll also find local handicrafts made from coconut shells and coral.

Practical Information

Climate: The day temperature is an even 27° C (80° F) for most of the year, tempered by cooling sea breezes. Dress is casual and light.

Currency: The Colombian peso.

Banks: Open 9 a.m. to 3 p.m., Monday to Friday.

WILLEMSTAD

Curaçao, Netherlands Antilles

Introduction

Often described as a fragment of Amsterdam set adrift in the West Indies, Willemstad is the most European of Caribbean cities. And somehow it manages to retain its old-world charm while forging ahead in the 20th century.

Curaçaoans seem particularly adept at reconciling the past and present. Lovely 18th-century Dutch colonial houses look out over St. Anna Bay (really an inlet connecting the Caribbean with the Schottegat harbour), while cruise ships and giant oil tankers glide by on their way to the world's second busiest port. Business is booming but landmarks are carefully preserved.

Willemstad is the capital of both the Netherlands Antilles and Curaçao. The island itself, 38 miles long and 7 miles wide, has a population of 160,000 made up of about 50 different nationalities. If you venture out into the countryside, you will find a few scattered wind mills, some old Dutch planta tion houses and a good deal of arid, windy land with cactu and *dividivi* trees. The scrawny *dividivi*, permanently bent at right angle by the wind, is something of an island trade mark.

The pragmatic nature of the Dutch has persisted here along with the gabled archi tecture. On cruise ship days the casino opens early to ac commodate eager gamblers and the shops, housed in gra cious, pastel-coloured build ings from another era, carr on through the usual lunch time pause. Many of the ol Dutch forts have been put t use as restaurants and on houses a hotel. Beauty an business manage to coexist i Willemstad.

A Brief History

15th–16th centuries
Curaçao is discovered in 1499 by Alonso de Ojeda, on of Columbus' lieutenants. Also along on the expeditio is Amerigo Vespucci, who goes ashore, meets th towering Caiquetio Indians and pronounces Curaça the "island of giants." Led by Juan de Ampues, th Spanish settle Curaçao in 1527 but they never mak very much of it.

7th–18th centuries	The Netherlands West India Company takes the island in 1634, chasing the Spaniards off to Latin America. Curaçao becomes the main Dutch trading base in the region. Peter Stuyvesant, better known for his subsequent assignment in New Amsterdam, is sent to the upcoming island as governor in 1642. The city of Willemstad grows up around Fort Amsterdam, as the Dutch build neat houses on carefully laid out streets resembling the ones they left behind. They also erect a series of forts. Jews from Spain and Portugal, fleeing the Inquisition, arrive in the 1650's to seek their fortunes in the tolerant Dutch colony. Willemstad flourishes as a trading centre—especially for slave-trading.
19th century	The British establish in 1800 a "protectorate" over Curaçao and take the island, briefly, during the Napoleonic wars. Treaty of Paris in 1815 restores Curaçao to Dutch hands. Slavery is abolished in 1863 and the island's economy goes into decline.
20th century	The Royal Dutch Shell Company selects Curaçao—with its fine harbour, political stability and choice location—as the site for a refinery to process Venezuelan oil. The petroleum industry brings prosperity to Curaçao; the people who come from all parts of the globe to work here bring a cosmopolitan tone. Curaçao and five other islands win autonomy from the Netherlands in 1954. They form the Netherlands Antilles, a parliamentary democracy with a governor appointed by the Dutch queen. And handsome, historic, worldly Willemstad is chosen as its capital.

Sightseeing

St. Anna Bay, actually a channel rather than a bay, runs right through the middle of Willemstad. On the east side is the Punda, the city's oldest district, on the west, the Otrabanda ("the other side"). Edged with fine Dutch colonial houses, the bustling bay provides the best show in town. A never-ending procession of small sailing boats, sleek cruise ships and lumbering oil tankers parades back and forth between the excellent deep-water port and the Caribbean Sea, with spectators nearly always around to watch the ships or browse in the shops near the **Queen Emma Pontoon Bridge.**

This floating bridge, which swings open on a hinge to let the ships by, was the ingenious idea of an enterprising American, Leonard B. Smith, the same man who brought ice and electricity to Curaçao. At first, back in 1888, they charged a toll: 2¢ for those wearing shoes but free for the barefooted, the laudable intention being to tax according to the ability to pay. But, it seems, the poor often borrowed or bought sandals so they could pay, while the well-heeled (financially) liked to take off their shoes and cross for nothing. The authorities eventually gave up and now all go free, shoes or not.

For many years, the Queen Emma was the bay's only bridge and every time it opened the traffic backed up for miles. In 1974, an arching, four-lane bridge was inaugurated for vehicular traffic. With it 160-foot high span, the **Queen Juliana Bridge** allows all but the tallest ships to sail right under it.

The buildings along St. Anna Bay house elegant shops and restaurants. The Dutch imprint here is unmistakable—narrow, gabled, three-and four-storey structure with red-tiled roofs. The til crossed the ocean as ballast c ships; for the return trip t vessels were filled with sa that the Dutch used to cu herring. As for the rainbo colours of the 18th-centur houses—the cool pastels, th vibrant blues and yellows— we have an early governor c Curaçao to thank. The poo man suffered from ferociou headaches and the glare of th tropical sun on the whit buildings hurt his eyes. So h ordered that every house b painted a colour, any colo but white.

Two forts guarded the er trance to St. Anna Bay. Th **Waterfort** on the east side wa built in 1634. A hotel no welcomes guests within i walls but the cannons remair Because of its vulnerable loca tion, the hotel has the uniqu distinction of carrying marir collision insurance.

Penha & Sons, near th pontoon bridge on the Pund side, is a lovely yellow buil ing and one of the city's olde: houses (1708). It sits at th corner of Breedestraat an Heerenstraat, the two mai shopping streets.

Imposing mustard wal surround **Fort Amsterdam,** th historic centre of Willemstac

Construction probably began before 1642, when Governor Peter Stuyvesant was in residence. Now it's the seat of government of the Netherland Antilles. The complex of buildings consists of various offices, the Governor's Residence, a gracious Dutch colonial mansion with 19th-century additions, and the Fort Church, which has a British cannonball lodged in its walls.

A very different house of worship, right in the middle of Willemstad's shopping district, is the Dutch colonial synagogue. Dating from 1732, **Mikve Israel Synagogue** is the oldest in the Western Hemisphere. Its congregation was founded some 75 years earlier by Sephardic Jews who came to Curaçao from Brazil by way of Holland. Bright yellow outside, richly furnished within, the synagogue has four magnificent bronze chandeliers, replicas of the ones in Amsterdam's Portuguese Synagogue. But perhaps the most striking feature is the floor—a carpet of white sand, symbolizing the desert where the Jews wandered in their search for the Promised Land.

The **Synagogue Museum** was once a rabbi's home and later a Chinese laundry. But the recent discovery of a 300-year-old *mikvah*, or ritual bath, in the courtyard led to extensive restoration of the 18th-century house. The museum contains many valuable historical objects connected with Jewish ritual and daily life.

A unique attraction is the **Seaquarium** complex, stretching along the largest beach on Curaçao. You can enjoy a fascinating collection of sea life, glass-bottom boat trips, water sports, and a variety of shops and restaurants.

Try to visit the **floating market** in the morning, when it's most lively, and take along your camera. Small boats from Venezuela bring fresh produce and fish, returning home after they have sold their merchandise. Haggling is still the order of the day—whether you're buying a piece of fabric or some exotic fruit.

The Wilhelmina drawbridge next to the market leads over to **Scharloo**, where the wealthy Jewish merchants lived. You'll see some of the finest homes in Willemstad here, ranging in style from early colonial to Victorian.

On the hill behind Scharloo stands the **Roosevelt House**, the one with the black-tiled roof and American flag. The building was a gift from the people of Curaçao to the United States in appreciation for assistance during World War II. The U.S. Consul General has his office and residence there.

First a Dutch plantation house, then a seaman's hospital, the **Curaçao Museum** has an interesting collection of colonial furnishings.

The celebrated Curaçao liqueur is made at **Chobolobo,** the Senior Liqueur Distillery. A small green orange (*laraha*) grown only in Curaçao gives the liqueur its special flavour. Every tour of the premises is followed by a tasting session. Be sure to take a look at Chobolobo itself, a typical 17th-century *landhuis* (plantation house).

The oldest synagogue has the oldest burial grounds in the Americas. **Beth Haim Cemetery** (house of life), consecrated in 1659, contains a number of very unusual old tombstones.

You will find the very best view of Willemstad at **Fort Nassau,** 200 feet above the inner harbour. From the fort or its restaurant you can look down on the toy city below. You can also see the gigantic Shell oil refinery, reduced to lilliputian dimensions by the distance.

Eating Out

In dining, as in most other things, Curaçao is resolutely international. But Dutch accents do predominate.

This is your chance to try *rijsttafel,* the multi-course Indonesian speciality that the Dutch have come to regard as their national dish. A *rijsttafel* (literally "rice table") consists of an enormous quantity of rice and up to 25 side dishes.

Here are some of the local specialities: *bakijaw* (salted cod); *bestia chiqui* (goat stew); *carco stoba* (conch stew); *chicharrón de pollo* (chicken with onions); *concomber stoba* (stewed meat with miniature cucumbers); *criollo* (anything cooked Curaçao style); *funchi* (cornmeal patties); *keshi yena* (Edam cheese stuffed with fish or meat and baked); *sancocho di galli* (chicken stew, country style); *sopito* (fish and coconut soup); *soppi juana* (iguana soup); *zult* (pickled pigs ears).

You'll find familiar Dutch beers or try locally brewed Amstel, the world's only beer made from distilled sea water. Juniper-flavoured Holland gin, *jenever,* is popular, but most tourists will probably prefer curaçao liqueur, made from the peel of a small, green orange grown only here.

Shopping

In Willemstad, shopping does not come under the heading of a sideshow: it's the main event. With its high quality merchandise, incredible array of goods and, of course, the bargains, Willemstad is really a wonderland.

The following are some of Willemstad's shopping highlights, divided (for the most part) by country of origin:

African printed cotton, dashikis for men, caftans for women; sculpture.

British woollens and cashmeres; English porcelain and bone china.

Curaçao handicrafts—driftwood carvings, silk-screened fabrics.

Dutch cheese, cigars, tile dolls and Delftware.

French designer fashion perfumes and cosmetics.

German cameras, optic equipment, porcelain, hummel figurines.

Irish linen and crystal.

Italian leather goods an clothing.

Japanese cameras, binoculars, electronic gear, hi equipment.

Jewellery from all ove Fine pieces of 14 and 18 kar gold, precious gemstones.

Oriental silks and antique

Scandinavian crystal, chin and silver.

Spirits—especially Cari bean-made rums and liqueur

Swiss watches—almost many as in Switzerland.

Practical Information

Banks: 8.30 a.m. to 4.30 p.m. Monday through Friday.

Credit cards and traveller's cheques: Major credit cards and traveller cheques accepted almost everywhere. U.S. and Canadian dollars a also widely accepted.

Currency: Netherlands Antilles *florin* or *guilder (NAf)*. One guilder divided into 100 cents.

Telephoning Home. To call the U.S. direct from Willemstad, di 00 + 1 + U.S. area code + local number. To phone Willemstad from tł U.S., dial 011 + 5999 + local number. To call the U.K. direct from Wi lemstad, dial 00 + 44 + area code + local number. To call Willemsta from the U.K., dial 010 + 5999 + local number.

DOMINICA

Lesser Antilles

Introduction

Dominicans call their island the land of the three R's—rivers, rainbows and romance. And that's no exaggeration. Some 365 rivers, one for every day of the year, tumble and cascade through the forest, and rainbows dance over the waterfalls.

As for romance, Dominica can certainly lay claim to being the most ruggedly beautiful of the Caribbean islands, with a mystique that hangs in the air like the perennial fine mist that the islanders term "liquid sunshine".

The small almond-shaped island, 29 miles (47 km.) long and 16 miles (26 km.) wide at its broadest, lies sandwiched between the French islands of Guadeloupe to the north and Martinique to the south, its shores washed by the Caribbean Sea on the west and the Atlantic Ocean on the east. A mountainous chain runs from north to south, rising to Morne Diablotin (Devil Mountain) at 4,747 feet (1,447 m.).

Nearly 300 inches of rain a year in the higher regions has led to the creation of a lush tropical rainforest covering most of the interior and harbouring a treasure house of unique and exotic flora and fauna. Delicate orchids and brilliant birds—among them the rare purple-winged sisserou and red-necked or jacquot parrots—provide a splash of colour in the dense green vegetation. Dominica's volcanic origin accounts for some strange natural phenomena too, such as a boiling lake and sulphur springs.

Dominica is the last refuge of the Carib race, the Indian tribe that settled throughout the Caribbean and gave it its name. Today they have abandoned the warlike tendencies that kept British and French colonists at bay for hundreds of years and engage in the peaceful activities of basket weaving and canoe-making on their reservation in the north-east of the island.

When the Caribs finally succumbed, the island seesawed between the two colonial rivals battling for supremacy in the Caribbean. In the end, the British held sway and after independence in 1978 Dominica remained part of the Commonwealth. English is the official language, but the French influence was strong enough to leave a *patois* as the everyday means of communication between the 80,000 islanders.

The very inaccessibility of Dominica's interior has remained its prime attraction. Largely passed over by the tourist boom of recent years, it offers escapists something more than the sun, sea and sand of other Caribbean isles. Nevertheless, there *are* beaches—gold or black sand—and experts swear by the scuba-diving round coral reefs and 16th-century wrecks.

But bountiful nature can also be unkind; devastating hurricanes in 1979 and 1980 destroyed homes and crops, leaving desperate economic problems in their wake. Yet the Dominicans still retain that special bond with their luxuriant land, as the inscription on their coat of arms illustrates: "Apres Bondie, C'est la Ter" ("After God, the Earth").

A Brief History

Early history	Carib Indians migrate to the Antilles from the South American mainland and settle on Dominica, ousting the peaceful Arawaks.
15th–17th centuries	On November 3, 1493, Christopher Columbus sights the island and names it Dominica, Sunday, after the day of its discovery. British and French try to settle in the 17th century, fiercely resisted by the Caribs.
18th century	With the 1748 Treaty of Aix-la-Chapelle, Britain and France agree to leave Dominica as neutral territory, in the possession of the Caribs. Nonetheless, the fertile soil attracts both French and British planters who attempt to establish themselves. The Peace of Paris in 1763 formally gives Dominica to the British, but the island continues to be juggled between the colonial powers.
19th–20th centuries	In 1805 the French burn down the capital, Roseau, and only relinquish their hold on the island upon payment of £12,000. Between 1833 and 1940, Dominica is governed by the British as part of the Leeward Islands; then it is transferred to the Westward Islands as a separate colony. On November 3, 1978, 485 years to the day after its discovery by Columbus, Dominica gains full independence within the Commonwealth.

Three hurricanes in 1979 and 1980 leave despair and destruction, with 60,000 homeless and the largely agricultural economy in disarray. But Dominica rebuilds, developing its tourist trade with a special emphasis on its unique attractions.

Sightseeing

Any point on the island is only a comfortable day trip away, and there are some fascinating hikes into the mountain interior to explore the primordial rainforest. Capital and main port is Roseau, lying in the delta of the Roseau River, on the south-west coast.

Roseau

Sadly, the hurricanes have taken their toll of historic and colonial buildings, and your main impression of the capital will be a jumble of wooden and concrete one- or two-storey structures with balconies overhanging the pavements. Along the river banks, you'll find reeds in profusion which gave the town its name. The Caribs used them to make poison-tipped arrows and they are now the essential component of the basket-weaving industry.

Bay Front runs along the harbour and is the site of the animated Saturday morning **market**. Look out for the **Post Office**, one of the oldest sur-

viving buildings in Roseau, as is **Government House**, dating back to the 1840s. The **Cathedral** (1854) testifies to the importance of Roman Catholicism on the island and boasts carved wooden benches 100 years old.

Behind the town rises the peak of **Morne Bruce**, the summit affording a good view back over Roseau and the harbour. You can reach it by car along a twisting road or climb the footpath from the **Botanical Gardens** on the southern edge of town. These are a splendid introduction to the island's flora—orchids, begonias, ginger lilies, bright red flame trees—all of which you will later see on your trips into the mountains and forest.

Into the Interior

Situated 5 miles (8 km.) north-east of the capital, **Trafalgar Falls** can be reached by car to the village of Trafalgar and then a 15-minute walk. In a setting of dripping greenery not one, but three cascades crash and splash into a rocky pool sprouting ferns and or-

chids. An observation platform gives optimal viewing.

Sulphur Springs, near the
falls, are bubbling pools of
grey mud belching sulphurous
fumes. The smell of rotten
eggs can be picked up over a
mile away!

The road up the valley
branches off to **Laudat**, starting point for forays into the
**Morne Trois Pitons National
Park**. Marked nature trails
lead into the dense under-
growth, where the trees and
plants are labelled for easy
identification.

The park's most challeng-
ing trek takes you up a rough
6-mile (9-km.) track to the

Valley of Desolation. The area lives up to its name with a stark landscape stripped of its vegetation by volcanic upheavals, the last major one in 1880. The eruption also created the **Boiling Lake**, which geologists believe is a flooded crack in the earth (fumarole) rather than a volcanic crater. Escaping gases from the molten lava beneath the lake bring the water temperature to between 180 and 197° F (82 and 92° C) at the edge and to boiling point in the middle. A cloud of steamy vapour hangs suspended over the lake.

A rather easier trail leads to the ethereal **Emerald Pool**, a delightful grotto fed by a clear waterfall, lined with ferns and home to myriad lizards and birds.

You can also climb to 3,500 feet (1,100 m.) to the **Freshwater Lake**, its surface dappled with floating purple water-hyacinths. From a grassy knoll, you have a magnificent view of the Atlantic on one side and the Caribbean on the other.

North of Roseau, the **Layou River Valley** has been densely cultivated with an almost unbelievable variety and profusion of crops (everything grows well on this island).

Look out for plantations of grapefruit, banana, passion-fruit, limes (that go into the famous Roses Lime Juice), tobacco and cocoa.

The West Coast

From Roseau, the road runs north to the island's second town, Portsmouth. The scenic drive is both exhilarating and heart-stopping, punctuated as it is by hairpin bends, steep gradients and tunnels, with spectacular views round every turn.

In **Portsmouth** itself, gaily painted wooden houses with flower-filled gardens line the streets that run parallel to Prince Rupert Bay—said to be the best anchorage on the island.

South of town, you can take a trip down **Indian River,** gliding in a dugout canoe under a canopy of thick tropical jungle and through mangrove swamps.

On the **Cabrits Peninsula**, jutting into the sea between Douglas and Prince Rupert bays, stand the ruins of 18th-century **Fort Shirley**. The restored complex contains a hospital, barracks, storehouses, lookout posts and batteries, with a few cannon still facing out to sea. The whole area, endowed with the Caribbean's last tropical dry woodlands, freshwater swamps, marine habitats and superb recreational opportunities, has been turned into a national marine park.

The East Coast

The Atlantic coast has a wilder, more untamed aspect, with beaches of pebbles or black sand, reddish cliffs dropping sheer into the sea and tropical vegetation crowding down to the water's edge.

The island's main airport, Melville Hall, lies to the north, linked to Roseau on the west coast by a road cut through the mountain interior. The coastal road from here takes you further north to a string of gold-sand beaches and south through several small communities, where you can observe villagers building canoes, fishermen bringing in their catch or mending nets, and bananas and other produce being loaded onto boats.

The few remaining Caribs in the Caribbean live in the **Carib Reserve**, a fertile 3,700-acre stretch of land running inland from the coast. Three villages make up the reservation. Huts with traditionally thatched roofs and plaited walls shelter craft shops, where you can buy baskets and other souvenirs made by the Caribs. In Salibia, visit the **church**, where the altar is made from a dug-out canoe. The fanciful shape of a solidified stream of lava protruding into the sea at Sineku has earned it the name **Snake Staircase** (L'Escalier Tête Chien) and has inspired some colourful Carib legends.

Eating Out

Dominica's cuisine is a blend of Creole and African influences, making good use of the island's fish and wildlife. As in most Caribbean kitchens, dishes are smothered in a hot sauce; the Dominica variety is known as *bello hot pepper*.

Seafood and fish dishes are plentiful. *Lambie* is the flesh of the conch shell. *Titiri* are fried patties made from tiny freshly spawned fish. The shells of red and black land crabs come stuffed with their own highly seasoned meat. Grilled dolphin is an island staple, usually served in a tangy tomato and onion sauce.

That old French favourite, frogs' legs—but here with gigantic proportions—is featured as "mountain chicken" or *crapaud*. You may also get the chance to sample smoked *agouti* (the meat of a small rodent), pig and wild pigeon.

For accompaniment you can choose between breadfruit fritters, *coush-coush* (a kind of yam) or *dasheen* (a local variety of spinach).

Drinks

Rum is the basis of many an exotic cocktail. Refreshing drinks combine fresh coconut milk and grenadine.

Best of all, try the island's numerous fresh fruit juices, among them mango, soursop, papaya, passionfruit, guava or even just orange or lime.

Shopping

Native handicrafts top the list.

The Caribs make reed baskets interwoven with banana leafs (to ensure their resistance to water) and carve small souvenirs in wood.

Look out also for hats and bags of vetiver grass, shell carvings and shell-encrusted picture frames, place mats and souvenirs made from bamboo or coconut.

The Dominicans also make pretty straw *khus-khus* mats with geometric patterns or flower or fish motifs.

Practical Information

Banks. Hours are from 8 a.m. to 1 p.m., Monday to Friday, and again on Fridays from 3 to 5 p.m.

Climate. Day-time temperatures average between 70 and 85° F (21 and 26° C). Evenings and the mountain regions can be considerably cooler, so bring along a sweater, too.

Currency. The Eastern Caribbean dollar (EC$).

Telephoning Home. To call the U.S. direct from Dominica, dial 0 + 1 + U.S. area code + local number. To phone Dominica from the U.S., dial 011 + 809 + 44 + local number.

PUERTO PLATA

Dominican Republic

Introduction

The Dominican Republic occupies two-thirds of the big island of Hispaniola. The western third is Haiti. Two mountain ranges, the Cordillera Central and the Cordillera Septentrional, stretch across the land, cradling fertile valleys. Columbus loved the place when he discovered it in 1492 and wrote an enthusiastic description that still holds true today. "You wouldn't believe such bays exist," exclaimed the great explorer, who had seen enough bays to know what he was talking about.

More than bays, there are great arcs of sandy beach set on the country's northern Amber Coast (Costa de Ambar) washed by the Atlantic Ocean. The amber is real. This beautiful fossilized resin from trees that lived 20 million years ago is mined in the nearby mountains. The world's largest deposits are found here. There are more glorious beaches on the south coast around La Romana.

The Dominican Republic has other "firsts". Pico Duarte, the highest peak in the West Indies, towers to 10,0 feet. Santo Domingo, the ca ital, is the oldest city in tl New World and was the gra dest, too, until Spanish gall ons pushed on even further plunder the golden wealth the Aztecs and Incas. The C lumbus clan took a propri tary interest in the place. C lumbus' brother, Bartolom was governor and founder Santo Domingo and his so Diego, became 16th-centu viceroy. Such a treasure Spanish hands was too mu for the prowling English. 1586 Francis Drake, Eliz beth I's "little pirate", lite ally strung up his hammo in Santo Domingo's San María la Menor, the olde cathedral in the New Worl and whiled away his time lil a naughty schoolboy, mal ciously whittling the nose c a statue while he waited fe a ransom. The rich beautie of the town gave their jewe to the cause, but the pric was not met and the city wa razed by fire.

The following centuries sa brief domination by tl French—who spread fro their own glittering color of Saint-Domingue (Haiti) take over the whole islan —then revolts leading self-government, a furthe

riod of Spanish rule, Hai-
an control and finally,
aky independence. Today
e republic of some 6 mil-
on people is run by a presi-
nt, senate and chamber of
puties, with free elections
ery four years. Exports in-
ude sugar, cacao, tobacco,
uxite and nickel. Columbus
rought the sugar cane. Fields
it with waving pinkish
lags", as the flowers are
lled, grow near Puerto Plata.

High unemployment and
e effects of recession have
t the Dominican Republic,
one of the most stable and
productive Latin-American
countries.

The island's natural beauty
is proving a monetary god-
send, as the country turns
more and more to tourism.
With horse-drawn carriages
clopping through the cobbled
streets and bougainvillea sizz-
ling against sunlit buildings,
not to mention its own international airport, Puerto Plata
is an entrancing seaward gateway to the Republic's holiday
playground, backed by the big
tourist resort of Playa Dorada.

DOMINICAN REPUBLIC

A Brief History

Early History | Christopher Columbus discovers the island on December 5, 1492 and names it La Española or Hispaniola. It populated by Taíno and Arawak Indians. Bartolom Columbus is appointed governor in 1496 and foun Santo Domingo. Diego, Columbus' son, becomes vic roy in 1509. Great Spanish explorers call in on their wa to new lands—Cuba, Mexico, Florida, Peru, Puert Rico.

16th–19th centuries | Sir Francis Drake sets fire to Santo Domingo in 158 burning down the town. The French take over, and the claim is eventually legitimized by the Treaty of Ryswic (1697). The Dominicans revolt in 1809 and Spain is control again. But unrest seethes and the Dominica finally announce independence in 1821. The followir year the Haitians invade. They keep power until 184 when yet another revolution leads to the founding of th Dominican Republic. The country does not, howeve achieve real stability.

20th century | The United States Marines occupy the Dominica Republic from 1916–24. General Trujillo comes power in 1930. His dictatorship lasts until he is assass nated in 1961. Instability and civil war result in a secon American military intervention in 1965. Since 1966 th country enjoys political stability with regular election allowing foreign investment to develop. Today, th republic flourishes as a popular tourist destination.

Sightseeing

Puerto Plata, with a population of 45,000, is the biggest Amber Coast town. It was founded by Columbus in 1502. The explorer named it "Port of Silver", not for the sweeping brightness of the beaches, but for the softer silvery light

which clothes the mountain at nightfall.

Cruise ships enter under th walls of **San Felipe fortres** (Fortaleza de San Felipe) a the end of the Malecón, buil to guard the island from Carib Indians—and British pirates Constructed around 1540, it' been marvellously restorec and is well worth a visit.

The town is a little dream of colonial architecture. Take the *teleférico* up 800 metres (2,500 ft.) to **Isabel de Torres** peak, where a giant statue of Christ the Redeemer stretches protective arms over city and harbour. There's a superb view, gardens, a café and gift shops.

East a little is **Playa Dorada** with great golfing on a Robert Trent course and luxurious tourist facilities. Further east lies **Sosúa,** on a lovely bay settled by Jewish refugees in the 1930s. The town has a flourishing smoked meat and dairy industry. Call in, too, at Río San Juan to explore the **Gri Gri Lagoon** by boat. **Cabarete Beach,** some 15 km east of Sosúa, is known worldwide as an excellent windsurfing paradise. Many guesthouses and small hotels cater to the sports-minded person. Sunshine tempered by cool breezes, dressy evenings livened by the *merengue* beat (set by a three-man accordion-and-percussion band) and days under the coconut palms are what the coast's all about.

Samaná is a charming fishing port even further east, whose 7,000-strong population is English-speaking. This peninsula, long isolated geographically from the rest of the country, is home to descendants of fugitive American slaves. They arrived vi Pennsylvania in 1824 and sti use the antiquated English their forebears, with a caress ing Southern accent. Plac names are a legacy of thei gratitude to the Quakers wh helped them. There's even township called Philadelphia The game fishing has bee celebrated since the lat Franklin Roosevelt came here There are two docks— one for cruise ships.

A popular excursion from Puerto Plata heads west, pas the Costambar resort area Imbert and Luperón, to th ruins of La Isabela (50 km.) founded by Christopher Co lumbus in 1493 on his secon voyage.

Eating Out

There's a Spanish flavour, o course, but if you don't wan to go too far, internationa cuisine is available every where.

Typical snacks includ *quipes,* a type of sandwich of Arab origin, *catibías,* frie yucca, and *pastelitos,* pattie of meat or cheese (fish durin Lent). You'll probably be of fered *tortilla de jamón,* a han

melette; *chicharrón,* fried
ork rind; and *galletas,* a type
f cracker.

Main dishes include *cocido,*
meat and vegetable soup;
ancocho, a meat and vegeta-
le stew; and *pipián,* goat tripe
tew. Goat also appears in
elicious (though bony) fri-
assées. Of course, there's fish
long the coast, often worked
to imaginative combina-
ions (sea bass stuffed with
rabmeat, or tuna steaks). So-
úa has unexpected speciali-

ties like *pastrami,* chopped
liver and *matzos.* A popular
sweet, *dulce de leche,* is made
from milk.

Santo Domingo abounds in
all the lush fruit of the Caribbean. *Presidente* is the fine
local beer. *Bermudez* and *Brugal* rum are some of the best
you'll ever taste: try them in
cool, tropical mixes. Imported
alcohol proves expensive, but
Dominican coffee is excellent
and well worth buying to take
home.

*Glorious miles of open beach (here, near Sosúa) make the Dominican
Republic a holiday paradise.*

Shopping

Amber, the national gem, comes in a multitude of colours from crystalline through pale yellow to dark brown and near black. Sometimes tiny fossilized insects, leaves or even drops of water are imprisoned in the stone. It is worked into all kinds of jewellery and small decorative objects.

Larimar (Dominican turquoise) looks specially good set in silver. **Coral** and a variety of **seashells** are also made into jewellery.

Straw weaving produces attractive hats and baskets, and the embroidery reaches a high standard. **Mahogany,** another of the country's treasures, is carved into figurines, bowls and a variety of boxes.

When thinking of gifts to bring home, don't forget that smooth, golden **rum,** aromatic **coffee** or the superb **cigars.**

Practical Information

Currency: The Dominican peso is divided into 100 centavos. It is illegal to change currency at places other than banks or hotels. When leaving the country, tourists may change 30% of their legally converted pesos back into foreign currency. The US dollar has a better exchange rate than other foreign currencies. Traveller's cheques and credit cards are accepted in hotels, restaurants and in many shops.

Health: Don't drink water from the tap. The drinking water provided in major hotels and tourist restaurants is probably safe but water in small local restaurants should be avoided.

Hours: Shops open from 8.30 a.m. to noon and 2.30 to 6 p.m., Monday to Saturday; banks from 8 a.m. to 12.30 p.m. daily. Shops and banks are increasingly opening without interruption from 8 a.m. through 6 p.m. particularly in resort areas.

Telephoning Home. Puerto Plata (area code 809) is linked to the U.S. network. For U.K. visitors to ring home, dial 011 + area code + local number. To ring Puerto Plata from the U.K., dial 010 + 1 + 809 + local number.

SANTO DOMINGO

Dominican Republic

Introduction

The Dominican Republic, lying at the very heart of the Caribbean between Jamaica, Cuba and Puerto Rico, covers two-thirds of the island of Hispaniola, the rest being occupied by Haiti. Two mountain ranges, the Cordillera Central and the Cordillera Septentrional, stretch across the land, cradling fertile valleys, while the rest is hills and lowland.

First and oldest capital in the New World, Santo Domingo is particularly well endowed in monuments and testimonies of the colonial heritage of Spain. Sightseeing in old town and new is a pleasurable experience, shopping interesting and imaginative, and bathing and sports activities superb around Santo Domingo and outside. The Dominican Republic suffers its share of economic woes, but has nevertheless within the Caribbean had one of the most healthy growth rates in recent times.

Simple grace of Spanish Colonial architecture in Santo Domingo.

A Brief History

15th-16th centuries

On December 5, 1492, Christopher Columbus discovers the island he names La Isla Española (Hispaniola). The inhabitants are Indians from the Taino and Arawak tribes. On August 4, 1496, Colombus' brother, Bartholomew, founds the city of Nueva Isabela, later called Santo Domingo de Guzmán. The city becomes the first centre of European culture in the New World and base of the Spanish empire in the Americas. Santo Domingo is used as departure point by the most famous explorers of the time like Diego de Velázquez (Cuba), and Juan Ponce de León (Puerto Rico). In 1509, Columbus' son, Diego, becomes viceroy. Splendid buildings are constructed and the colony flourishes. The Catedral Primada de América is begun in 1514. After the conquest of Mexico and Peru, however, Santo Domingo declines in importance, never to regain its former eminence.

When Sir Francis Drake takes the town in 1586, there is no money to pay the ransom demanded. He sets it afire—but Santo Domingo survives.

17th-18th centuries

In the early 17th century, French, English and Dutch pirates settle on Tortuga Island, just off the northern coast of today's Haiti. They use the island as a base for smuggling. By the terms of the Treaty of Ryswick (1697) the western third of Hispaniola is ceded to France and the eastern part remains under Spanish control. Under the Treaty of Basel in 1795, the entire island devolves to the French, but Spanish rule is re-established in 1809.

19th century

In 1821 the Dominicans proclaim their independence from Spain (the so-called "Ephemeral Independence"). The new Dominican Republic is too weak to stand alone and Santo Domingo is occupied by Haitians (1822–1844). Revolution breaks out and independence is finally obtained on February 27, 1844. Santo Domingo becomes the official capital. A succession of revolutions and new regimes continue to devastate the country.

20th century

The U.S. Navy occupies the Dominican Republic between 1916 and 1924. General Rafael Leonidas Trujillo Molina takes power from 1930 until his assassination in

1961. In 1930 Santo Domingo is destroyed by a hurricane but the city is soon rebuilt with broad boulevards monuments and ostentatious buildings. Santo Domingo is christened Ciudad Trujillo in 1936, reverting to its original name after the dictator's death. Civil war leads to a second American military intervention in 1965. The difficult world economic situation is affecting the Dominican Republic that has enjoyed healthy growth rate in recent years.

Sightseeing

Although much of this city of over one million is vibrantly modern, the **old town** contains monuments of unique historical interest.

Central point is the **Catedral Primada de América,** Santa María la Menor, the oldest cathedral in the New World. Completed in 1540, the exterior is Renaissance and the interior contains Gothic vaulting. The main entrance has a huge door, weighing 2½ tons, that dates back to the founding of the cathedral.

Inside you'll find the reputed remains of Christopher Columbus in a massive **mausoleum** of marble and bronze topped with a bronze statue. They open the tomb once a year, on October 12, the anniversary of the explorer's discovery of the New World.

In the first chapel to the right of the altar, Francis Drake slung his hammock and slept during his stay in 1586. You can see where he maliciously chipped the nose off a statue.

Calle Las Damas, the oldest street in the city, lined with colonial buildings, is named after the ladies-in-waiting of María de Toledo, Columbus' daughter-in-law. It leads to the Fortaleza Ozama (fortress), dominated by the imposing **Torre del Homenaje** (Tower of Homage). Constructed at the beginning of the 16th century, this square, no-nonsense building contains a wooden spiral staircase. Ships entering the harbour used to be saluted from here—whence the name. The fortress is supposed to be haunted. It certainly looks grim enough.

Heading north on Calle Las Damas, you pass the **Hostal Nicolás de Ovando** on your right, a fine 16th-century house incorporated within a hotel. The door is considered an admirable example of colonial Iberian Gothic.

The **Museo de las Casas Reales** (Royal Houses Museum) is diagonally across Calle Las Damas. Note the exquisite entrance with the heraldic shield of Emperor Charles V. The museum merits a visit for its excellent material on Dominican history from earliest times, including Indian relics and models of Columbus' ships.

The **Alcázar** (castle) stands on a slight rise. It was built about 1510 for Diego Colum-

bus, son of the discoverer. When the Columbus family died out in Santo Domingo, the Alcázar fell to ruin. Now well restored, it houses a first-class museum with furniture, tapestries, paintings, musical instruments and a very fine 16th-century Flemish carving of the *Death of the Virgin*.

The **Atarazana,** just beyond, consists of eight 16th-century buildings—an early New World trade centre. Now galleries, boutiques and restaurants have moved into this charming colonial neighbourhood.

Sculpted in stone over the

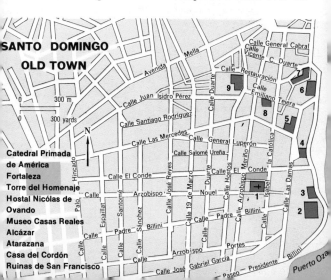

SANTO DOMINGO OLD TOWN

Catedral Primada de América
Fortaleza
Torre del Homenaje
Hostal Nicólas de Ovando
Museo Casas Reales
Alcázar
Atarazana
Casa del Cordón
Ruinas de San Francisco

entrance to the **Casa del Cordón** (House of the Cord) is the belt of St. Francis. It was here that rich women of the city brought their jewels to have them weighed as a contribu-

tion to the ransom demanded by Sir Francis Drake.

At the end of Calle Emiliano Tejera are the **Ruinas de San Francisco,** probably the oldest monastery in the New World. Its dedication to St. Francis is marked, again, by a gracefully carved replica of the white cord of the order.

Live chickens for sale are part of the fun of everyday business.

New Town

The modern city has an entirely different atmosphere. Startlingly up-to-date buildings decorate the **Plaza de la Cultura.** Among them is the marble and mahogany Teatro Nacional and the grey, corrugated Galería de Arte Moderno (Museum of Modern Art). A forest of contemporary statuary rises in front of it. Well worth a visit, the **Museo del Hombre Dominicano** (Museum of the Dominican Man) has a good collection of pre-Columbian artefacts, necklaces, ornaments and amulets, as well as objects from the colonial period.

Eating Out

There's a Spanish flavour to everything in Santo Domingo, from the architecture to the clothes (neat and elegant), and, no less, to the food.

Snacks

Some typical snacks to pick up along the way are *quipes,* a type of sandwich of Arab origin, *catibías,* fried yucca, and *pastelitos,* meat patties which become fish patties during Lent.

Meat

The Dominican national dish is *sancocho,* a stew of different meats and local vegetables cooked in a broth. If you prefer Creole cooking, try fried chicken with rice, under its Spanish name *(arroz con pollo).* Roast sucking pig *(lechón asado)* is often found in the Dominican Republic.

Fruit

All the lush fruit of the Caribbean is there for your enjoyment—mangoes, papayas, pineapple, coconut and fresh oranges. A popular sweet is *dulce de leche,* made from milk.

Drinks

The local beer is excellent, but of course the most famous drink in the Caribbean is rum—Santo Domingo's brands are Bermudez and Brugal.

Shopping

Carving and weaving are part of the country's tradition, and mahogany, one of its treasures.

Of special interest for visitors is the jewellery made from amber (found here in very large quantities) or from larimar, the "Dominican turquoise", an attractive blue stone often combined with silver.

Santo Domingo's market offers the best bargains—you can find embroidery and straw work, baskets, bowls, hats and sandals.

Dominican rum, coffee or cigars make fine souvenirs.

Practical Information

Currency: The Dominican *peso* is divided into 100 *centavos*. It is illegal to change currency at places other than banks or hotels. Traveller's cheques and credit cards are accepted in hotels, restaurants and a great number of shops. When leaving the country, tourists may change 30% of their legally converted pesos back into foreign currency.

Hours: Shops: 8.30 a.m.–12 noon and 2.30–6 p.m., Monday to Saturday. Banks: 8 a.m.–12.30 p.m. Post Office: 7 a.m.–12 noon and 2–6 p.m., Monday to Friday. On Saturdays, at variable hours. More and more banks and shops are opening without interruption.

Post Office: At Calle Emiliano Tejera, opp. Alcázar de Colón.

Telephoning Home. Santo Domingo (area code 809) is linked to the U.S. network. For U.K. visitors to ring home, dial 011 + area code + local number. To ring Santo Domingo from the U.K., dial 010 + 1 + 500 809 + local number.

GRAND CAYMAN

Cayman Islands

Introduction

Sleepy, peaceful and British to the back teeth, the Cayman Islands dot the sea about 180 miles north-west of Jamaica. There are no cries for independence here. Things run smoothly under a British governor, Queen Elizabeth II's photograph is hung with pride on office walls and the language is English.

The Caymans, three islands of which Grand Cayman is the largest and Cayman Brac and Little Cayman the lesser members of the family, have spent most of their history quietly being ignored. This is no longer true, for tourists have discovered the beaches and the gentle atmosphere, like a small town, where everybody knows everybody else. Besides, the islands have become a financial centre—with over 500 banks. There is no income tax, no profit tax, no capital gains tax, no estate and death duties. Consequently, international business thrives here. This financial success story, which began less than two decades ago, has led to tremendous economic expansion.

In spite of affluence, in spite of the tourists who now come in increasing numbers, the place has retained its sober gait. Americans feel at home since the American influence is strong. The British may think that this is the way an English country village could be if only someone pepped up the economy and turned on the sun.

GRAND CAYMAN

Legend has it that the first settlers were two deserters from Cromwell's army, Bodden and Watler, names found all over the islands today. The pirates came and went, delighting in the remoteness of Grand Cayman and its absolute flatness, which makes it practically invisible against the horizon—in short, a perfect hideaway.

Wherever there's water, there's an excuse for a dip.

A Brief History

16th century	Columbus discovers the Caymans in 1503, calling th group "Las Tortugas" after the great number of turtle in the surrounding seas. Early Spanish settlers of th Caribbean area rename them the "Caimán" island possibly mistaking the native iguanas for alligator
17th–18th centuries	In 1670 the Caymans are formally ceded to Grea Britain by Spain. About the same time, the islands' fir permanent settlers arrive, an assortment of debtor buccaneers hiding from the Royal Navy, deserters from Cromwell's army and sailors shipwrecked on the is lands' reefs. They make their living by working sma plantations (later with the help of slaves) or by fishing
19th–20th centuries	By an Act of Parliament in 1863, the Governor an legislature of Jamaica are given certain legislativ powers in the Islands. When Jamaica chooses inde pendence in 1962, the islands elect to become a Britis Crown Colony. Today, the Caymans are an inter national financial centre, with a booming economy an one of the highest per capita incomes in the Caribbean

Sightseeing

Most of the points of interest in the islands are on Grand Cayman. **George Town** (written in two words), the capital, is thriving but very quiet. There are no great sights and although it is pleasant to wander around the well-planned streets (where all the cars stop to let you pass), you will no doubt soon want to head north for **Seven Mile Beach** (they're exaggerating, it's only 6 miles, really), where the big hotels are located and clean white sand stretches to an invitingly blue sea.

Continue north along th coast road to the world's firs **green turtle farm.** It provides legal source of turtle products such as meat, hide and tortois shell, and aims at protectin an endangered species. You can eat turtle on Cayma without suffering pangs o ecological guilt.

Afterwards you may as wel go to **Hell**. The name refers to the Dantesque area of jagged limestone formations. Its ma jor industry revolves aroun selling postcards and stamp and postmarking them to prove you have been to Hell East of George Town, th oad runs to **Pedro Castle**, riginally built by an Englishman who arrived in the islands n 1765. Local—unsubstantited—stories also associate it vith the pirate Henry Morgan nd a 17th-century Spaniard, edro Gómez.

At **East End**, sprays of water shoot like geysers through he sea-torn rocks and, further n, the wrecks begin. Over 325 f them have been counted round Grand Cayman, not ll the result of natural ci cumstances. The most southrly, off the east coast, is the *Ridgefield*, perfectly visible rom the road. Though the hip was practically empty when lured onto a reef in 1943, at least she carried the bonus of 100 cases of beer.

Grand Cayman's central road which strikes off to the left some distance after **Betty Bay Point**, takes you to the north side and then west as far as **Cayman Kai** and **Rum Point**. The silky sand has been divided up and very pleasant beach houses have gone up. The whole landscape shines blue and silver, it's New England in a Caribbean setting. The gardens are beautifully planted (amazing what will grow in sand), the holiday houses verging on the luxurious.

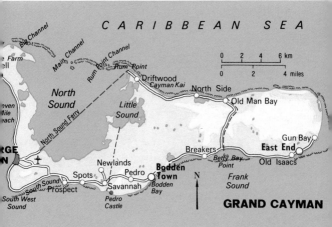

GRAND CAYMAN

The swimming in the Cayman Islands is good, so is the snorkelling, and the diving has a strong claim to being the best in the Caribbean. For underwater photography, head for Spanish Bay Reef where they have all the gear and expertise.

Beyond the reefs are the big fish such as bluefin, marlin and wahoo. Bonito, amberjack and barracuda are closer to shore and inside the reef you will land grouper and yellow-tailed snapper. Boats can be rented, ranging from a 60-foot yacht to a dinghy. Experts say the best fishing guides are on Cayman Brac and Little Cayman.

Once every year Caymanians honour the buccaneers with Pirate Week (usually late October). Then there are parades, banquets, treasure hunts, coconut-shucking contests and pirate ship cruises. A make-believe governor is "captured" as part of the fun and a gala ball is held to wind it all up.

Turtles can be seen at the turtle farm—or in your plate!

Eating Out

Grand Cayman abounds in good restaurants, many of which specialize in American or continental dishes. But you will also come across the best of Caribbean cuisine, including Cayman specialities featuring turtle meat or fresh seafood.

Specialities

Turtles were once abundant in the islands, and turtle recipes are still traditional here. Nowadays, most of the meat comes from Grand Cayman's green turtle farm. Try tasty turtle soup or stew, or the truly memorable turtle steaks.

Conch, a shellfish that resembles oyster meat, turns up in hearty stews and chowders and also as a marinated cocktail. Spiny lobster often appears as an appetizer, garnished with seaweed.

Codfish and ackee is another local favourite, sometimes offered as a breakfast dish. The rosy ackee fruit is poisonous until it ripens and bursts open, revealing a delicate yellow interior. When cooked, it tastes somewhat like scrambled eggs.

Your vegetable might be white sweet potato, breadfruit, cassava root, or fried plantain, a larger, coarser cousin of the banana. Rice is frequently served with curry and coconut milk or with red beans (rice 'n peas).

For dessert, sample some of the exotic local fruits: mango, papaya (paw paw), coconut, sweetsop and soursop. You'll also find these fruits turned into tantalizing pies, cakes and puddings.

Drinks

The light, aromatic rum of the Caribbean is rightly famous, and forms the base of many cocktails and punches. The popular piña colada consists of rum, coconut cream, crushed pineapple (or juice) and crushed ice. Most bartenders have their own personal recipe for rum punch: a refreshing concoction of lime juice, sugar syrup and crushed ice, with a sprinkling of nutmeg or bitters.

Shopping

There are two shopping categories on the Caymans—local handicrafts and imported duty-free articles. You'll see crystal, perfumes, cameras, woollens and silver.

The Caymans are considered a developing area by the

U.S. Customs, so certain local crafts may be exempted from duty. Cayman shopkeepers can advise you on existing legislation. Among local handicrafts, look for the jewellery fashioned from shells and local semi-precious stones lik Caymanite.

Straw work is another pop ular native craft, and you' find a broad range of wove goods, including hats, duster and hammocks.

Practical Information

Banks and currency exchange: Open 9.30 a.m. to 3 p.m. Monday t Thursday, till 5 p.m. on Friday.

Credit cards and traveller's cheques: Major credit cards are widel accepted by most hotels, better restaurants and shops. Traveller' cheques are also accepted, preferably those in U.S. dollars.

Currency: Cayman Islands dollar = 100 cents. Coins: 1, 5, 10, 25 cent Notes: 1, 5, 10, 25 dollars. Prices are usually quoted in Cayman dollar but shops will also accept U.S. and Canadian dollars.

Post Office: The General Post Office in George Town is open 8.30 a.n to 3.30 p.m. Monday to Friday, 8.30 a.m. to 11.30 a.m. on Saturday

Shops: Generally open 8.30 a.m. to 5 p.m. Monday to Saturday, som supermarkets till 9 or 10 p.m. on Friday and Saturday.

Telephoning Home. Grand Cayman (area code 809) is linked to the U.S network. For U.K. visitors to ring home, dial 0 + 44 + area code + local number. To call Grand Cayman from the U.K., dial 010 + 500 80 + local number.

GRENADA

Lesser Antilles

Introduction

Spice is a way of life in Grenada. One of the most southerly—and some say the most beautiful—of the Caribbean chain, it is the only spice-growing island in the western hemisphere, producing a quarter of the world's supply of nutmeg, as well as cinnamon, cloves, bay leaves, saffron and mace. Even the breezes wafting over the aptly nicknamed "Isle of Spice" are heady with their fragrance.

In prehistoric times, Grenada rose from the sea in volcanic eruption to take its place near the end of the island necklace that links the tip of Florida to the Venezuelan coast and separates the Caribbean from the Atlantic. Its largest neighbours are Trinidad and Tobago, 145 kilometres (90 mi.) to the south. To the north lie the Grenadines, a group of tiny islands, of which Carriacou, Petit-Martinique and several islets belong to Grenada.

St. George's, Grenada's tiny capital and chief port, is often acclaimed as the world's most picturesque. Built on hills surrounding the sheltered blue lagoon of its inner harbour, the mellowed bricks, wrought-iron balconies and red-tiled roofs of English Georgian and French provincial houses preserve the flavour of its colonial past.

Grenada bases its economy almost entirely on the export of nutmeg and cocoa. Long years of British rule left the island with little but the English language; the lavish carnival costumes, exuberant style of painting and sinuous rhythms of music and dance are the gift of Africa. Most of Grenada's population of 110,000 are black or mulatto descendants of African slaves.

The vibrant lifestyle of Grenada's inhabitants matches the luxuriance of the island's natural beauties. Dense carpets of tropical rainforest drape the volcanic mountains in a tangle of coconut palms, lianas and flowering shrubs. Waterfalls cascade down the hillsides to shady groves of nutmeg nestling in the valleys.

Tourism is a potential not yet fully exploited. A period of turbulence since independence and the island's relative remoteness have kept it off the beaten track, but those who have been there rank its rugged volcanic beauty supreme among the enchanting islands of the Caribbean. Grenada is perfect for escapists—who don't want to escape too far.

A Brief History

Pre-European history	By A.D. 300, the Arawak Indians from South America have settled throughout the Caribbean. They are driven out centuries later by the warlike Caribs, also from South America.
15th to 17th centuries	In 1498, Columbus discovers Grenada on his third voyage. He calls it Concepción, but later Spanish sailors rename it after their native Granada. The French then turn this into Grenada, but the British have the last word, pronouncing it Gre-NAY-da.

Early attempts by both British and French to subdue the Caribs on Grenada fail, and it is not until 1650 that the French establish a foothold on the island. They carry out a campaign of extermination against the Caribs. When defeat is certain, the last small group of Caribs jump to their deaths from a northern cliff.

Slaves are brought in to work the sugar plantations. |
| 18th century | The British oust the French from Grenada in 1762 but are driven out again in 1779. France then holds the island for four years, until the Treaty of Versailles (1783) awards it to Britain.

In 1795, a slave uprising provokes bloody reprisals. |
| 19th century | Slavery is abolished in all British colonies in 1833. Contract workers from India and Africa begin arriving to replace slave labour on the Caribbean plantations.

In 1843, nutmeg is introduced to Grenada from the Dutch East Indies and soon takes over from sugar as the island's principal export.

Grenada is formally declared a Crown Colony of Britain in 1877. |
| 20th century | An elected legislature is created in 1924 and the island is made a British Associated State in 1967. Grenada achieves full independence in 1974 but remains within the British Commonwealth.

A coup d'état in the spring of 1979 deposes Prime Minister Sir Eric Gairy and installs Maurice Bishop at the head of a People's Revolutionary Government.

In the autumn of 1983, Maurice Bishop is killed during an attempted takeover by the extremist elements of his own party. Cuban involvement precipitates military intervention by the United States. |

Sightseeing

St. George's

Begin your visit to Grenada's capital and chief port by exploring the **Carenage,** the curving waterfront of St. George's inner harbour, where attractive 18th-century warehouses line the quay. High on a hill overlooking the harbour, you'll see Fort George, an impressive structure erected by the French in 1705.

From here it's a short distance to the **Botanical Gardens and Zoo,** majestically heralded by a clump of royal palms. The gardens bloom with an array of tropical flowers, and you may sight some brilliantly plumed Caribbean birds.

Sendall Tunnel leads from the Carenage to the **Outer Harbour** and quayside **Melville Street,** a busy shopping centre. One street inland, you'll find **Market Square,** site of a wonderful typically West Indian open-air market. Among the wares for sale in the area are all manner of straw goods, carvings and paintings, as well as a profusion of local spices.

Walk along Church Street, so-called for the many churches there. Notice the **clock tower** of the Anglican Church which has become something of a town symbol, as well as that of the Presbyterian Kirk.

Up on Richmond Hill, **Fort Frederick** is a magnificent lookout point. Construction was begun by the French in 1779, but it was the British who applied the finishing touches in 1783.

Excursions

Points South

Heading south from St. George's, the **Royal Drive** was named in honour of Queen Elizabeth. You'll probably want to stop on the way at **Morne Jaloux Ridge** to admire views fit for a queen.

The road winds at first through green hills (known as *mornes* in the West Indies) past neat little settlements and farming country. As you approach the deeply indented southern coastline, the landscape grows wilder and more desolate, until finally you reach **Point Jeudy,** where black volcanic rock rears out of a surging sea.

At **Point Saline,** on the south-west tip of the island, the black volcanic sand pounded by the Atlantic forms a dramatic contrast to the white sandy beaches that stretch northwards up the Caribbean coast. One of them, **Grand Anse Beach,** has won renown for the silvery whiteness of its 2-mile expanse.

Spice Country

The scenic route to the northern spice plantations follows the west coast, with bays and headlands of uncommon beauty. You'll see wooden huts, brightly painted boats and long seine nets hanging out to dry in some of the prettiest fishing villages in the Caribbean.

Hidden among the red roofs of **Gouyave** (formerly Charlotte Town), is a **factory** where spices are sorted and dried in preparation for shipping all over the world. Chief among factory products are nutmeg and the mace made from its filament.

To see spices growing on a traditional plantation, head inland a short distance to **Dougaldston Estate,** a centre for the cultivation of nutmeg and cacao.

Other highlights of the north include Sauteurs and nearby **Morne du Sauteurs** (Leaper's Hill), the rocks from which the last of the Carib Indians plummeted to death in 1650 rather than surrender to the French. The cliff is not

as spectacular as one would imagine, but the rocks about 12 metres (40 feet) below look sufficiently sinister.

Just east lies **Levera Bay** and its inviting beach. Columbus reputedly saw this very place as he sailed past the northern tip of the island in 1498.

On the eastern coast, **Grenville,** Grenada's second-largest town, seems more like a casual village than a city. It has a lively market, however, and its own spice factory.

The inland road back to St George's from here is spectacular. Numerous hairpin turns take you through tropical rainforests and past gorges of stunning beauty. The road passes within hailing distance of **Grand Etang National Park** and its extinct volcano, 549 metres (1,800 feet) high, that cradles a beautiful blue lake of 5 hectares (13 acres).

The region is open to exploration, and camping is permitted.

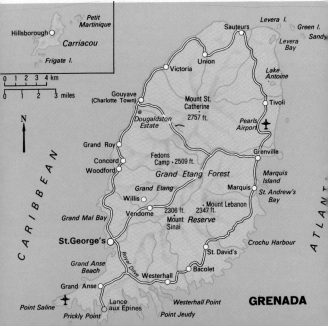

Eating Out

Imagine a fresh catch of fish and shellfish, a multi-coloured choice of glistening tropical fruits and vegetables and an aura of spice. These are the basic ingredients of Caribbean cooking, a happy marriage of fresh products and time-honoured recipes evolved from the culinary traditions of Africa, Spain, France, India and England.

Starters

Among the wide variety of first courses are *pastelles,* plantain or banana leaves stuffed with a corn meal and savoury meat filling. *Accras,* lightly fried codfish balls, come with a piquant sauce.

Delicious soups include cream of breadfruit, avocado and cream of pumpkin. Highly spiced pigeon-pea soup is usually made with coconut milk and a little ham or salt-pork. A standard Caribbean dish, *callaloo* includes dasheen leaves, okra, onions, garlic, chicken stock, salt-pork, coconut milk, crab meat and hot pepper seasoning to taste.

Main Courses

Seafood. Always ask for the catch of the day in the Carib-bean. Coquilles of fish—shells filled with scallops or bill-fish—may appear temptingly *au gratin* in a wine-flavoured sauce with mushrooms. Crab backs are crab shells stuffed with a spicy crab-meat filling.

Lambi—chewy conch meat —is served cold with lime, having been chopped and stewed beforehand.

Meat. An outstanding meat dish is pepperpot, which orig-inated with the South Amer-ican Indians. It's a succulent stew of pork, beef and chick-en, though the key ingredient is casareep, a spicy mixture of grated cassava, cinnamon and brown sugar.

Sancoche is a "soup" of pork and pig's tail, with lots of beef and stock, cassava, yams, potatoes, chives, peppers and perhaps coconut milk.

Vegetables. Plantains, simi-lar in appearance to a green banana, but much firmer and not nearly as sweet, can be cooked as a savoury vegeta-ble. *Christophene,* a kind of squash, is delicately sautéed or cooked *au gratin* in cream sauce. Both *dasheen* (the tuberous part) and bread-fruit may be boiled, sautéed or fried. *Coo-coo* technically means a side dish, but here usually implies corn meal or semolina.

Desserts

Fruit provides a host of refreshing desserts. Fruit salads come laced with a dash of liqueur or rum. Good ices are made from a tangy fruit called soursop. Coconut is used liberally in cakes, puddings, cream-filled pies and tarts.

Drinks

On the Isle of Spice, you will not be surprised to find your rum punch, omnipresent drink of the West Indies, sprinkled liberally with nutmeg. *Piña colada* combines rum, coconut cream and pineapple juice in a drink so rich it seems more like a sweet.

Non-alcoholic drinks include *sorrel,* made from a plant called rosella and *mauby,* from roots and bark.

Shopping

The most obvious buys on the Spice Island are baskets woven of straw or palm fronds and filled with ginger, cinnamon, nutmeg and so on. You'll also find all sorts of hand-crafted goods, from hand-blown glass to straw hats, bags and mats. Batik caftans and overblouses, as well as resort wear, in African or Liberty cottons are very attractive.

Look, too, for shell objects and jewellery, china and ceramics. A few shops stock excellent British woollens and cashmeres – if you can face choosing winter clothing in the tropics. There are also a couple of galleries selling the best of island art.

Practical Information

Currency: East Caribbean dollar (EC$), 100 cents = EC$1. Also referred to as "Bee Wee" (British West Indian) currency.
Notes: EC$1, 5, 20 and 100. Coins: 1, 2, 5, 10, 25, 50 cents and EC$1

Language: English is spoken by all Grenada's inhabitants, but often sprinkled with local colloquialisms.

Telephoning Home. Grenada is not fully integrated into the International Direct Dialling network, and most long-distance calls must be routed by the operator.

THE GRENADINES

St. Vincent, Lesser Antilles

Introduction

Dangling at the southern end of the Caribbean like the beads on a necklace is a chain of idyllic islands untouched, undiscovered, unpolluted—as perfect as the day they were created. Chalk-white beaches lapped by crystal seas make the glistening Grenadines the ultimate escape spot—even by Caribbean standards.

So remote are these islands that opinions differ as to just how many of them there are. Counting all the islets and rocky outcrops, some only a few yards across, there are about 600, of which some 125 constitute the core of the Grenadines. Some are rich in vegetation, with sheltered harbours and coves offering exceptional sailing and sunbathing. Others are rocky and uninhabited, protected from "invasion" by sheer, breathtaking cliffs. All demonstrate natural beauty at its awesome best.

The Grenadines occupy the 35-mile (50-km.) stretch between the well-known Caribbean islands, St. Vincent and Grenada. The islands are so close together that, whichever one you are on, there is always another in sight. Yet this abundant archipelago is home for just 18,000 people, concentrated on a handful of the larger islands. Under St. Vincent's domain (the northern half) come Bequia, Mustique, Canouan, Mayreau, the Tobago Cays, Union, Palm and Petit St. Vincent. All are renowned for their superb water sports and fantastic and varied scenery.

To the south lie the islands of Carriacou and Petit Martinique, geographically part of the Grenadines, but politically part of Grenada.

The names of the islands in the Grenadines hint at their tug-of-war past between English and French colonists. The people, too, share French and English names. To the south, French is more in evidence, although you will also find many a name prefixed with "Mac", coming from the Scottish boat-builders who once pioneered these islands.

One of the Grenadines has achieved international renown as the holiday haunt of Princess Margaret. A true gem of an island, Mustique is the private playground for some very public people. As well as Princess Margaret, celebrities such as Mick Jagger, Raquel

Welch, Cheryl Tiegs and Kenny Rogers have homes here.

Bequia (pronounced BECK-wee), closest to St. Vincent, is more public and more "civilized"—although the only means of getting there is still by boat. In Port Elizabeth, Bequia's main town, there is even a tourist office—mainly to put the many passing sailors on the right tack.

For city dwellers seeking solitude, tranquillity and extraordinary beauty, there are few island groups that compare with the Grenadines.

A Brief History

7th century	The French claim the Grenadines, although the main island of St. Vincent is the prime target for colonists. The Grenadines come under a Norman feudal lord, Jacques Diel du Parquet. Native Caribs resist colonization. Escaped African slaves intermarry with islanders, creating a new race of Black Caribs.
8th century	St. Vincent changes hands frequently between French and English. A revolt by French and Caribs against the rulers of the moment, the English, ends bloodily in 1795. In revenge, the English banish 5,000 Caribs from Bequia and ship them to Honduras two years later. Portuguese and East Indians are imported to work sugar plantations after the emancipation of slaves.
9th–20th centuries	King George V and his brother Prince Alfred visit the Grenadines in 1880, describing them as the "Cyclades of the Grecian archipelago or the islets of the inland sea of Japan". St. Vincent and Grenada both become British Associate States in the 1960s but then gain independence in the 1970s. The Grenadines are split up between Grenada and St. Vincent, with the dividing line on the northern extremity of Carriacou. Yachtsmen, and then tourists, discover the Grenadines, but the islands remain relatively secluded.

Sightseeing

At the top of the necklace, there is **Bequia,** a small, tidily developed island just 9 miles (15 km.) from mainland St. Vincent. All visitors arrive in Port Elizabeth's colourful **Admiralty Bay.** Once in the harbour, you are surrounded by activity, as if a permanent yachting regatta were under way. On the beach, fishermen mend their nets and hand-build their boats, maintaining age-old traditions and Bequia's most important industry.

The quaint waterfront at **Port Elizabeth** is lined with bars, restaurants and shops. There's also a tourist board near the dock, that will help you fix inland tours and settle you with cars and drivers by the day.

The main sights on Bequia can be covered in half a day. **Old Fort** affords a good view of Admiralty Bay; **Paget Farm** is a quaint whaling village (whaling with hand-thrown harpoons is still practised in the Grenadines); **Vista Point** offers views of St. Vincent and other Grenadine islands; there are a couple of hotels at **Friendship Bay; Moon Hole,** a troglodytic residential development, has literally been

carved from the cliffs. The beautiful **Princess Margaret Bay** is noted for its coral reef and excellent snorkelling. Because the road is poor, it's best to go there by boat. An inexpensive water taxi service is available from Port Elizabeth.

Heading south, the next island of note is magical **Mustique** (MUS-teek), measuring 3 miles by 1½. The name comes from the French word for mosquito, but this shouldn't put you off. It hasn't deterred some of the world's richest and most famous people from building very impressive private villas on the island. But for all its publicity, Mustique looks more like a desert island than a gathering place for the jet set.

Unless you rent one of the villas or know someone on the island who owns one, you are unlikely to go further than the sandy beaches and turquoise waters of **Britannia Bay,** a famous yachtsmen's and sailors' haunt. The exception is the island's only hotel, **Cotton House,** a sprawling 18th-century plantation house designed by Oliver Messel. This exceedingly luxurious establishment bears all the hallmarks of rustic elegance, with louvered windows, Spanish silver screens

and a fountain of scallop shells.

Canouan, the next island down, claims some of the best beaches in the Caribbean (and that is saying something!). Long hot ribbons of powdery white sands blend with warm clear water and coral. The few hundred inhabitants are mostly farmers and fishermen. The island has only a couple of hotels, but is currently being developed as a discreet resort.

South of Canouan are the **Tobago Cays,** four uninhabited islets surrounded by truly spectacular coral reefs. This is the perfect paradise for escapists. There is sailing, snorkelling, swimming and picnicking in complete seclusion—a rare tropical Eden, normally reached by chartered yacht or a daily connection from Union.

West of the Cays is **Mayreau,** only 1½ square miles (4½ sq. km.) of island, with no roads and a small local population. Atop the highest hill, the single village snuggles round a delightful little church. Salt Whistle Bay harbours the island's only hotel. The beach here is one of the most sheltered in the Grenadines, perfect for children.

On **Union Island** you're almost back to civilization! There's an airport, a bank and even a small hospital. But don't worry, as elsewhere in the Grenadines, the main charm is sheer escapism. The island's silhouette is quite distinctive, with the impressive **Mount Parnassus**, "the Pinnacle", soaring 900 feet (300 m.) from the sea. **Clifton Harbour,** the main town, is small but commercial.

On the resort-hotel island of Petit St. Vincent and Palm life is casual but chic. The 110-acre (45-ha.) flat **Palm Island** was named after the 8,000 elegant coconut palms lining its beaches. The island is again, privately owned, but in the resort every kind of water sport is available.

The southernmost St. Vincent Grenadine, **Petit St. Vincent** (P.S.V.), is more hilly than Palm Island. The carefree lifestyle and simple seclusion makes this one a favourite with yachtsmen.

Sports

Needless to say, water sports, in particular sailing, snorkelling, skin-diving and swimming, top the bill in the Grenadines. The beaches, too numerous to list, are one more idyllic than the next—silvery white, blissfully uncrowded. The sparkling water simply invites you in, but do take all the usual precautions: don't swim too far out or on your own, keep a watchful eye on small children, and heed warnings about dangerous beaches.

Skin-divers and snorkellers will be well rewarded anywhere in the Grenadines, but the most recommended waters are off Young and Palm islands and the Tobago Cays.

Avid sailors discovered the Grenadines long before anyone else did, and they continue to favour the islands for the challenging, yet relaxing sailing possibilities. Yachts are available for charter on St. Vincent, and you can usually find sailboats, motorboats, catamarans, wind-surf boards for hire on most islands.

On land, depending on the island, you can play tennis, horse-ride or go hiking in the beautiful interiors.

Underwater Wonderland

A host of exotic creatures inhabits the watery depths of the Caribbean. Common sights include elkhorn, finger and brain coral, which look exactly as their names imply. In addition, you may see fire and pillar coral, as well as sea fans. Take care not to step on the razor-sharp coral, and refrain from breaking off samples, a practice frowned on by the authorities.

Fish are not at all shy about parading their gorgeous colours past snorkellers and divers. Look for the bright-blue-and-yellow Queen Angelfish, the orange-and-blue Honeytail Damselfish and striking Queen Triggerfish. The blue Ocean Surgeon has a neat "incision" marked in black on its gill, and the Sergeant-Major sports pretty blue, yellow and black stripes.

Eating Out

The richly fertile soils and seas of the Grenadines produce wholesome, succulent fresh food to suit most palates. As always in the Caribbean, ask for the catch of the day, which may then be seasoned with a tangy sauce. One of the more unusual fish dishes could be *lambi,* chewy conch meat chopped, stewed and dished up cold with lime.

But to start, why not try *pastelles,* or *doucana,* local banana leaves stuffed with corn meal and savoury meat or grated coconut and raisins, folded, tied and boiled. Or there's a generous selection of exotic soups: cream of breadfruit, avocado, cream of pumpkin or pigeon-pea soup, made with coconut milk and ham or salt pork.

Main course meats are abundant, and good cuts of beef, pork and lamb, along with the chef's favourite sauce, are always on the menu.

Chicken, duck, turkey and guinea fowl (*pintadeau*) are served stuffed and roasted or spiced with sauces.

For afters, sample some of the excellent Caribbean fruit salads which nearly always come with a dash of rum or liqueur. Bananas too, fried or in a cake, make a good sweet. Beer's the usual accompaniment, wine tends to be pricey—but don't forget the rum the Caribbean is famous for!

Shopping

Naturally, shopping on a string of getaway islands is no top of the list. But on the larger Grenadines, bags, baskets and rugs woven with straw or sisal are available.

Similarly, local clothes designed for the local climate may be a good buy. Batik and tie-dye fabrics make colourful resort wear. Particularly useful are the green palm-frond sunhats, woven for you right there on the beach.

On the more touristic islands, luxuries such as jewellery, china and crystal are on sale. Caribbean costume dolls, coral necklaces, wooden carvings and postage stamps are also popular souvenirs.

Practical Information

Banks: Monday to Thursday 8 a.m. to noon or 1 p.m., Friday 8 a.m. to noon or 1 p.m and 2 or 3 to 5 p.m.

Currency: Eastern Caribbean Dollar (EC$) = 100 cents. Coins: 1, 2, 5 10, 25, 50 cents and EC$1. Notes: EC$1, 5, 20, 100.

Shops: Monday to Friday 8 a.m. to noon and 1 to 4 p.m., Saturday 8 a.m to noon.

Telephoning Home: The Grenadines (area code 809) are linked to the U.S. network.

POINTE-A-PITRE

Guadeloupe

Introduction

Proudly styling itself the Caribbean's "Emerald Isle", Guadeloupe is actually two islands linked by a drawbridge across a narrow, salt-water channel, the Rivière Salée. From the air, or on a map, it resembles a butterfly.

This largest of the islands in the French West Indies (FWI) spreads its wings midway along the Lesser Antilles chain. Columbus named it after his favourite Spanish monastery, Our Lady of Guadeloupe in Estremadura. To the Carib Indians then living there, it was simply Karukera— "Island of Beautiful Waters". Today its natural unspoiled charm complements the sophistication of Martinique, the other main French island, 100 miles (160 km.) to the south.

Guadeloupe's two component islands are notably dissimilar and confusingly named. Grande-Terre is smaller, drier, flatter and more important because it has Pointe-à-Pitre, Guadeloupe's commercial centre and largest city. Basse-Terre is higher, bigger, greener and has the political capital, also called Basse-Terre, which lies at the foot of the famous Soufrière volcano. In fact, the islands' names refer not to their topography, but to the winds which strike them.

Officially part of France, Guadeloupe enjoys all the niceties of French living: terraced cafés, creamy cheeses and freshly-baked croissants, French wines. But it's all spiced with an intriguing Caribbean flavour—the contribution of its tropical island setting and that fascinating culture known as Creole. Voodoo superstition and cockfighting are as much a feature of life here as the unmistakably French coins in your pocket.

One of the island's major problems is the high population density. About 350,000 people live here, with some 30,000 on its administrative dependencies (Saint-Martin, Saint-Barthélemy, Marie-Galante, Les Saintes and Désirade). Two-thirds are classified as mulattoes, including some 16,000 Asian Indians. Blacks form 28 per cent of the population and Creole whites born here, 8 per cent. The racial mixture gives rise to a range of subtly different skin tones and facial features.

Guadeloupe teems with life, yet it retains a relaxed and leisurely pace which enhances the tranquil delights of this island paradise.

A Brief History

Pre-European history	Indians from the Orinoco basin in South America migrate up the Antilles chain, reaching Martinique and Guadeloupe before A.D. 200. They are followed by the Arawaks, another wave of Amerindians from the Orinoco, who settle throughout the Caribbean by A.D. 300. For centuries they have the islands to themselves but their tranquillity is shattered by the arrival of the Caribs. These Indians, also from South America, attack the Arawaks, driving the men off island after island and appropriating their women.
15th–17th centuries	Christopher Columbus discovers Guadeloupe in 1493. But half-hearted attempts during the 16th century to establish a Spanish foothold on the island are repulsed by the warlike Caribs. The French move into Guadeloupe in 1635, but it takes them another five years to prevail against the Caribs. Sugar-cropping begins booming as early as the 1640s and slaves are brought in to work the plantations.
18th century	Britain conquers Guadeloupe in 1759 and holds it for four years. The British occupation gives Guadeloupe's sugar-based economy a boost: more slaves are imported, new cane-grinding windmills are built, and a port is established at Pointe-à-Pitre.
	The island is returned to France in 1763 and the following year is declared a French province. In the 1790s, a slave revolt, sparked off by the French Revolution, is followed by a second brief occupation by Britain. Victor Hugues, representing the new French Republic, drives the British off the island, proclaims slavery abolished and sets about guillotining the old guard colons.
19th and 20th centuries	Responding to a revolt by the former slaves, Napoleon Bonaparte's forces arrive in Guadeloupe in 1802 and reintroduce slavery. The British return to occupy the island in 1810, but it reverts to France at the end of the Napoleonic Wars.
	In 1838, the philanthropist Victor Schoelcher (you'll see his name in many streets) succeeds in having a law passed in France abolishing slavery. Ten years later, the

law is implemented in Guadeloupe, freeing 87,50 slaves. Contract workers begin to arrive from India an Africa to replace slave labour on the plantations.

In 1871 Guadeloupe is granted representation in th National Assembly in Paris and both Guadeloupe an Martinique become full *départements* of France in 1946 Later, under an administrative reshuffle, they ar renamed *régions*, each with a *préfet* named in Paris an 4 deputies and 2 senators sitting in the nationa legislature.

Sightseeing

Pointe-à-Pitre
A tiny fishing village three centuries ago, this city is named after a Dutchman, Pieter, said to have been the most popular fish pedlar on the waterfront. Today weathered banana schooners chug past yachts, and gargantuan passenger liners dock in this lively tropical port which is Guadeloupe's principal city and gateway to the world.

In the heart of the town, the **Place de la Victoire** sprawls in the shade of sandbox trees planted by Victor Hugues to commemorate his defeat of the British in 1795. During his reign, a guillotine shortened many lives here, but now its numerous cafés are a popular haunt of young people.

Pointe-à-Pitre's cathedral, the **Basilique Saint-Pierre et Saint-Paul,** features unusual metal columns and balconies Originally built in 1873, it wa destroyed by three hurricane in this century and restorec each time. Its simple beauty i enhanced by locally designed stained-glass windows.

Don't miss the bustling open-air **market** close by the wharves. Colourful mounds of fruit and vegetables lie heaped beside land crabs dried fish, spices and nuts. The vendors, wearing straw hats or brightly patterned Madras handkerchiefs, will sell you almost anything from a baby pig to a "spiritual spray" for your home.

Excursions

Around Grande-Terre
Three formidable cannons greet you at the wooden drawbridge entrance to **For Fleur d'Epée** which commands access to Pointe-à-Pitre's har-

our. Late in the 18th century, British and French forces ought bloody hand-to-hand battles for this strategic hill.

A few miles down the coast t **Gosier,** contingents of fierce invaders used to put ashore. Today this is Guadeloupe's "riviera", with resort hotels strung along the beaches and tennis courts laid out among the coconut palms.

Further east, between the pleasant seaside village of Sainte-Anne and the sleepy fishing village of Saint-François, lie some of the best of Guadeloupe's white sandy beaches where the coral reefs are clearly visible beneath the limpid water. Inland is a peaceful region of green hills, or *mornes* as they're known in the West Indies.

One of the scenic highlights of the entire Caribbean, **Pointe des Châteaux,** at the eastern tip of the butterfly's wing, is a wildly beautiful cliff formation with rocks shaped like castles lashed and eroded by Atlantic waves. You may well get sprinkled by sea spray as you walk along the rocky bluff to the large cement cross erected at the summit. From here the view is magnificent: the large island in the distance is Désirade, the small Petite-Terre islets are much closer.

The sparsely inhabited northern part of Grande-Terre is sugar cane and cattle country. Notice the windmills, mostly in ruins, that used to grind cane. Near the once-flourishing sugar port of Le Moule, resort hotels take advantage of several sandy beaches protected by breakwaters from the heavy Atlantic surf that pounds most of Grande-Terre's east coast. Most dramatic is the northern **Porte d'Enfer** (Gate of Hell), where the waves have sliced a huge chasm into the limestone shoreline.

At the end of a bumpy dirt road as far north as you can go in Guadeloupe, **Pointe de la Grande Vigie** offers spectacular views; on a clear day, you can see across 25 miles (40 km.) of blue ocean to Désirade, and even further to Antigua and the green peaks of Montserrat.

Further south the beaches of tan sand at **Anse Laborde** and **Anse de Souffleur** have gorgeous turquoise waters. Vast mangrove swamps extend from the fishing village of **Port-Louis** all the way down Grande-Terre's west coast to Pointe-à-Pitre. They're almost unreachable except by boat, but rewarding for fishermen and birdwatchers.

Around Basse-Terre

Half-way along the eastern coast of Basse-Terre, surrounded by fields of sugar cane and thick groves of banana trees, lies the village of **Sainte-Marie,** the spot where Europeans first encountered Guadeloupe late in the 15th century. The village was named by Christopher Columbus, whose bust stands in a roadside square. Curiously, there is no likely-looking landing place for a boat here. Locals shrug and suggest that the shoreline must have changed in the 500 years since Columbus.

Just south of the farming town of Capesterre, twin rows of majestic royal palms line the so-called **Allée Dumanoir,** named after the man who planted the trees. Further along and inland, the three **Carbet Falls,** which have to be reached on foot, cascade amid a tangle of ferns and tree vines. Just off the road to the falls is the **Grand Etang,** a placid lake surrounded by forest.

At **Trois-Rivières** stop to see fascinating rock engravings carved about 1,000 years ago by the Arawak Indians. A delightful archaeological park has been created around these huge mysterious rocks.

Guadeloupe's political cap-

tal, **Basse-Terre,** is much smaller and sleepier than Pointe-à-Pitre. You may be reminded of a minor town in the French provinces except for its tropical seaside setting at the foot of Mount Soufrière's green slopes. The mighty **Fort Saint-Charles** dates back to 1645.

La Soufrière, temperamental and magnificent, even if its peak is almost always shrouded in clouds, is a "semi-active" volcano. At 4,183 feet (1,468 metres), it dominates the lush and rugged south of Basse-Terre. In the summer of 1976 it began acting up with low-grade "vapour explosions" which provoked worldwide newspaper headlines and the evacuation of 72,000 volcano-zone residents at great cost; but nothing happened and visits to the sulphur springs and lunar landscape of its upper slopes remain a safe and enjoyable thrill.

Guadeloupe's **Natural Park** covers more than 74,000 acres (30,000 hectares) of Basse-Terre's mountainous and densely forested interior. In the midst of the tropical rainforest, **Cascade aux Ecrevisses** (Crayfish Falls) is a lovely picnic area where you can swim in the rocky, fern-lined pool beneath the waterfall.

Eating Out

The French islands offer the best eating in the Caribbean. Piquant Creole dishes as well as the imported staples of French cuisine make dining out a real treat.

Appetizers
Accras—fritters stuffed with salt codfish, sea urchins, shrimp, meat or vegetables. *Accras à pisquettes* is stuffed with a tiny transparent local fish.

Harengs fumés à la Créole—smoked herring flamed in rum, served with a sauce of hot pepper, vinegar, oil and onion, accompanied by cucumber or avocado.

Main Course
Matété de crabes—sautéed crab meat with onions, garlic, lemon juice and seasoning.

Crabes aux ti bananes vertes—boiled crab and green bananas with an aromatic sauce.

Lambi—conch extracted from its shell, tenderized and served boiled or sautéed in oil with lemon and garlic.

Blaff—stewed or "soused" fish with lemon or lime, garlic, hot red pepper, India wood *(bois d'Inde)* and other spices.

Calalou—soupy stew containing smoked ham, bacon

or crab with chives, onions, parsley and special calalou greens, garlic and hot pepper.

Ti nin lan morue *(bananes vertes et de la morue)* — green bananas, cod, sweet potatoes, piquant green peppers, cucumbers and garlic-laced bits of pork.

Dessert

Look for the Creole speciality, a hot tart of grated coconut and delicate pastry. Coconut cake is another favourite and there are creamy French-style *pâtisserie* products.

Drinks

Ti punch, Creole for *petit punch,* is the ubiquitous drink — a short snort of rum, sugar cane syrup and a dash of lime. Other rum punches include *planteurs* (with fruit juices), *au coco* (with coconut milk) and the daiquiri.

Shopping

If you're not French, thin French. Outstanding bargain are in perfumes, Parisian fash ions, silk items, porcelair crystal, liqueurs and vintag wines.

Other good buys: clot hangings of Creole scenes, tor toise-shell and other seashe jewellery, straw mats and hat particularly from Saint-Bar thélemy, local rum án conchshells.

A standard Guadeloup souvenir is a puffed-up, por cupine-spined puffer fisl *(poisson lune),* which, if larg enough, can become an off beat lampshade.

Note: for all non-residents a 20 per cent discount fo purchases made with trave ler's cheques is common ii Pointe-à-Pitre shops.

Practical Information

Currency: The French *franc* (abbreviated *F* or *FF*) is divided into 10 *centimes* (cts.). The coins and banknotes in circulation in the FWI ar exactly the same as those used in France.

Language: French is learned at school but Creole is widely used fc everyday purposes.

Tipping: a 10% tip is the norm.

CAP HAÏTIEN

Haiti

Introduction

Haiti is a land of high, mist-shrouded mountains and plunging valleys, of voodoo and Christianity, of enormous cultural wealth and the direst material poverty.

Here, you won't find the usual Caribbean holiday spot. It may share the dramatic scenery of some islands and the excellent beaches of others, but a visit to Haiti is, as the inhabitants describe it, a cultural experience in the widest sense of the term.

The Republic of Haiti occupies the western third of the Caribbean island of Hispaniola, which it shares with the Dominican Republic. It is one of the world's most densely populated countries.

Its 5½ million people are proud of their country's status as the oldest Black republic in the western hemisphere. All the magnificence of a splendid and turbulent history is there to see in the former mansions of the coffee barons and in the grandiose ruins of palaces and fortresses.

Perhaps there is a folk memory of a distant past, of a lost Eden predating the freebooters, slave owners, heroes, warriors and megalomaniac emperors. It is often reflected in the art, which seems to blossom everywhere—in galleries, churches, on the walls of buildings and even spread along the pavements.

The language of the Haitians is Creole, derived from French with an admixture of Spanish, West African languages and even a little English.

A lost innocence is certainly reflected in the dignity and gentleness of the people whose courtesy and hospitality have been unaffected by tourism. Haiti may disturb you, move you or fascinate you. It certainly will not leave you indifferent.

A Brief History

Pre-Columbian	The name Haiti means "high country" in the language of the peaceful Arawak Indians who inhabit the land before the arrival of the Europeans.
15th and 16th centuries	Columbus sights the island on December 5, 1492, and names it Española, "Spanish Island". The Arawaks welcome the newcomers with gifts of gold, but within

	two generations are wiped out by disease, slavery and slaughter. West African slaves are imported.
17th century	French and English buccaneers set up their headquarters on Tortuga island from 1625. Later the French found the mainland settlement of Cap-Français, now called Cap Haïtien. Spain relinquishes the western third of Hispaniola—today's Haiti—to France in 1697.
18th century	The area, then called Saint-Domingue, becomes the richest of France's Caribbean possessions. In 1791, half a million slaves seize their freedom. When the English move in, the French call on a former slave, Toussaint Louverture, who ousts the invaders and becomes governor and commander-in-chief.
19th century	Stung by Toussaint's success, Napoleon sends 80 warships and captures him in 1802. Three of Toussaint's generals continue the struggle and defeat the French troops. On January 1, 1804, one of the generals, Jean-Jacques Dessalines, proclaims the country independent, and himself Emperor of Haiti. He is assassinated in 1806. The two other generals, Henri Christophe and Alexandre Pétion, set up rival kingdoms. In 1822 Haiti seizes the eastern part of the island from the Spanish. When the Dominican Republic is formed in 1844, Haiti enters a long period of unrest and civil strife.
20th century	The United States occupies the country from 1915 to 1934. In 1957, Dr. François Duvalier, "Papa Doc", is elected president. He rules with the support of the secret police, Tontons-Macoutes, until his death in 1971. His son, Jean-Claude or "Baby Doc", takes over as President for Life but has to flee the country in February 1986.

Sightseeing

Cap Haïtien, "Cap" as it is known locally, is Haiti's oldest and most historic city and the springboard for excursions to the fascinating ruins of Sans Souci palace and what has been described as the eighth wonder of the world, the great Citadelle Laferrière.

"Cap" is a quiet town despite its 55,000 people. Founded by pirates in 1670, it's the second biggest city after the capital, Port-au-Prince. It was near here that Columbus landed in 1492.

Looking at its crumbling mansions, fortifications and Baroque architecture, it's not hard to believe that it was once a centre of gaiety and wealth under the French. Much of the town was destroyed by an earthquake in 1842.

Yet there is enough old-world appeal for you to imagine the elegantly dressed ladies of colonial times strolling along the promenade. Today, you can escape the bustle of the harbour and explore the back streets with their pastel-coloured houses and Creole atmosphere.

As a foretaste of your visit to the Citadelle look in at **Fort Picolet**, said to have been designed by Louis XIV's military engineer, Vauban. A visit there will reinforce the flavour of old French colonialism.

"Cap" was also the base of General Leclerc, whose ill-fated expedition to recapture France's richest colony spelled the end of French rule. He lived with his wife, Pauline Bonaparte, Napoleon's sister, in what is now a ruined palace.

There are one or two fine beaches near "Cap". The most accessible are **Cormier,** with a good hotel and tourist facilities, and **Coco Beach** noted for its beautiful sea and sand.

If you want to see what a typical Haitian village looks like, ask a boatman at Coco Beach to take you to **Labadie.** The villagers may greet you with *"Bonjour Blanc"*. It's not racism but good manners, for *Blanc* (white) simply means "stranger".

Excursion

Prepare yourself well for the visit to Sans Souci and the Citadelle, for rainclouds inevitably gather later in the day. You'll need strong shoes, a sweater (it is dank and cool in the Citadelle) and a hat—and don't forget your film because you cannot buy any there. It's a 10-mile (16-km.) drive to the nearest village of Milot.

Sans Souci is a fantasy from the megalomaniac mind of King Henri Christophe I of Haiti (1767–1820) who in 14 years built eight forts and nine palaces. Begun in 1807, as a Caribbean counterpart to Frederick the Great's palace of the same name in Potsdam, it was the scene of King Henri's bizarre court rituals. Now the chandeliers, the tapestries and the mahogany wainscoting are long gone, the lovely pink brick is crumbling, the fountains are dry and all that is left is a gigantic and eerie stage set with a magnificent double staircase.

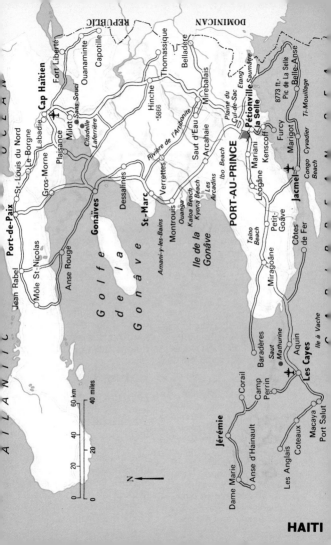

HAITI

Reaching the remote and fantastic **Citadelle Laferrière** involves a bone-shattering drive and a walk or horseride. It is not recommended for the elderly.

The Citadelle looms from the tropical forest like a haunted battleship, its massive 140-foot (43-m.) ramparts seem to hang in the grey air.

Started in 1804 during a French invasion scare, the fortress was built by 200,000 men, women and children. Some 20,000 people lost their lives in the herculean task of hauling building materials through steep forest paths to a height of 3,000 feet (about 1,000 m.).

It was designed for more than 15,000 soldiers to withstand a year-long siege. Some 45,000 cannonballs heaped in the galleries still wait to be fed to hundreds of rusted cannons that never fired a shot in anger.

From the Citadelle's **Upper Court,** where King Henri is supposed to have ordered a troop of soldiers to march over the parapet to their deaths as an example to others, you can see the mountains and valleys of Haiti in all their magnificence.

The Citadelle is the final resting place of King Henri who in a last grand gesture shot himself here—some say with a golden bullet. His motto on his tomb says: "I am reborn from my ashes".

Voodoo

Voodoo is not black magic but an animistic religion from Africa. It was the unifying force of Haitian slaves in their struggle for freedom, and today exists side by side with Christianity.

A voodoo ceremony can last from a few hours to a few days—or even months around December and January. It is led by a *hougan* (priest) or a *mambo* (priestess) assited by *hounsi.*

The increasing frenzy of drumming, dancing and chanting follows a number of rituals, all designed to establish contact between the living and the spirits of the dead.

Eating Out

Haitian Creole food is excellent—a combination of tropical ingredients and French flair.

There are plenty of crayfish and other fish, prepared in delicate and spicy ways. Try crayfish flamed in rum with a helping of *du riz et djon-djon* —rice flavoured with local black mushrooms.

Another delicacy is *tassot*, sliced turkey or beef marinated and fried—and you'll almost certainly come across *griot*, a snack made of pork, which is first boiled in its marinade and then fried in its own fat. It's served with a fried banana. Pickled vegetables, known as *pickles* or *confit*, often accompany the meal. Meat is sometimes served with a sauce of bitter oranges, but beware of *ti malice*, a sauce that can take the roof off your mouth, the main ingredient being vicious little chillis.

You may see people hard at work with a pestle and mortar—they'll probably be making *mamba*, fresh-ground peanut butter which is grilled in cakes and sold at the roadside. Eat it with cassava bread, which you might have to ferret out as it is not always served in hotels.

Pain patate is a delicious end to a meal. It's made of sweet potatoes and sometimes

168

served with a mango jam. And to round it all off there is the superb Haitian coffee.

Drinks

The French influence is felt in the Haitian way of distilling rum. Known as Barbancourt Five Star, this relatively mild rum is distilled in the same way as Cognac.

Rum, as elsewhere in the Caribbean, is the heart of many a cocktail, made even more exotic by the choice of tropical fruit juices and nectars.

There are a number of tropically flavoured liqueurs, good local beer and imported wines.

Shopping

Haiti is justly famous for the quality of its **paintings** and **carvings,** and these will certainly catch your eye. There are dozens of galleries, some of them well known and selling the work of prominent artists, especially of Haitian Primitives.

There is an artistic sense too in the **craft work,** from metal sculptures cut from the tops of oil drums to baskets, embroidery, inlaid wood and horn.

For a true flavour of the country, Haiti's **rum and liqueurs** are recommended.

Practical Information

Banks: Open from 9 a.m. to 1 p.m., Monday to Friday.

Clothing: There is a marked difference in temperature between the coast and the hills where there is a likelihood of drizzle. Take a sweater, a hat and stout shoes for excursions. Don't offend the locals by wearing beach clothes in town.

Currency: The unit of currency is the gourde, divided into 100 centimes. The U.S. dollar is accepted everywhere. Most hotels and larger shops will accept credit cards and traveller's cheques.

Telephoning Home. To call the U.S. direct from Cap Haïtian, dial 00 + 1 + U.S. area code + local number. To phone Cap Haïtian from the U.S., dial 011 + 50 93 + local number. To call the U.K. direct from Cap Haïtian, dial 00 + 44 + area code + local number. To call Cap Haïtian from the U.K., dial 010 + 50 93 + local number.

PORT-AU-PRINCE

Haiti

Introduction

With a population of some 900,000, the capital of Haiti sprawls across the rough triangular plain emerging from the mountains that overlook the Gonâve Gulf.

A visit to Port-au-Prince—even for a few hours—is more than a mere stopover; for Haiti, as the inhabitants themselves describe it, is a cultural experience in the widest sense of the term. Voodoo and Christianity, riches and poverty, sunshine and mist, mix to produce startling contrasts.

The republic's 5½ million people are squeezed into a surface area of 27,750 square kilometres (10,714 sq. mi.), making Haiti one of the world's most densely populated countries. It's also the oldest independent Black nation in the Western hemisphere—dating its freedom from January 1, 1804—and its citizens are proud of the fact.

Haiti's lilting Creole language is derived from French with an admixture of Spanish, West African tongues and a touch of English. Even French speakers need some time to adjust.

This is not the usual sort of Caribbean holiday spot. No clichés can encompass it. There are beaches, some very good, some undeveloped. There is art blooming everywhere—in galleries, along the walls of buildings, spread on the sidewalks. There is luxury too, in the calm of Pétionville villas and hotels. On the other hand, you will see signs of poverty that may make you feel very uncomfortable.

Haiti may disturb you, move you or fascinate you. It is practically certain it will not leave you indifferent.

A Brief History

Pre-Columbian	The name Haiti means "high country" in the language of the peaceful Arawak Indians who inhabit the land before the arrival of the Europeans.
15th and 16th centuries	Columbus sights the island on December 5, 1492, and names it Española, "Spanish Island". The Arawaks welcome the newcomers with gifts of gold, but within two generations are wiped out by disease, slavery and slaughter. West African slaves are imported.

7th century	French and English buccaneers set up their headquarters on Tortuga island from 1625. Later the French found the mainland settlement of Cap-Français, now called Cap Haïtien. Spain relinquishes the western third of Hispaniola—today's Haiti—to France in 1697.
8th century	The area, then called Saint-Domingue, becomes the richest of France's Caribbean possessions. In 1791, half a million slaves seize their freedom. When the English move in, the French call on a former slave, Toussaint Louverture, who ousts the invaders and becomes governor and commander-in-chief.
9th century	Stung by Toussaint's success, Napoleon sends 80 warships and captures him in 1802. Three of Toussaint's generals continue the struggle and defeat the French troops. On January 1, 1804, one of the generals, Jean-Jacques Dessalines, proclaims the country independent, and himself Emperor of Haiti. He is assassinated in 1806. The two other generals, Henri Christophe and Alexandre Pétion, set up rival kingdoms. In 1822 Haiti seizes the eastern part of the island from the Spanish. When the Dominican Republic is formed in 1844, Haiti enters a long period of unrest and civil strife.
20th century	The United States occupies the country from 1915 to 1934. In 1957, Dr. François Duvalier, "Papa Doc", is elected president. He rules with the support of the secret police, Tontons-Macoutes, until his death in 1971. His son, Jean-Claude or "Baby Doc", takes over as President for Life but has to flee the country in February 1986.

Sightseeing

Port-au-Prince

Port-au-Prince's most important landmark, clearly visible from the sea, is the **Palais National**. Built in 1918, and modelled after the Capitol in Washington, it formerly contained the offices and apartments of the Duvaliers. Adjacent is the large open area of the Place des Héros de l'Indépendance, generally known as the Champ de Mars (many squares and streets in Haiti have two names, an official and a popular one), with statues of the national heroes—Dessalines, Henri Christophe and Alexandre Pétion. Directly in front lies the Place du Marron Inconnu (Square of the Unknown Slave) with Albert Mangonès' fine **statue** of a man, holding a conch shell to his lips to call his brothers to revolution.

Nearby, in the **Musée du Panthéon National,** an underground crypt shelters the remains of the founding fathers of Haiti. Beyond the impressive modern vault are exhibited early Haitian relics, portraits and historical documents. Among them are the anchor from Columbus' ship, the *Santa María,* Toussaint-Louverture's elaborate watch and the silver pistol with which King Henri Christophe killed himself.

Administrative offices surround the area. Haiti has developed the unusual and practical habit of colour-coding its buildings. Yellow indicates the army, a green roof points out government buildings. The large yellow edifice to the right of the statue as you look towards the palace is the François Duvalier barracks.

A few blocks north is the Anglican Cathédrale Sainte-Trinité filled with murals by Haitian painters. Two Americans—Dewitt Peters, an English teacher and water colourist and Selden Rodman, writer and critic—were instrumental in the extraordinary burgeoning of Haitian art in the '40s. Directors of the Centre d'Art in Port-au-Prince, they persuaded the Anglican bishop, Alfred Voegeli, to let Haitian artists decorate the interior of his church with **biblical murals.** The results are astonishing. Philomé Obin, Rigaud Benoît, Castera-Bazile and Gabriel Levêque all produced moving religious painting; Wilson Bigaud's *Marriage at Cana* steeped in an eerie green light, is a masterly mixture of Christian and Haitian symbolism.

Once you've seen the Sainte Trinité murals, you will probably want to explore Haitian art further. The **Musée d'Art Haïtien** behind the Presidential Palace on the Place des Héros displays many leading Haitian artists. The shop at the back of the gallery sells interesting objects, such as wood carvings, iron sculpture and weaving.

Two other prominent churches in Port-au-Prince are **La Cathédrale Notre-Dame,** the official religious centre of Haiti, and **l'Ancienne Cathédrale Catholique,** built in 1720 under French rule.

The city's second major

Voodoo

Voodoo is not black magic but an animistic religion from Africa. It was the unifying force of Haitian slaves in their struggle for freedom, and today exists side by side with Christianity.

A voodoo ceremony can last from a few hours to a few days—or even months around December and January. It is led by a *hougan* (priest) or a *mambo* (priestess) assisted by attendants called *hounsi*.

The increasing frenzy of drumming, dancing and chanting follows a number of rituals, all designed to establish contact between the living and the spirits of the dead.

You can join up to see a voodoo ceremony as part of a shore excursion.

landmark is the so-called **Marché de Fer** (Iron Market), a fantastic construction in red and green, topped by minaret-style cupolas. It is situated downtown on Boulevard Jean-Jacques Dessalines, usually referred to as Grand'Rue. The story goes that the structure was ordered for a city in the Orient, built in France by the same engineers responsible for the Eiffel Tower and then shipped to the wrong place. Be that as it may, the colourful market is a beehive of activity

where you can buy just about anything from pimentoes to shoe-laces, from naïve paintings to live chickens. It's hot, noisy, smelly and fun. Incidentally, you should haggle.

West are the International Exhibition Grounds, the modern centre of Port-au-Prince with offices, airlines and post office set near the harbour and edged by Truman Boulevard. The International Casino is situated here, so is the Tourist Office and the Théâtre de Verdure, where dance troupes perform twice a week. There is also a *gaguère* or cockpit and a civic fountain, prettily lit at night. The whole area is popular with Haitians for a quiet stroll in the cool of the evening.

Casino Pier on the waterfront is the departure point for daily trips to **Sand Cay Reef** and the Beau Rivage Marina has an excursion daily to Le Grand Bac, where there is excellent swimming and snorkelling.

A colourful phenomenon around Port-au-Prince, "tap-tap" buses look for all the world like circus wagons. Covered with paintings and symbols, each proudly bears a pious message, like "Heart of Jesus" or "The Eternal is very big". If you ride one, you have to bang twice to get off.

Pétionville and Beyond

With its cooler temperatures and welcome breezes, **Pétionville** is where most of the richer citizens of Port-au-Prince live. It's also the location of some of Haiti's finest hotels and restaurants, as well as of many galleries selling paintings and carvings and the Haiti perfume factory.

Pétionville Square is also known as Place Saint-Pierre, after the church of Saint-Pierre set slightly to one side. From here the road goes to Bou-TILLIER where the **Jane Barban-court castle** is situated. This ersatz château containing old distillery vats offers free samples of various rum liqueurs.

Further on, at 3,000 feet, is a lookout point offering a superb **view** of Port-au-Prince and as far east as the ETANG SAUMÂTRE, the brackish, alligator-infested lake on the border of the Dominican Republic.

In **Kenscoff** (about 5,000 ft.), the air is so cool that you may need a sweater. Poinsettias line the road. Flowers and vegetables are grown in quantity in the area, garden produce of a temperate climate thriving in small hillside patches.

Still higher up, winding along a poor road best suited to jeeps is **Furcy**, where the air is so clean, the silence so complete and the scent of the pine trees so strong in the mountain air, you could imagine yourself in the Alps. Floating in a distant blue haze that lends mystery to many views of Haiti is Pic de la Selle, the country's highest peak.

Eating Out

Haitian Creole food is excellent—a combination of tropical ingredients and French flair.

There are plenty of crayfish and other fish, prepared in delicate and spicy ways. Try crayfish flamed in rum with a helping of *du riz et djon-djon*—rice flavoured with local black mushrooms.

Another delicacy is *tassot,* sliced turkey or beef marinated and fried—and you'll almost certainly come across *griot,* a snack made of pork, which is first boiled in its marinade and then fried in its own fat. It's served with a fried banana. Pickled vegetables, known as *pickles* or *confit,* often accompany the meal. Meat is sometimes served with a sauce of bitter oranges, but beware of *ti malice,* a sauce that can take the roof off your mouth, the main ingredient being vicious little chillis.

You may see people hard at work with a pestle and mortar

—they'll probably be making *mamba,* fresh-ground peanut butter which is grilled in cakes and sold at the roadside. Eat it with cassava bread, which you might have to ferret out as it is not always served in hotels.

Pain patate is a delicious end to a meal. It's made of sweet potatoes and sometimes served with a mango jam. To round off a meal try the superb Haitian coffee, a delicious tropical liqueur or a glass of the mild and excellent Barbancourt Five Star rum.

Shopping

Haiti is justly famous for the quality of its **paintings** and wood **carvings.** Dozens of galleries sell the work of prominent artists, especially the Haitian Primitives.

The superb **craft work** ranges from metal sculptures cut from the top of oil drums to baskets, embroidery, inlaid wood and horn.

Haiti's **rum** and **liqueurs** are among the best in the Caribbean.

Practical Information

Banks: Open from 9 a.m. to 1 p.m., Monday to Friday.

Clothing: There is a marked difference in temperature between the coast and the hills where there is a likelihood of drizzle. Take a sweater, a hat and stout shoes for excursions. Don't offend the locals by wearing beach clothes in town.

Currency: The unit of currency is the gourde, divided into 100 centimes. The U.S. dollar is accepted everywhere. Most hotels and large shops will accept credit cards and traveller's cheques.

Transport: Taxis are not metered and the fare must be agreed in advance. *Publiques* (group taxis), *camionnettes* (open minibuses with benches) and *tap-taps* (brightly decorated trucks with benches) are very cheap, but for the more adventurous only.

Water: In hotels and tourist restaurants the water supplied in carafes is perfectly safe. Do not drink tap water and do not drink from streams or rivers.

ILES DES SAINTES

Lesser Antilles

178

Introduction

Totally unspoiled and serenely beautiful—Les Saintes belong to that rare species of island which figures in everyone's holiday dreams but rarely appears on the itinerary.

French, but spiced with an intriguing Caribbean flavour, the eight tiny islands of Les Saintes bask in the scorching sun just over 6 miles from Guadeloupe.

They form part of the scattered French West Indies (FWI), or Antilles Françaises as they are called in France, and are dependencies of Guadeloupe. French Antilles citizens enjoy the same state benefits as all Frenchmen, drink the same famous wines, eat the same cheese and pâtés on baguettes just as crustily delicious as those turned out by every baker in the *métropole*. And yet, you'll sense immediately that this idyllic part of the world isn't, nor could ever be, metropolitan France.

The atmosphere is richer, more exotic: Africans, Asians, Indians and whites of various origins have become absorbed and transformed into the fascinating culture known as Creole. By world standards this racially varied society is a model of harmony.

What will strike you first the marvellous range of subtl different skin tones and faci features. The famous FW women, inevitably wearin bright earrings and flashin colours, manage to be bot graceful and sensuous as the walk. This is true even whe they glide along country road with large bundles balance on their heads. Little gir learn this sure-fire postur improver very early in life.

As on most tropical island the pace of life tends to b lazy. During the hottest hour things come to a virtual stan still, though the Caribbean s esta is an hour or two short than its Mediterranean cou terpart. Slip into the casua drift of things West India Whether eating, touring shopping, taking your tim will always be rewarding.

But when the sun go down and the music starts u there's nothing lazy about th dancing. This is where the *b guine* began and still belong along with all manner of othe Caribbean rhythms just popular and even more fren zied.

They say that if you ca understand the dancing, you' have begun to understan the Creole soul. It's certainl worth trying.

A Brief History

re-European history	Arawaks (Amerindians from the Orinoco) and Caribs (other South American Indians) visit the islands, but lack of water and hot dry climate do not encourage settlement.
5th century	On 4th November 1493, Christopher Columbus discovers an archipelago to the south-west of Guadeloupe; he baptizes it Los Santos in honour of All Saints Day. The islands do not awake the interest of Portuguese or Spanish and so drift into oblivion.
7th century	The French move into Guadeloupe in 1635. Thirteen years later, Sieur Houël, Governor of Guadeloupe, decides to establish a colony on Los Santos, which become Les Saintes. The 30 colons, under Dume, take possession of Terre de Haut, but lack of water makes them leave. In 1652 a new occupation is led by Hazier du Buisson. The settlers are attacked by Dominican Caribs but later these become valuable allies, as the islands become a stake in the rivalry between European powers—particularly in the wars between France and England, beginning in 1666. On the 4th of August Lord Willoughby invades the Saintes waters with 8,000 men in 18 warships. Les Saintes are defended by two French ships commanded by Baron and Beauville. A violent tempest annihilates most of the British fleet, but they are not defeated until Dulion arrives on the 15th August with 200 Dominican Caribs, who oblige the English to surrender.
8th century	On 12th April 1782, in the channel of Les Saintes, a British fleet led by Admiral Rodney marks a historic victory against France's Admiral de Grasse. This disastrous French naval defeat is kown as the Battle of Les Saintes. Following this "Trafalgar of the Antilles", the English hold sea power over the archipelago.
9th century	After a short English occupation, Les Saintes are returned to the French in 1816. They construct Fort Napoléon in 1867. In 1871 Les Saintes and several other small islands become administrative dependencies of Guadeloupe.

Sightseeing

Only 3 of the 8 Saintes are inhabited. The harbour of the main island, Terre de Haut, is dotted with yachts and fishing boats, reminiscent of a mini Rio de Janeiro or various Aegean and Mediterranean ports. Red-roofed houses nestle on the surrounding hills. Under a trim white beacon, a sign says: *"Terre de Haut est heureuse de vous accueillir et vous souhaite un agréable séjour"* ("Terre de Haut is happy to welcome you and wishes you a pleasant stay"). They mean it. Little children carrying trays offer you delicious coconut tarts—a filling treat for a franc or two. Everybody seems to be smiling, and almost everyone is barefoot.

You'll soon notice that this is first and foremost a fishing island—nets, lobster traps, gutting knives, rods and lines are everywhere; it's no surprise to learn that the inhabitants, mostly descendants of Bretons who settled here 300 years ago, are considered the best fishermen in the Antilles.

Epic naval battle was named for beautiful, tranquil Les Saintes.

ILES DES SAINTES

Both they and their long bright boats are called Saintois. The islanders often wear a distinctively flat hat known as a *salako* and don't mind being photographed by polite visitors.

To begin with, you can take a guided minibus tour (local drivers generally speak French only), that covers all 3 miles of road on the island. It includes hilltop Fort Napoléon, unscathed since it was built after the days of Anglo-French warfare in the region. (Some modern art work is displayed inside.) On the Cabrit islet across the way you'll see a 19th-century fort

named, inevitably, after th Empress Joséphine.

After strolling for the fiv minutes it takes to examin the little village, wise tourist head directly for **Pompierr beach** (there's a nominal ad mission charge). This migh be your idea of a paradise a semicircular sandy strip backed by sea grapes and tro pical shrubs, gentle aqua marine surf, a coral reef clos to shore plus some rocks and seaweed for rewarding snor kelling, and a view out to some huge "pierced rocks' (*roches percées*) that partly shelter the entrance to the cove.

There's more shade, from coconut trees, at the delightful unnamed beach on the little **Pain de Sucre peninsula** across the island. Among other beach possibilities is Anse Crawen which is a *naturisme* haunt and said to offer the best off-the-beach snorkelling and skin-diving. Underwater exploring in the transparent depths of the Les Saintes archipelago ranges from good to outstanding. For a negotiable sum, boatmen will take you around the isles, pointing out where the great 1782 naval encounter occurred between French and British fleets, known as the Battle of Les Saintes.

Regardless of the time of year you visit these islands, you'll spend most of your time outdoors on or near the water—and a word of caution is necessary. The rays of the tropical sun here can cause you serious trouble. In no more than 15 to 20 minutes, fair skin can be painfully broiled, *even* in the shade of a coconut tree. For the first few days you'd be well advised to take the sun in extremely small doses.

Swimming conditions vary enormously on all the islands. You'll have no trouble in identifying the many perfectly safe, protected shores where hardly a ripple disturbs the surface. Otherwise, there are some beaches or sections of beaches where swimming is less recommended or even dangerous for all except experts.

Good tidings about the shark situation: no incident involving a swimmer, snorkeller or diver has been reported anywhere in the FWI. Nonetheless, swimming after dusk is not advisable.

Beware of the *mancenillier*, a poisonous tree: do not touch them, nor eat the fruit, and do not shelter under one if it rains. They are clearly signposted.

Eating Out

Doing as the French West Indians do, after your *ti rhum punch* (little rum punch), you can choose from some of the following Saintes seafood specialities. *Blaff* is raw fish, "soused" with lemon or lime juice, garlic, hot red pepper, India wood and other spices. *Ouassous* are giant riverine crayfish, a great delicacy that is becoming rare in the FWI. The *lambi* is conch, the Caribbean's favourite mollusk, extracted from its large shell, tenderized, cut up and served boiled or sautéed in oil with lemon, garlic and seasoning. *Court-bouillon à la Créole* is fish slices marinated in lemon, crushed garlic, hot pepper and salt, then boiled with chives, tomatoes, more garlic and lemon and *fines herbes*. For dessert, try *tourment d'amour* (love's torment): a tart filled with coconut jam.

Shopping

There are several souvenir shops on the islands, where you can find pell-mell the typical Saintes straw hats, *sala kos*; beautiful conch shells, stuffed iguanas and seashell jewellery. An unusual buy is locally distilled bay rum, renowned as a medication against rheumatism.

Practical Information

Currency: The French *franc* (abbreviated *F* or *FF*) is divided into 100 *centimes* (*cts*). The coins and banknotes in circulation in the FWI are exactly the same as those used in France. Coins: 5, 10, 20, 50 cts; 1, 2, 5, 10 F. Notes: 20, 50, 100, 200, 500 F.

Language: French is learned at school but Creole is widely used for everyday purposes.

Tipping: a 10% tip is the norm.

Telephoning Home. To call the U.S. direct from the FWI, dial 19 (wait for dial tone) + 1 + U.S. area code + local number. To phone the FWI from the U.S., dial 011 + 596 + local number. To call the U.K. direct from the FWI, dial 19 (wait for dial tone) + 44 + area code + local number. To call the FWI from the U.K., dial 010 + 596 + local number.

MONTEGO BAY

Jamaica

Introduction

Mo' Bay (as you are soon likely to call it) entered the touristic scene early in the century when a certain Dr. McCatty, advanced for his time, advocated the bracing virtues of salt-water bathing. He and his friends formed the Doctor's Beach Club. That was in 1906. Nowadays nobody doubts the benefits—or pleasures—of sea-bathing and Montego Bay has become part of Caribbean history.

Sugar and bananas take second place here to the tourist industry. Although a good part of the "international set" has now moved on. Mo' Bay still has plenty of visitors.

Jamaica's second largest city supposedly got its name from the Spanish word *manteca*, meaning "lard". Passing ships took on supplies of pork and beef fat from this coastal

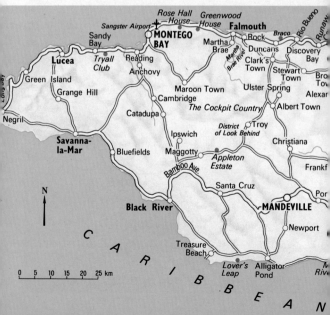

point and some old documents refer to it as Lard Bay.

Today's Mo' Bay has expanded along a generous stretch of the northern coastline. You'll find two excellent golf courses, superb hotels, well-stocked shopping plazas, an occasional sugar plantation and some of Jamaica's best beaches. Inland, there's the mysterious Cockpit Country, a strange potholed landscape with sharp peaks carpeted in green.

Like all of Jamaica, Mo' Bay offers a profusion of colours, scents, sounds and legends. You'll see orchids galore, red-orange poinciana, sunshine yellow *poui* and flaming poinsettias. The island's 200 or so species of birds twitter away among the casuarina, breadfruit or banyan trees—the latter likely to be inhabited by "duppies" or ghosts, for Jamaica has more than its fair share of superstitions.

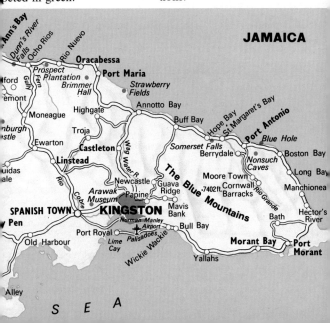

A Brief History

Pre-hispanic times	Arawak Indians from South America come to Jamaic about A.D. 700. These gentle people farm and fish an make some crude pottery. Their words for Jamaica canoe, hammock and tobacco have passed into th English language.
15th–16th century	Columbus anchors at Montego Bay in 1494. When h sails off, he takes along an Arawak, probably the firs Jamaican to try his luck abroad. In 1509, the Spanis establish a settlement on the north coast, near St. Ann' Bay. A few years later they move south to set up shop i what is now Spanish Town. Almost all the Arawaks di off under Spanish rule; African slaves are brought in t replace them.
17th century	The British take over Jamaica in 1655, but pirate continue to rule the waves. Montego Bay first appear on a map that same year. Few people want to live there though: it's too vulnerable to buccaneer attack and to close to the wild Maroons, former Spanish slaves wh live in the hills.
18th century	Era of sugar and slavery. By 1785, Jamaica has a whit population of 25,000 and 250,000 slaves. Uprisings ar common and many planters fortify their homes. Th British sign a treaty with the Maroons in 1739, putting stop to the intermittent warfare. Montego Bay develop apace and even has its own newspaper by 1773 Fire destroys a good part of the town in 1795.
19th century	Jamaica's last and most serious slave rebellion occurs i Montego Bay in 1831. Property and crop damage i extensive; the reprisals, swift and savage. Slavery i abolished by Parliament in 1834 but the system does no actually die out for another 50 years or so.
20th century	Jamaica goes through some tough times and severa periods of great social unrest. In 1944 it attain autonomy; in 1962, independence. But Jamaica doe not completely cut its ties to Britain, deciding to remai part of the Commonwealth.

Sightseeing

Montego Bay falls naturally into three areas—the town itself, the coastal strip with hotels, beaches and shopping plazas and the hills behind.

The **Cage,** right in the centre of town on Sam Sharpe Square, dates from 1807. It used to be a gaol for runaway slaves; now it houses a small museum of slave artifacts. On Sundays, the plantation slaves were allowed to come to town to sell their produce but they were supposed to leave after a bell rang at 2 o'clock. Any slaves still on the streets after the second bell at 3 would be locked up in the Cage.

Also on Sam Sharpe Square is the **Old Court House,** which bears the date 1804 over its main doorway. This was the scene—after the slave rebellion of 1831—of hundreds of trials and sentences carried out in a summary fashion. Those found guilty were strung up outside the courthouse to serve as examples.

The handsome Georgian **Parish Church of St. James** has no such gruesome associations. Built between 1775 and 1782, it was faithfully reconstructed after an earthquake in 1957. Inside you'll find fine mahogany furnishings and two monuments by the prominent British sculptor John Bacon; outside are tropical gardens. There's another Georgian landmark, a red-brick house, at 16 Church Street.

Fort Montego, built around 1750, was a failure from the start. It could not even command the harbour entrance from its site—but luckily the fort was never needed. About the only time a shot was fired from the fort, it was a case of mistaken identity: an English schooner that sailed into harbour in the half-light of evening was thought to be a French privateer.

For a nice view over Montego Bay, pay a visit to Richmond Hill. There's a good restaurant up there, too.

The Montego Bay area stretches 26 miles east to the **Martha Brae,** one of Jamaica's rafting rivers. Vessels made of long bamboo rods, with a seat for two at the stern, are piloted skilfully downriver by barefoot raftsmen. The trip along the winding waterway takes about an hour. Feathery bamboo fringes the river, as you drift through banana plantations, fields of sugarcane and yams. Birds a-plenty—small green parakeets, woodpeckers and the energetic banaquit serenade you on your way. The adventure begins at Rafter's Village and ends at Rock; a bus takes visitors back to the starting point.

A mile to the west, **Falmouth** boasts an admirable concentration of Georgian buildings.

There are several estates which can be visited in the area. **Greenwood House,** built in the early 1800s, used to be be owned by a member of Elizabeth Barrett Browning's family. It's beautifully furnished and contains a collection of early musical instruments, as well as one or two well-authenticated "duppies" (ghosts).

Rose Hall, restored from a ruin at great expense, was the home of the infamous "white witch". Built in 1760, this was always one of the finest houses in Jamaica, with its mahogany panelling, precious fruit-woods and superb staircase. But a 19th-century mistress of Rose Hall gave it such an ominous reputation that for years no one wanted to live there. A mixture of fact, rumour and superstition would have us believe that Annie Palmer, a beautiful but restless young bride, arrived about 1820. Before long she poisoned her first husband,

strangled her second and then stabbed number three. Along the way, she allegedly assassinated the odd lover and terrified the local slaves with her "white" black magic. She was only 29 when they buried her at Rose Hall. The "white witch" had been strangled by an unknown hand.

Inland from Montego Bay, near Anchovy, you can observe and photograph rare birds at **Rocklands Feeding Station,** founded by naturalist Lisa Salmon. Hummingbirds fly right down to drink from hand-held bottles. The feeding takes place around 4 p.m.

Eating Out

Visitors to Jamaica find the food delicious, surprising and very often spicy. In the early days, when many products had to be dried, pickled or salted for shipping to the island, spices were added to perk up or disguise the flavours.

One of those early imports, salted cod, has been incorporated in the national dish: salt fish and ackee. The ackee also came from abroad, brought by Captain Bligh (*the* Captain Bligh). This rosy fruit, when cooked, resembles scrambled eggs.

Two popular Jamaican starters are pepperpot soup, made with kallaloo (a type of spinach), okra and coconut milk, and Solomon Gundy, a well-seasoned pickled herring. The quaintly named "stamp and go" turns out to be fish fritters.

If you attend a buffet at one of the hotels, look for jerk pork. The recipe for this highly peppered meat smoked over pimento wood originated with the Maroons—but they used to make it with wild boar.

Rice 'n peas (actually red beans) has been dubbed "the Jamaican coat-of-arms" because it turns up so often on the table. Breadfruit (also introduced by Captain Bligh) is boiled, fried or roasted for a starchy vegetable.

When it comes to fruit, Jamaica really goes exotic. Naturally, there are oranges, pineapples, bananas and mangoes, but you'll also have a chance to sample such off-beat delights as *paw paw* (papaya); sweetsop and soursop, rough-skinned fruits best blended into milky drinks; naseberry, an almond-flavoured treat; or a collection of highly unusual "apples" which bear little resemblance to the Golden Delicious you left behind.

Shopping

Whether you're looking for Jamaican products or duty-free imports, the shops of Mo' Bay should be able to accommodate. Plan to visit one (or more) of the shopping plazas. You could also check the St. James Craft Market for baskets, carving, embroidery and straw goods (don't forget to bargain there).

Start off with **resort wear.** After all, Caribbean fashion got its start here and the Jamaicans are still in the forefront of the movement. Women's clothes tend to be well cut and flattering with that special island look. Many are made of striking silk-screened fabrics, which you can also buy by the yard.

You will find some very good **painting, sculpture** and **carving** by island artists in the galleries and shops of Montego Bay. **Jewellery** fashioned around Jamaican gemstones—such as coral and coral agate —is attractive and original. Or what about that surefire solution: **rum.**

For duty-free shopping, take along proof of your visitor's status.

Practical Information

Banks: Open 9 a.m. to 2 p.m. Monday to Thursday; 9 to 12 and 2.30 to 5 on Friday.

Credit Cards and **Travellers' Cheques:** Accepted almost everywhere.

Currency: Jamaican dollar (J$) = 100 cents. Coins: 1, 5, 10, 20, 25 and 50¢; bills: J$1, 2, 5, 10, 20, 50, 100. It is illegal to import or export Jamaican currency. Save the receipt from the bank for reconversion when you leave. All transactions made on the island must be paid for in Jamaican dollars, except purchases from in-bond shops.

Shops: 9 a.m.–5 p.m. Monday to Saturday, excluding Thursday; to 1 p.m. on Thursday.

Telephoning Home. Montego Bay (area code 809) is linked to the U.S. network. However, direct dialling is not as yet available to the U.K.

OCHO RIOS

Jamaica

Introduction

Properly speaking a growing village, "Ocho Rios" now refers to a golden strip of north-central Jamaican coast about 60 miles long. It's a region known for decades for its superb beaches and elegant resorts.

The name Ocho Rios may have come from the Spanish for "eight rivers" but is more likely to be a corruption of *las chorreras,* "spouts", referring to the many waterfalls in the region.

This part of Jamaica is important in New World history, with the intrepid explorer Christopher Columbus figuring prominently. He landed here, possibly at Discovery Bay, during his second voyage. He also spent a year (1503–04) marooned at St. Ann's Bay, later the site of the island's first permanent European settlement. Columbus described Jamaica in glowing terms, as "the fairest island that eyes have beheld".

At the time, Jamaica was inhabited by the Arawak Indians, a gentle agricultural people who gave the island its name, "Xamayaca", land of wood and water. The Arawaks disappeared during the period of Spanish rule and African slaves were brought in to replace them. In 1655, the British took over—and stayed for the better part of three centuries, running the flourishing sugar industry, until its decline in the late 1800s.

Jamaicans today are a rich cultural and racial mix (there's a bit of Chinese, Lebanese and East Indian in there, too). They speak English with an Irish—some say Welsh—lilt and their speech is studded with creole words, like *labrish* (discussion), *nyam* (eat), and unusual greetings like "Walk Good" (good day, keep well). The ultimate Jamaican expression is "Soon come"—which really means, if you're very patient and don't try to push anybody around, you'll get what you want in the end because intentions are basically good.

With its swaying palms, magnificent beaches, lush woodlands, delightful waterfalls and masses of flowers—all surrounded by the sparkling aquamarine waters of the Caribbean—Ocho Rios comes pretty close to almost anyone's idea of an island paradise.

A Brief History

Around 700	Arawak Indians arrive from South America. Gentle, primitive and shy, they farm, fish and live in small villages.
5th–16th centuries	Columbus lands on the north shore of Jamaica on his second voyage to the New World. During his fourth voyage (1502–03), Columbus and crew are forced to spend a year at St. Ann's Bay, while waiting for the governor of Hispaniola to send a ship for them. Spaniards found a settlement at Sevilla la Nueva near St. Ann's Bay in 1510. (Discouraged by recurring bouts of fever in that swampy site, the colony later moves to the island's south shore.) The Arawak population plummets from about 60,000 to 0 in the century and a half of Spanish rule. African slaves are brought in to replace the Arawaks.
17th century	The British land in Kingston Harbour (1655) and capture Jamaica. The Spanish governor, Don Cristobal Ysassi, heads for the hills, where he carries on a guerrilla resistance for five years. It's said that he hid out in the Runaway Caves, west of Ocho Rios, before sailing for Cuba. Treaty of Madrid (1670) sets an official seal on England's claim to Jamaica. Golden Age of Piracy—with the likes of Henry Morgan controlling the seas.
18th century	Era of sugar and slavery. Jamaica becomes the world's largest sugar producer. By 1785 Jamaica's slaves number 250,000; its white population, 25,000. Slave uprisings occur frequently, followed by cruel reprisals.
19th century	Slavery is abolished by an act of Parliament in 1834 but does not really come to an end till late in the century.
20th century	Decline of sugar industry. Development of banana trade helps faltering economy. Hard times for Jamaica. Alexander Bustamente and Norman Washington Manley emerge as national leaders in the island's fight for independence. Jamaica is granted its own constitution and self-government in 1944. After 1945, many Jamaicans immigrate to Great Britain. On August 6 1962, Jamaica becomes independent but remains part of the British Commonwealth.

OCHO RIOS

Sightseeing

Shaw Park Gardens are one good place to start a tour of Ocho Rios, firstly, because of the stunning view of Ocho Rios Bay and the surrounding countryside and, secondly, for the gardens themselves—lush greenery, brilliant local flora, a sampling of Jamaica's birds and some dramatic waterfalls.

Fern Gully, an old riverbed that has been turned into a road, is another area of natu-ral beauty. It meanders along for about 4 miles through a shadowy valley of tall ferns framed by liana and hard wood. Though car fumes have given the fern a hard life, this is still an enchanted place.

Near Lydford are the Reyn old's bauxite mines. Bauxite the crude ore of aluminium, is Jamaica's most important in

Luxury accommodation a few steps from the beach at Ocho Rios

lustry. Following the road on to Moneague, it passes the site of a disappearing lake. In 1818, water covered hundreds of acres and flooded out a sugar factory; but by 1900 the lake had vanished. Legend has it that once the lake rises, it stays high until it has claimed a life by drowning.

West of Moneague are the remains of **Edinburgh Castle,** built in 1763 by a red-haired Scotsman with a macabre pastime. Lewis Hutchinson used to shoot down anyone and everyone who passed along the lonely road by his castle, decapitate the bodies and throw them into a pit. Tried and sentenced to be hanged, Hutchinson was totally unrepentant. He left £100 at the foot of the scaffold for a monument to his memory.

Back along the coast to the west, **Dunn's River Falls** is quite simply the loveliest, most refreshing spot around. Clear, cool water from the rain forest above comes cascading down over limestone terraces through pools to the sea. Best of all you can climb the falls assisted by experienced guides. Of course, you wear a swimming suit for the occasion and get doused with water, but it's all very easy and pleasant. Once a week, music and dancing begin in early evening, along with a Jamaican "feast".

St. Ann's Bay, the capital of the parish of the same name, is the birthplace of Marcus Garvey, one of the great black leaders of this century. It's also the site of Jamaica's first Spanish settlement, Sevilla Nueva, founded in 1510. Columbus was marooned nearby a few years earlier, and there is a bronze monument to the explorer to commemorate his stay. The church behind the statue contains stones from Sevilla Nueva's first church.

At the Gem Factory in St. Ann's Bay, you will be shown all the steps necessary to transform a raw stone into a finished piece of jewellery. You can also buy souvenirs.

The last Spanish governor of Jamaica is supposed to have hidden out in the **Runaway Caves** before setting sail for Cuba. First used by the Arawak Indians, these limestone caves became a pirate and smugglers' haunt in later years and then a place of refuge for runaway slaves. They were rediscovered in 1838 and 7 miles of passageway have been explored to date. A visit to the caves includes an eerie boat ride in the Green Grotto, 120 feet underground.

To the east of Ocho Rios, **Prospect Plantation** specializes in beef, lime trees and pimento (the source of allspice). But this working plantation also produces a full complement of tropical fuits and vegetables, from savas to pawpaws. Informative guided tours are conducted by the cadets from Prospect Estate Cadet Training Centre, an institute devoted to developing leadership in young Jamaicans. You visit the estate in a "jitney", an open buggy pulled by a tractor, while listening to colourful explanations of the life cycle of a banana plant. And you'll see the plantation's Great House. Jamaica's first hydro-electric power station was built here on the White River.

Further afield, **Oracabessa** is a small banana port that gained fame because of two celebrated British writers who lived there—Ian Fleming and Noel Coward. Fleming's *Dr. No* was filmed in Jamaica, part of it in the bauxite factory at Ocho Rios. Noel Coward's home, **Firefly,** stands on a beautiful headland overlooking the sea. Two baby grand pianos occupy the drawing-room, along with many of the playwright's mementoes, scores, scripts and paintings.

Eating Out

Jamaican food tends to be spicy. This stems from the country's early isolation when many products had to be dried, pickled or salted for shipping to the island, and spices were added to cheer them up—or to disguise the flavour. Jamaica has drawn from the culinary traditions of Africa, England and America but has modified each to suit the island's bountiful produce.

Starters

Two soups to try: pepperpot containing kallaloo (a type of spinach), okra and coconut milk, and the rich, creamy pumpkin.

Solomon Gundy is a well seasoned pickled herring, "stamp and go" are fish fritters. You'll find patties, meat filled pastries, everywhere.

Fish and Meat

The ingredients of Jamaica's national dish, salt fish and ackee, are not indigenous. The fish was originally imported from Norway as cheap protein food for slaves and the ackee was brought to the island (along with breadfruit) by the famous Captain Bligh. Incidentally, this rosy fruit i poisonous until it ripens and bursts open, revealing a delicate yellow interior. When cooked, it looks and tastes rather like scrambled eggs.

Jerk pork, an east coast speciality often served at buffets, is highly peppered pork that has been smoked over pimento wood. The recipe came from the Maroons, runaway slaves who lived in the hills, and was originally tried out on wild boar.

Vegetables and Fruit

Sweet potatoes, you'll find, are a perfect accompaniment to curry; chocho, the prickly fruit of an aggressive vine, has a mild watery taste somewhat like marrow; rice 'n peas (red beans) make a frequent appearance; green bananas turn up boiled as a vegetable, while plantains, their larger, coarser cousins are sliced and fried.

Naturally, you'll find oranges, mangoes and papaya. You will also come across sweetsop and soursop, rough-skinned fruits that can be eaten raw but are especially good in milky drinks. They're reputed to have aphrodisiac qualities. Sugarcane lengths are sold along the road. Ask to have the cane stripped: you chew on the stringy interior.

Drinks

All those fruits go into the blender to produce delicious drinks, with or without alcohol. Coconut water makes a good roadside refresher. The green fruit is beheaded with a clean sweep of the machete and you drink straight from the nut.

Red Stripe beer, the strong local lager, will quench any thirst. Most famous, of course, is Jamaica's light, aromatic rum. It's very popular in a planter's punch made with lime juice, sugar syrup and crushed ice.

Shopping

There are basically two types of article on sale: local goods—arts and crafts—and imported duty-free articles (called in-bond). You'll find clusters of shops catering to both kinds of shopper at Pineapple Place, Ocean Village and Coconut Grove in the tourist areas.

Take along proof of your visitor's status when you go duty-free shopping. You can carry away anything you buy except the "consumables", alcohol and tobacco, which are delivered to your point of departure.

Local products worth investigating include fashions, embroidery, shell work, handcrafted jewellery and carvings.

Rastafarian carving (an activity practised by members of the Rastafarian movement, most known for Reggae music) can be very good. Look especially for objects made of *lignum vitae,* a light-coloured hardwood. You'll also find a very attractive assortment o **resort wear.**

For a unique Jamaican sou venir, take home a **recording** of **reggae** or **calypso music.** O a bottle of golden **rum,** o **Rumona,** a rum liqueur, or Ti Maria, a coffee liqueur.

Practical Information

Banks: Open 9 a.m. to 2 p.m. Monday to Thursday; 9 to 12 and 2.30 to on Friday.

Credit Cards and **traveller's checks:** Accepted almost everywhere.

Currency: Jamaican dollar (J$) = 100 cents. Coins: 1, 5, 10, 20, 25 an 50¢; bills: J$1, 2, 5, 10, 20, 50, 100. It is illegal to import or expor Jamaican currency. Save the receipt from the bank for reconversio when you leave.

All transactions made on the island must be paid for in Jamaica dollars, except purchases from in-bond shops.

Shops: 9 a.m.–5 p.m. Monday to Saturday, excluding Thursday; t 1 p.m. on Thursday.

Clothing: Hats are really useful against the powerful sun—you can bu ideal broad-brimmed ones on the spot.

Telephoning Home. To call the U.S. or Canada from Ocho Rios, dial 0 + area code + local number. To call Ocho Rios from the U.S. or Canada dial 1 + 809 + local number. There is no direct dialling to the U.K from Jamaica.

PORT ANTONIO

Jamaica

Introduction

Refreshed by rain showers drifting over from the Blue Mountains, Port Antonio (pop. 10,000) is one of the greenest spots in Jamaica. It is a centre for the Jamaican banana trade and was an early mecca for tourism, celebrated before Montego Bay and Ocho Rios were ever heard of. They have since surpassed it in tourist numbers, but Port Antonio, in contrast, offers a feeling of exclusivity and charm.

Cradled by the bushy arms of the mountains, Port Antonio has two superb harbours, divided by the Titchfield Peninsula. The two harbours, rather unimaginatively named East and West, are flanked by Navy Island, once owned by the film star Errol Flynn. His name and anecdotes of hard living—and harder playing— have entered into the area's history.

Flynn was not the only well known figure to be captivated by Jamaica. Swiss industrialist Baron Heinrich Thyssen gave Pellew Island in San San Bay to his bride as a wedding gift and Ian Fleming spent many winters in Jamaica plotting the next adventure of Agent 007.

The waters off Port Antonio are noted for deep-sea fishing, with marlin, wahoo, kingfish, bonefish, yellowfish and dolphin (a fighting fish, not the porpoise variety) running within half a mile of the shore.

Or if bird-watching is more in your line, there are more than 200 species of birds in Jamaica—24 of them found nowhere else in the world. And the variety of plants is spell-binding, the vivid colours rarely found on an artist's palette.

A Brief History

8th century	Arawak Indians from South America settle on the island they name Xamayaca, "Land of Wood and Water". Daily life revolves round farming and fishing
15th–16th centuries	Columbus sights Jamaica in 1494 on his second voyage to the New World and describes his latest discovery as "the fairest island that eyes have beheld". Later his ship is marooned for a year at St. Ann's Bay, and a Spanish

settlement is founded. Fever forces the newcomers south to what is now Spanish Town. The Spaniards plant sugar cane, tobacco and bananas. Disease and Spanish massacres wipe out 60,000 Arawaks who are replaced by imported African slaves.

7th century   Jamaica is captured by the British in 1655 as a face-saving operation after failing to conquer the island of Hispaniola. The British land at what is now Kingston Harbour and the Spaniards surrender. However, the governor, Don Cristobal Ysassi, heads guerrilla resistance for five years. Britain's claims to Jamaica are rubber-stamped by the Treaty of Madrid in 1670. Runaway slaves, Maroons, harass the British. Pirates rule the waves with Henry Morgan engineering attacks against Spanish vessels. He is tried in London for piracy, pleads patriotic motives and is knighted and made Governor of Jamaica—a role he uses to crack down on his former fellow pirates.

8th–19th centuries   Sugar brings wealth to the whites, but misery to 250,000 black slaves, most of whom toil on the plantations. Uprisings result in cruel reprisals. Missionaries sympathetic to the black cause are terrorized and have their churches razed to the ground.

Slavery is abolished in 1834, but complete emancipation comes years later. Former slaves fight for better living conditions.

0th century   Africans revolt against low wages and lack of voting powers. Adult suffrage is granted in 1944 and electoral lists rocket from 20,000 to 650,000. Full independence comes on August 6, 1962. Jamaica remains part of the British Commonwealth, with a governor-general, senate and house of representatives. Today's economy is based on bauxite mining, sugar and tourism.

Sightseeing

Port Antonio does not have much in the way of historic monuments, but its natural beauty is second to none. The peninsula between the East and West harbours was the original site of the town, which was called Titchfield after the Duke of Portland's English estate. The town was

cals selling jerk pork in the park.

A walk up to **Bonnie View** is rewarded with a splendid panorama of the town and harbours. Head for the lighthouse and you will see **Folly Estate**—an enormous dilapidated mansion which the locals love to spin tales about. The story goes that the house collapsed when the American owner, Alfred Mitchell, arrived with his newly wed bride. The truth is that the house fell prey to sea salt which corroded the iron reinforcing rods, causing the roof to cave in in 1938.

Excursions

The **Nonsuch Caves** offer an easy expedition 5 miles (8 km) inland from Port Antonio. They are situated at the Seven Hills of Athenry, a working plantation of pimento trees, banana, coconut and citrus groves, formerly owned by the United Fruit Company. There is a view to the coast and a fine aspect of Blue Mountain Peak.

The caves once lay under water and preserve fossilized remains of ocean species. A guide takes you through the caves, which are well lit and have good paths.

No visit to Jamaica is com

protected by **Fort George,** the walls of which now enclose Titchfield School.

A stroll around King, Fort George and Musgrave streets will reveal some interesting architecture, especially **De-Montevin Hotel.** If you follow your nose along West Street, you'll find white-aproned lo-

lete without an exhilarating raft trip down **Rio Grande,** between the slopes of the Blue Mountains. This mode of transport was originally used for produce, until actor Errol Flynn turned it into a sport. A qualified rafter navigates the rapids, giving you the chance to wonder at the luxuriant jungle scenery, where a breast-eating Tarzan would not look out of place. **Rafter's Rest** marks the end of the 7-mile (11-km.) trip and provides

a bar and restaurant where fellow travellers can relive their experiences.

Breathtaking views can be enjoyed at many points along the coastline, which boasts more than its fair share of tempting white beaches. Don't miss a visit to **Blue Lagoon,** also known as Blue Hole, south-east of Port Antonio. It deserves every adjective that has ever been lavished upon it. Translucent water of the deepest ultramarine lies

surrounded by dark green vegetation. Have a drink, water-ski, hire a glass-bottomed boat to explore the sea life or simply capture the memory of it all with your camera.

Eating Out

Eating places to suit everyone's pocket and taste buds are abundant. Whether you opt for a five-course meal or a speedy street snack, do try and sample the local fare..Jamaican food is certainly not bland—nearly every dish contains hot peppers or spices which give it a kick of originality.

Salt fish and ackee, similar to scrambled egg with fish flakes, is the national dish. Barracuda, razor-toothed king fish, surgeons, parrots and grunts appear on the fish menu, as well as stuffed crabs, which make a succulent entrée.

Peppered pork cuts, known as jerk pork, are cooked over pimento wood fires at the roadside. Jerk chicken is also available. Curried goat ap-

pears on menus, while pigeon is served in season. Nearly all meat and fish dishes come with Jamaica's "coat-of-arms", a mixture of rice and peas (really red beans).

Kallaloo, a kind of spinach, boiled and baked bananas and the good old potato are among the common vegetables.

Bananas also star on the dessert list—but this time grilled and drowned in rum and lime. The more unusual fruits include sweet sop, served as a dessert or as a drink, paw paw—excellent for breakfast—and naseberry, a small fruit with weird jelly-like skin.

Drinks

King of liquid pleasures is rum, often served with dry ginger ale or coconut milk. Watch out for white overproof rum—if you're not used to drinking paint stripper you could be in for a shock. Gin, vodka and liqueurs made under local licence are cheaper than the imported varieties, but equal their quality. Tia Maria, made from the famous Blue Mountain coffee, is a rich velvet-smooth liqueur.

Don't despair if you are not a rum lover. Jamaica boasts beers from all the main beer-

You can water-ski, swim or simply dream at the lovely Blue Lagoon.

brewing countries, as well as a wide selection of wines, sherries and ports.

Fresh fruit juices such as mango nectar are real thirst quenchers and help wash down the aspirins after a bout on the harder stuff.

Shopping

A couple of hours wandering round the craft markets and shopping streets is a very good way of meeting the local people and getting into the swing of Jamaican life.

If you're thinking of taking away souvenirs, Rastafarian wood-carvings make original gifts and are usually not too expensive. Apart from beads and bamboo carvings, Jama can embroidery, decoratin everything from dresses to te towels, is very attractive.

Perfumes made from nativ flowers, bay rum and lime ar easy-to-carry gifts, while re cords or cassettes of calyps and reggae music will liven u a winter's night back hom (especially if you remembe the bottle of rum).

Jamaica has a good selec tion of duty-free article known as "in-bond". Thes include Japanese cameras Swiss watches and French per fumes. Most of these item you can carry away with you apart from consumables—to bacco and alcohol—whic are delivered to your point o departure.

Practical Information

Banks: Open 9 a.m. to 2 p.m., Monday to Thursday; 9 a.m. to 12 noo and 2.30 p.m. to 5 p.m. on Friday.

Currency: Jamaican dollar (J$) = 100 cents. Coins: 1, 5, 10, 20, 25 and 50¢; bills: J$1, 2, 5, 10, 20, 50, 100. It is illegal to import or expor Jamaican currency. Save the receipt from the bank for reconversion when you leave.

Shops: 9 a.m. to 5 p.m. Monday to Saturday, excluding Thursday to 1 p.m. on Thursday.

PORT ANTONIO

FORT-DE-FRANCE

Martinique

Introduction

The Indians called it *Madinina* —island of flowers, and they were right: hibiscus and bougainvillea, magnolia and oleander, anthurium, poinsettia and more, all compete to make Martinique one of the most colourful tropical gardens on earth. When Columbus discovered the island late in his career, he called it "the best, the most fertile, the sweetest, the most charming country in the world" and named it Matinino, probably after Saint Martin (or, some say, as an approximation of Madinina), a name which the French later adapted to Martinique.

This southernmost of the French West Indies lies between English-speaking Dominica and Saint Lucia. Its 1,100 square kilometres (425 sq. mi.) are crowded with 400,000 inhabitants. The islanders are vibrant, generous and passionate: the loveliness of Martinique's women is legendary, the number of children... astounding. Josephine, Empress of France and wife of Napoleon was born here.

Martinique is officially and proudly part of France; the island has been a *département* of that nation since 1946 with a senator representing her interests in Paris. And yet, despite the flocks of familiar French automobiles with yellow headlights, the francs and centimes, the gendarmes, cafés and Parisian-like little shops, you'll sense immediately that this isn't, nor could it ever be, metropolitan France.

The atmosphere is richer, more exotic: Africans, Asians, Indians and whites of various origins have become absorbed and transformed into the fascinating culture known as Creole.

Everyone agrees there's a special magic to Martinique. Smiling readily but somewhat shy about making the first approach, the islanders will often overwhelm you with kindness once contact is made. Honesty is taken for granted. You'll find a simplicity, a lack of complication, about many local people, yet something, too, of the sophistication associated with the French.

As on most tropical islands, the pace of life tends to be lazy. During the hottest hours things come to a virtual standstill, though the Caribbean siesta is an hour or two shorter than its Mediterranean counterpart. It would be folly for a visitor to expect American-style efficiency or speedy service; a

would be wisest to slip into the casual drift of things West Indian.

Whether eating or drinking, touring or shopping—or just plain dreaming—on Martinique you'll be able to share "our little corner in the Caribbean" as the tourist publicity proudly proclaims.

A Brief History

A.D. 100–300   Saloide and Arawak Indians from the Orinoco basin in South America start arriving in Martinique. New waves of peaceful Arawaks settle in the Antilles, only to be invaded by the war-like Caribs who slaughter the men and appropriate the women.

16th to 17th centuries   Columbus discovers Martinique on his fourth transatlantic journey in 1502. Serious attempts at colonizing the island begin in 1635 with Belain d'Esnambuc, a Norman nobleman, who leads a party onto the island. Warding off fierce attacks by the Caribs, he constructs Fort St. Pierre. By mid-century most of the Indians have fled to Dominica and St. Vincent. After 1640 the sugar industry booms. Thousands of slaves are imported from Africa to work the plantations.

18th century   Britain and France battle for domination of the Antilles. In 1794 Britain occupies Martinique for 8 years, preventing the unrest experienced by neighbouring Guadeloupe when slavery is abolished.

19th century   France reclaims Martinique from Britain through the Treaty of Amiens and reinstates slavery; but Victor Schoelcher, Martinique's greatest hero, dedicates his life to its abolition. After years of struggle, on April 27, 1848, 72,000 slaves are officially declared free.

20th century   Mount Pelée erupts devastatingly in 1902, leaving over 30,000 dead. Martinique, along with Guadeloupe, becomes a full *département* of France in 1946. Tourism and the export of sugar, rum and bananas continue to be the main sources of income.

Sightseeing

Fort-de-France

Clinging to its superb **harbour,** Martinique's capital is sometimes bustling, sometimes drowsy—but always captivating. Awesome green mountains form the backdrop while strikingly tall palm trees dwarf all but a very few buildings.

This is a city to savour on foot. Best is the teeming shopping area centred on the **rue**

Isambert market. In this caver nous emporium you'll have your pick of fresh Martinique pineapples, coconut slices of the pungent baby limes so loved in the West Indies. Among the bananas and Caribbean swee potatoes, you'll find bottles o old-time patent medicines fo sale. Cross the "canal" (the Le vassor River) to get to the **fis market** on the Boulevard Al lègre; it's fascinating to watch the vendors preparing thei wares for sale with machetes

but cast in bronze. Though you'd never guess it, the French fought bloody battles against the English and Dutch on La Savane. Near the park, notice the New Orleans-style iron grillwork on the buildings.

Alongside La Savane runs rue de la Liberté, and at No. 9 is Martinique's excellent **Musée Départemental.** In the three stories of this little air-conditioned museum you can see a wealth of items chosen to evoke a feeling for the island's history. Napoleon and Josephine get top billing, of course, as does the eruption of Mount Pelée. There are slave irons, traditional island costumes and an interesting French map of 1778 showing the *théâtre de la guerre* (theatre of war) between the Americans and the British.

Further along rue de la Liberté is the startling **Schoelcher Library** *(Bibliothèque).* This odd but attractive town house (there's a collection of Arawak and Carib relics) was on display at the 1889 Paris Exposition, then dismantled, brought to Martinique and reconstructed.

Tourists and Martiniquais like tend to gravitate towards the landscaped park called **La Savane** near the water's edge in the heart of the city. Beyond the outdoor shopping pavilions here, you'll come across a white marble **statue** of Napoleon's Josephine, holding a rose and facing the direction of her birth-place across the bay.

Pierre Belain d'Esnambuc, the Norman adventurer who first claimed Martinique for France, also has a statue here,

Saint-Pierre and the Volcano

It was a lovely seaside town, the first French settlement on Martinique, the "Paris of the West Indies". When 1,400-

metre (4,700-ft.) Mount Pelée began belching smoke and cinders far above Saint-Pierre in late April, 1902, authorities professed no concern. Evacuation was unthinkable—an election was coming up.

On May 4–5 a mass of mud and rocks was swept down by Pelée's White River *(Rivière Blanche)*, killing 25 people. At the same time a tidal wave lashed the shores near Saint-Pierre. Flames began spouting from the mountain's peak. On May 7 the governor of Martinique arrived with his wife to calm the residents—Saint-Pierre's total population was about 30,000.

At 8:02 a.m. on May 8, Pelé erupted titanically. A vas burning cloud of gas and steam bearing rocks, lava and ashe roared down the mountainsid onto the town. In just thre minutes Saint-Pierre was to tally wiped out. The only sur vivor was a prisoner in thick-walled dungeon who fo years afterwards was displaye abroad as a circus attraction.

The eruption of the volcan is documented in the excellen **Frank Perret museum.**

Excursions

South of Fort-de-France don' miss **Trois Ilets.** This is th home-town of Marie-Joseph

Rose Tascher de la Pagerie—better known as the famous Josephine, Empress of France and wife of Napoleon. In the **Musée de la Pagerie** you can see a photocopy of her wedding certificate and ponder how even the greatest military geniuses have a place in their hearts for the love of a woman.

Continuing round the coast past Point du Bout, with its resort hotels, and the pretty village Les Anses d'Arlets, you'll suddenly be confronted by a gigantic and ominous-looking bulk rising straight up out of the sea. Two miles off-shore, **Diamond Rock** *(Le Rocher du Diamant)* was occupied by the Royal Navy as a strategic base during the struggle for Martinique in 1804. Watching the wheeling gulls and listening to the lapping surf, it's difficult to believe that the rock was under French bombardment for 18 months.

Eating Out

Just as you'd expect, Martinique offers some of the best eating in the Caribbean. The piquant Creole dishes as much as the imported staples of French cuisine make dining a treat.

North American visitors are thrilled to find real *croissants,* non-plastic Camemberts, crusty French bread *(baguettes),* château wines and any number of good French restaurants. But Creole dishes should be sampled, too. Some specialities:

Accras—Creole fish fritters; hot and delicious.

Potage à la crème de coco—cream of coconut soup.

Matoutou de crabes—sautéed crab with sauce and seasonings.

Lambi—conch, boiled or sautéed in oil and served with lemon, garlic and assorted seasonings.

Blaff—fresh fish, with lime, garlic and hot red pepper.

Calalou—a fragrant stew containing dozens of ingredients, including smoked ham, bacon or crab with chives, green vegetables, onions, parsley, garlic and hot pepper.

Ti nin lan morue—cod with green bananas, sweet potatoes, peppers, cucumbers and pork.

For **dessert** try a hot tart of grated coconut and delicate pastry—a Creole speciality. And for **drinks** its rum, rum, wherever you go. Rum with sugarcane syrup and lime (Ti punch), dark rum, white rum and various rum cocktails. Of the local mineral waters, the *Didier* brand is particularly good.

Shopping

Much of central Fort-de-France is fertile territory for shoppers.

Best buys: perfumes and other French luxury items; you'll also find neckties and the best Parisian silk scarves on sale at reasonable prices.

Good buys: the island's typical *poupée martiniquaise,* a doll in Creole madras costume on sale everywhere; tapestries, wicker trays and boxes, coral and tortoise-shell objects and the memorable dark (aged) or white rum.

Facing the ferry pier on the Fort-de-France waterfront is an outdoor pavilion where you might try bargaining for straw hats and baskets, conch shells, huge wooden forks or seashell necklaces. Some of the sales ladies at this colourful, soft sell market wear traditional Martinique costumes.

Fort-de-France's main shopping streets, tourist-oriented or not, are between the Savane and the Levassor River.

Practical Information

Banks: All banks change traveller's checks and currency. They are usually open from 8 a.m. to 3 p.m. in summer and from 8 a.m. to noon and 2.30 to 4 p.m. in winter, Monday to Friday.

Credit cards and traveller's checks: You may be able to get as much as a 20% non-resident discount on purchases if you make payment with a credit card or a traveller's check.

Currency. The french *franc* (abbreviated *F* or *FF*) is divided into 100 *centimes (cts).* The coins and banknotes in circulation in Martinique are exactly the same as those used in France. Coins: 5, 10, 20, 50 cts, 1, 2, 5, 10 F. Banknotes: 20, 50, 100, 200, 500 F.

Shops: In general stores are open from 8 a.m. to noon and 2 to 5 p.m. Supermarkets, department stores and bookshops—8.30 a.m. to 12.30 p.m. and 2.30 to 5.30 p.m.

CHICHEN ITZA
TULUM

Mexico

Introduction

Two archaeological sites on the Yucatan Peninsula provide fascinating day trips from Cozumel or Cancún: Chichén Itzá was the last great Mayan city, the final flowering of a talented and perplexing civilization; Tulúm, commanding a glorious view over the sea, is believed to be the only fortified Mayan city built on a coastline.

History

1500 B.C. –A.D. 300	**Pre-Classic Maya.** Village life develops, along with the first ceremonial centres. The Maya learn much from the Olmecs, the most advanced people of the time.
300–900	**Classic Maya.** A period of intense intellectual and creative activity in Mesoamerica with considerable cultural interchange between the Maya and the people of Veracruz, Teotihuacán and Oaxaca. Mayan cities are founded in Guatemala, Honduras, southern Mexico and the Yucatan. Chichén Itzá is established in 431 Mayan civilization reaches its height around 600. But by the end of the 9th century building comes to a halt in all the important Mayan centres and one by one the cities are abandoned.
900–1517	**Post-Classic Maya.** The Toltecs (from central Mexico) and the Itzá (from the Gulf Coast) take over Chichén Itzá. The city is refounded in 987. Chichén Itzá is the scene of a Mayan renaissance and it dominates the Yucatan, in league with Mayapán and Uxmal, until around 1200. Then Mayapán usurps leadership. Trade expands as far as central Mexico, Panama and Nicaragua. Tulúm is important in Mayan maritime trade. In the middle of the 15th century, the Yucatan is torn by civil war, and Mayapán is destroyed. Many Maya migrate to the Petén region of Guatemala.
16th century	The Spanish arrive in 1518. In 1526, Francisco de Montejo sets out to conquer the Yucatan. The ruins of Chichén Itzá are occupied by his son in 1537. The Spanish conquer the Yucatan by 1546, but many lives are lost to both the Spanish and the Maya.

Sightseeing

Chichén Itzá

Chichén Itzá, the largest of the Mayan archaeological sites, has hundreds of monuments, though only about 30 of them have been restored or uncovered. The earliest structures date from around A.D. 600 (Late Classic Period), but most were built or rebuilt during the time of the Toltecs.

Dominating the northern section, the **Pyramid of Kukulkán** is dedicated to the Plumed Serpent, a deity introduced by the Toltecs as Quetzalcóatl. The impressive structure consists of a flat-topped pyramid, 75 feet high, crowned by a square temple. What the Mayans really built, though, was a calendar in the shape of a pyramid. Each of its four sides has 91 steps, which together with the top platform adds up to the number of days in the year ($91 \times 4 + 1 = 365$). Nine tiers on each side are subdivided by a central stairway, giving the number of months in the Mayan year ($9 \times 2 = 18$). The 52 panels on each side represent the years in the Calendar Round, the Mayan equivalent of a century.

Most amazing of all is what happens every spring and fall on the days of the equinox: the afternoon sun creates a pattern of light and shade on the north-west stairway resembling a serpent (Kukulkán) descending the stairs—the god's descent to earth. Inside, an earlier pyramid encloses a statue of the rain god, Chacmool, and a fabulous red jaguar set with pieces of polished jade for eyes and spots.

The **Temple of the Warriors** is a large complex with some gory friezes of jaguars and eagles offering human hearts to a god. On the top level you'll find a huge Chac-mool and two serpent columns.

Chichén Itzá's main **Ball Court** is the largest in Mesoamerica. The game played here involved hitting a hard rubber ball through elevated stone rings using hips, thighs and elbows—no hands or feet. It was a very serious affair in which the captain of the winning team had the privilege of offering his head and life to the gods. The gruesome ceremony is depicted in a bas-relief on the side wall.

South of the highway stands **El Caracol** (snail), the astronomical observatory. Small openings along the wall mark the cardinal directions and other significant astronomical points.

Chichén Chob (known as the Red House), **the Nunnery** (so named because it reminded the Spanish of a convent) and the well-restored **House of the Three Lintels** in Old Chichén are among Chichén Itzá's most venerable structures. All are Mayan without Toltec influences. A stone causeway leads from the main plaza of Chichén Itzá to the **Sacred Cenote,** a deep well, jade-green in colour.

A few miles away from the main archaeological site is the **Cave of Balancanché,** an underground shrine that lay sealed and forgotten for at least 1,000 years.

At Chichén Itzá, you can visit the archaeological museum and attend a sound and light show—modern man's way of bringing the ancient city of the Maya back to life.

Tulúm

When a Spanish ship sailed past Tulúm in 1518, the chaplain on board was so impressed by the walled city that he compared it to Seville. An important link in the network of Mayan maritime towns, the city flourished between 1200 and 1500. Most of the present structures date from then.

El Castillo, a pyramidal construction topped by a temple, is most impressive when seen from the sea. Serpent columns like those at Chichén Itzá flank the main entry. The **Temple of the Descending God** takes its name from the figure over the door, possibly representing rain or the setting sun. Oddly enough, the temple walls slant outwards. Other buildings at Tulúm share this feature; a few have doors that slant in.

Some fine carvings decorate the façade of the **Temple of the Frescoes.** Note especially the head of a man (or god) on the corner of the gallery.

Xel-ha provides a good occasion to combine water sports and archaeology. The narrow, rock-lined lagoon is famous for its clarity and changing colours. Snorkellers and skin divers delight in the underground garden and in a submerged shrine, part of the Mayan coastal city once connected by the causeway to Tulúm and Coba.

COZUMEL
PLAYA DEL CARMEN/CANCUN

Mexico

Introduction

Back in the days of the ancient Maya, Cozumel was called "Land of the Swallows." It was a holy island dedicated to Ix Chel, the Goddess of Fertility, and Mayan women were expected to make the arduous journey there at least once in their lives. The Itzá, who took over the Mayan heritage, also considered Cozumel a sacred place, a sort of Garden of Eden where the Mayan people began.

Modern-day pilgrims to the captivating island are likely to be underwater enthusiasts, for the reef running alongside Cozumel ranks near the top of the world's diving sites. The water is remarkable for its transparency (you can see up to 300 feet), its treasures (sunken galleons abound) and its colour (ranging from deep blue to aquamarine).

Those who prefer to spend their time above water will find plenty to see and do topside, starting with the beautiful beaches, sports on land and on sea, a lazy little town, some obscure Mayan ruins and a marvellously relaxed atmosphere—nothing too pushy or commercial.

Cancún is a different sort of place. All new. Though the Mayans had some settlements here as long ago as A.D. 300, the site was virtually virgin territory when the Mexican government decided—with the help of computers—that Cancún was the perfect place to build the perfect resort.

Although Cancún is an island, it doesn't have the same away-from-it-all feeling as Cozumel. On the contrary, it aims to be modern and up-to-date with its carefully planned layout, first-class facilities and deluxe accommodation. Still, Cancún has its share of powdery beaches, palm trees and unfailingly sunny skies. And despite all the new construction, ample space and wilderness remain—and they plan to keep it that way.

Both islands are fun to explore by bike, moped or jeep. You can visit the local Mayan ruins or make a day's outing to the fascinating sites of Chichén Itzá or Tulúm. Towering pyramids, glyph-dated stones, an ancient ball park, art depicting the Maya at work and at war—all are tantalizing remnants of the extraordinary civilization that flourished here long ago.

History

Prehispanic times	Mayan-speaking people appear on the scene about 2000 B.C. Maize is cultivated. The Maya build ceremonial centres and great cities in southern Mexico, the Yucatan and Guatemala. The civilization reaches its peak about A.D. 600. It goes into decline some 300 years later, and many cities are abandoned. The Toltecs, Itzá and other peoples settle in the Yucatan, and the Mayan civilization takes a new direction.
16th–17th century	In 1518, a Spanish expedition headed by Juan de Grijalva lands on Cozumel. The following year, Hernán Cortés stops by the island before setting off on the conquest of Mexico (1521). Cozumel's next Spanish visitor, Francisco de Montejo, is commissioned by the King of Spain to conquer and colonize the Yucatan. Francisco's son takes on the fight which lasts until 1546. The Maya make a last desperate effort to repel the invaders but are ultimately defeated. Franciscan friars come to the Yucatan to convert the heathen and are impressed by the Maya civilization. But continuing idolatrous practices prompt them to stage an auto-da-fé in which all Mayan books are burned.
18th–19th century	The generally tranquil 18th century ends on a note of agitation as new, revolutionary ideas from the United States, Europe and Latin America begin to take root. The Yucatan gains its freedom from Spain in 1821 and joins Mexico two years later. However, centuries of isolation have fostered a sense of separateness in the region. Widespread dissatisfaction with the Mexican government leads the Yucatecans to declare their independence in 1840. A brief reunion, secession and then civil war shake the land in these turbulent years. But what follows is even worse: the devastating Caste War, opposing whites and Indians, from 1847 to 1867. By the end of the century, when the fighting finally stops, the Yucatan has lost half its population.
20th century	World demand for *henequén* (hemp) helps put the Yucatan back on its feet and modern communications and transportation end centuries of isolation. Tourists begin to arrive in the 1950s, bringing further changes.

Sightseeing

Cozumel

Locals usually call **San Miguel de Cozumel** "the town" — logical enough and certainly simpler since it's the only one on the island.

You'll find it to be a pleasant and unpretentious place. Pastel buildings house boutiques and souvenir shops. Open-air restaurants line the waterfront. And there are plenty of diving shops chock-a-block with underwater gear. After you've browsed through the shops, visited the museum (some Spanish relics and Mayan figurines) and stopped by the aquarium to have a look at the giant sea turtles, well, you've seen it all.

North of town lies a stretch of sandy coastline and most of the island's hotels. On the beach in front of the Cozumel Caribe you'll find a marker indicating the spot where Cortés stepped ashore in 1519.

But the beaches are better south of town. If you like amenities with your sand and sea, try Playa San Francisco which has lounge chairs and a restaurant. The calm green waters of the **Chancanab Lagoon,** connected to the sea by a subterranean channel, are ideal for novice snorkellers. Even without diving in you can see all the many reef fish flitting around the coral grottoes.

The other side of Cozumel, the **windward coast,** has miles and miles of magnificent fine sand, all quite empty. It's great for beachcombing and sunbathing but somewhat dangerous for swimming.

A very bumpy road leads past Playa San Francisco to the Mayan ruins of **El Cedral.** There you'll find a small crumbling temple with frescoes inside. The island has other Mayan sites, but it's probably not worth the effort to visit them.

Cozumel's highpoint for underwater enthusiasts is the **Palancar Reef,** 6 miles of submerged mountainous terrain, generally acknowledged to be one of the world's best dives. This is a place for experts. Master divers conduct tours through the sensational scenery — four kinds of coral, including the rare black variety, abundant marine life and undersea wrecks. And you'll be able to see it all clearly, since visibility ranges from 1 to 300 feet.

A delightful Cozumel institution, Robinson Crusoe

Tours, offers a day's outing to a beach like San Francisco or Isla Pasión for sunbathing, swimming, snorkelling and a bountiful beach barbecue. Before the region was declared a national wildlife preserve, the guides used to catch the lunch themselves. But now you can rest assured that the fish you meet will not be the ones you eat.

From Cozumel, the options for excursions are numerous and varied. Fishermen can hop over to **Boca Paila Flats** on the mainland for fantastic bonefishing. Then there's **Isla Mujeres,** the Isle of Women, named by the Spaniards after

the terracotta figurines they found on the island. Like Cozumel, it was dedicated to the Goddess of Fertility.

Today, turtles and lobsters are the tiny island's specialities, and believe it or not you can take a ride on a turtle. Perhaps the chance of a lifetime. Isla Mujeres also offers excellent snorkelling; the best spots are Playa Garrafón and Los Manchones reef. And the island has a few Mayan temples. One, perched high up over the sea, doubles as a lighthouse.

Playa del Carmen/Cancún

Playa del Carmen makes an excellent entry point to the Yucatan — whether you're heading for the computer-planned resort of Cancún or the Mayan ruins of Tulúm and Chichén Itzá. And those who prefer to skip the excursions can just relax on the beautiful beach.

Cancún is an island paradise that works. The Mexican government put a good deal of time and effort into the development of the resort. They chose the island for its beauty, fantastic weather, fine sands, clear seas, coral reefs — and its accessibility. Then they supplied the indispensable infrastructure: good roads, local buses, an up-to-the-minute communications network, water purification plant, convention centre, marinas, championship golf course and, naturally, luxurious hotels and condominiums. The architects of Cancún's master plan tried to think of everything that would make a visitor's stay here enjoyable and trouble-free. It seems they succeeded. Cancún has been popular ever since it opened.

Actually, there are two Cancúns, connected by a causeway. Isla Cancún is the resort proper; Ciudad Cancún on the mainland serves as the support city.

Cancún takes top honours in water sports. You're likely to see devotees of windsurfing, spinnaker flying and parasailing struggling to stay upright or airborne, as the case may be. As for beaches, you can opt for the sheltered waters of **Playa Bahía de Mujeres** or the surf of the open Caribbean — 12 miles of silky white sand to chose from. **Playa Chac-mool** and Playa Tortuga are public, i.e., not connected to hotels.

There are some respectable Mayan ruins in the jungly southern part of the island, accessible by car or boat tour. The **El Rey ruins** — flat-topped buildings and a few pyramids—date from the Late Post-Classic Period (1200–1517). The nearby site of San Miguel is just being opened up. Before you set off though, it's a good idea to pay a visit to Cancún's new archaeological museum, which will provide you with background on the world of the Maya.

Eating Out

Though the Yucatan has its own specialities, you can also get anything from a pizza to a Polynesian banquet in the restaurants of Cozumel and Cancún. Seafood is noteworthy, especially the red snapper, lobster and shrimp.

Yucatecan cuisine, based on Mayan cooking, tends to be spicy and robust rather than fiery. They usually serve the *chile habanero*, the local pepper, on the side so you can dose the hotness yourself. *Achiote* (a paste made of betel-like seeds) and sour orange are the most common seasonings. Some Yucatecan dishes and drinks to look for:

cazón—baby shark

cochinita (pollo) pibil—suckling pig (chicken) with spicy barbecue sauce, baked in banana leaves (*pib* means barbecue in Mayan)

filete de venado—venison steak

horchata—drink made from rice, sugar and vanilla

Ixtabentum—Mayan aperitif based on fermented honey

huevos motuleños—tortillas with fried eggs, beans, ham and peas

panucho—fried tortilla, beans, chicken or turkey, lettuce and onion

papadzules—tortilla rolled around hard-boiled egg, covered with tomato sauce

pipián—pumpkin-seed sauce

pollo muebil—chicken-stuffed tamale baked with *achiote* sauce

pollo (pavo) en escabeche—marinated chicken (turkey)

sopa de lime—chicken soup with lime

torta del cielo—rich almond cake served on special occasions

Shopping

Both Cozumel and Cancún are free ports so you'll find a wide selection of imported goods in the shops. Perfume, china and crystal are among the better buys.

For **handicrafts** there's the Arts and Crafts Market in the centre of San Miguel de Cozumel, offering goods from all of Mexico; in Cancún, the Ki-Huic market in Ciudad Cancún. But many other shops in both islands carry hand-made Mexican articles.

Filigree **jewellery** of gold and silver is a popular buy, as are the following items:

Hammocks, a Yucatecan speciality, come in single and double size (known as matrimonial).

Resort **clothing** is fun and not too expensive, but be sure to check the workmanship and size carefully before buying.

Guayaberra shirts, open-necked and pleated, basic clothing for men in the Yucatan.

Huipil, traditional woman's dress, a cotton shift with embroidered neck and hem.

Poncho, the Yucatan version is triangular.

Pottery and **sculpture,** reproductions of Mayan classics.

Rebozo, silk shawl worn by Mayan women.

Sisal rugs, bags and other items made of the locally grown henequén.

Practical Information

Archaeological sites. Open-air sites open from 6 a.m. to 5.30 p.m.; museums and interiors have shorter hours.

Banks. 9 a.m. to 1.30 p.m., Monday to Friday.

Currency. The monetary unit of Mexico is the *peso*, often abbreviated "m.n." *(moneda nacional)* or "$". The peso is divided into 100 *centavos*.

Telephoning Home. To call the U.S. from Cozumel/Cancún, dial 95 + area code + local number. To phone Cozumel from the U.S., dial 011 + 52 + 987 (988 for Cancún) + local number. To call the U.K. from Cozumel/Cancún, dial 98 + 44 + area code + local number. To call Cozumel from the U.K., dial 010 + 52 + 987 (988 for Cancún) + local number.

MONTSERRAT

Leeward Islands, Lesser Antilles

Introduction

Almost 500 years after its discovery, a hint of Irish lingers still upon the speck in the Caribbean which Columbus named Montserrat. For Irish Catholics were among the first to populate this pear-shaped utopia which has come to be known as "the other Emerald Isle". Today Montserrat is the only Caribbean island which keeps St. Patrick's Day (March 17) as a public holiday. Irish names like Fagan, Kelly, Maloney and O'Donaghue are still heard on the island, and the occasional redhead tells as much of a story as the shamrock adorning Government House.

Seven miles (11 km.) long and nearly 11 miles (18 km.) across at its widest point, Montserrat is a mere dot in the northern Leeward chain, lying about 27 miles (43 km.) southwest of Antigua. It is volcanic in origin, with sulphur vents active in the mountainous interior and some beaches of black sand. A former plantation colony, it is cloaked in virgin forest, with only about half for the remaining land suitable for cultivation.

Tourism predominates in the economy, with 70 per cent of the workforce employed in the service sector. But, apart from a few hotels and villas and reasonable facilities for sport, Montserrat remains essentially undeveloped and prides itself on being one of the few unspoiled venues in the eastern Caribbean.

A Brief History

15th–16th centuries	Christopher Columbus discovers this tiny volcanic island in the Leeward chain in 1493. Its saw-toothed profile—the island has a mountainous spine running north to south down its length—reminds him of the hills surrounding the Abbey of Montserrat near Barcelona, and he names it accordingly.
17th century	In the early 1600s, European settlers arrive—Spaniards first, followed by the British. In 1632 Irish Catholics, believed to be fleeing religious oppression on nearby St. Kitts, start arriving. Soon the French, too, begin taking an interest. In 1665, they take the fort, and the governor and his family are deported. The French remain in occupation for four years.

18th century	The British regain possession and continue to fortify the island. But in 1782 the French invade again. The island is only finally secured for Britain by the 1783 Treaty of Versailles, which ends the Anglo-French wars.
19th century	The British and Irish turn Montserrat into a plantation colony with sugar as the main crop. After the abolition of slavery in 1834, sugar is replaced by limes and, eventually, other orchard and market garden crops.
20th century	Montserrat, together with Antigua, St. Kitts-Nevis and Anguilla, is incorporated into the Territory of the Leeward Islands in 1956 and joins the Federation of the West Indies two years later. Independence is offered in 1966, but the island chooses to remain a British Crown Colony.

Sightseeing

On the south-west coast of the island, the diminutive capital city of **Plymouth** (population 2,500) has a distinctly British colonial air. On the main street, the formality of Georgian houses built from ballast rock from the U.K. contrasts with the typically West Indian hubbub of the Saturday Market and of the waterfront, where inter-island craft of all kinds are tied up.

The 18th-century **Government House** is an obligatory first stop—to visit the public rooms, sign the visitor's book and see the gardens with their immaculate lawns and brilliant tropical shrubberies. On nearby Richmond Hill, the **Montserrat Museum** is housed in a restored sugar mill.

On the outskirts of town, **St. Anthony's Church** was first constructed in 1640. It was rebuilt in 1730, after a battle with the French, and the tamarind tree outside is said to be over 200 years old. On a hilltop 1,200 feet (356 m.) above the town, the **Old Fort** built in 1664 remains an impressive vantage point.

Beyond Plymouth, the scenery is magnificent, varying from secluded coves and beaches to thickly forested mountainsides. Most spectacular perhaps is a trip to **Galway's Soufrière,** east of the town, where the mountain guide will no doubt boil an egg in the sulphur water bubbling forth from the still active volcano.

Also in the south, **Great Alps Waterfall** offers a fascinating spectacle. An hour's walk from the road, the horse-shoe-shaped falls cascade 70 feet (21 m.) into a crystal-clear mountain pool. A more hazardous climb—not to be ventured without a guide—is to **Chance's Peak** further north. At 3,000 feet (914 m.) the highest point on Montserrat, the Peak with its viewing tower provides the best panorama of the island. Further north still, the golden expanse of **Carr's Bay** is the most popular bathing beach.

Eating Out

Montserrat's rich volcanic soil ensures a plentiful supply of fresh fruit and vegetables, including tropical favourites such as mango and papaya. Seafood is also readily available. Among local specialities, you will find the famous "mountain chicken"—actually the legs of the huge land frog found here and on Dominica—and goat water, a sort of exotic Irish stew consisting of goat's meat simmered with yams, breadfruit, pumpkin and cassava.

Shopping

Hand-woven or knitted fabrics, worked from the locally grown sea-island cotton, are among the best buys here. Craftwork of all kinds —woven goods, pottery, leatherwork, jewellery—make good souvenirs. Colourful Montserrat stamps—collectors' items—are available from the Post Office or Philatelic Bureau in Plymouth.

Practical Information

Climate: Temperatures in Montserrat range from the low 70s F (20s C) to about 90°F (35°C), although the island is always cooled by trade winds; humidity is low.

Currency: The local unit is the Eastern Caribbean dollar (EC$). The U.S. dollar circulates widely.

PANAMA CANAL
BALBOA · CRISTÓBAL

Introduction

The Panama Canal has operated without a hitch for more than seven decades. A miracle of early twentieth-century engineering, the multi-lock canal runs north-west to south-east across the mountainous isthmus of Panama. It extends for a distance of 50 miles, linking the Atlantic and Pacific oceans and reducing the long journey around Cape Horn to a mere 8 or 9 hours' passage—instead of weeks or months.

The first trans-Panama crossing was made on August 15, 1914. This simple historical event marked the conclusion of a legendary feat, overshadowed by tragedy. For the construction of the canal cost dearly: a total of 387 million U.S. dollars was spent and many lives were lost to malaria, yellow fever and other tropical diseases.

The feasibility of a transoceanic canal was debated from the day in 1513 when Balboa first sighted the Pacific. Charles I of Spain, Simón Bolívar and the governments of the United States and Great Britain all gave thought to the problems involved. But it was a French company that first sought permission from Colombia to undertake the task.

Ferdinand de Lesseps builder of the Suez Canal made initial surveys in 1881 He urged construction of a sea-level channel, despite the fact that this would necessitate wholesale blasting of the mountainous terrain. Digging began, only to be brought to a halt after 18 miles by financial problems, inadequate machinery and the high death toll.

The United States government opened negotiations with Colombia for the rights and property secured by the French, but Colombia failed to come to an agreement. In 1903 Panama declared independence, ceding the Canal Zone to the U.S. in perpetuity. The breeding grounds for disease-carrying mosquitoes were destroyed and work on the canal proceeded.

U.S. Army engineers under the direction of George Washington Goethals rejected the French sea-level plan in favour of a new design incorporating a series of locks to raise and lower ships in transit. This avoided costly and time-consuming blasting operations. Each of the locks was provided with twin chambers to allow ships to move in opposite directions at the same time. Despite the complicated mechanics, everything functions smoothly and no significant modernization has ever been required.

Every year some 15,000 ships pass through the "big ditch", each bringing the Panama Canal Company an average of 20,000 U.S. dollars. However high it may seem, the toll is a bargain, as the Cape Horn journey would cost far more.) Until the canal reverts to Panamanian control at the end of 1999, the company is to pay the Republic an annual sum of ten million dollars. In the meantime, the canal remains Panama's biggest tourist attraction—and a lasting monument to American technical skill.

A Brief History

16th century	The Spanish explorer, Rodrigo de Bastidas, discovers Panama in 1501. Vasco Nuñez de Balboa becomes governor of the first permanent settlement; in 1513 he sights the Pacific Ocean. Panama City is founded on the Pacific coast in 1519 and the Camino Real (Royal Road) is opened, linking Caribbean to Pacific and facilitating the shipment of treasure from Peru to Spain. Panama is incorporated into the Viceroyalty of Peru in 1542. Sir Francis Drake leads a series of raids on the area and the Spanish counter by building a comprehensive system of fortifications.
17th century	In 1671 the pirate Henry Morgan attacks the Caribbean coast, taking the fort of San Lorenzo and penetrating the isthmus all the way to Panama City. He burns the town to the ground and it is rebuilt two years later on a more easily defensible site.
18th century	Panama is joined to the Viceroyalty of Granada (present-day Colombia) in 1717. Admiral Sir Edward Vernon captures Portobelo in 1739 and San Lorenzo the following year.
19th century	During the gold rush of 1849, hordes of would-be prospectors travel from the east coast of the United States to the west by way of Panama. A railway is constructed from Colón to Panama City, facilitating the journey

across the isthmus. During the second half of the century,
revolution breaks out some 50 times, but Panama remain
tied to Colombia. A French company begins excavatio:
of the Panama Canal in 1882, only to give up after seve:
years of technical and financial problems, outbreaks o
malaria and yellow fever. The United States governmen
buys out French rights and property.

20th century

The U.S. supports Panama's successful bid for indepen
dence in 1903. The Canal Zone—a strip of land extendin
five miles to either side of the canal—is granted to the
U.S. in perpetuity. The area is cleared of disease-carryin
mosquitoes and work on the canal goes forward, reachin
completion in 1914. In time Panama rejects the perpetua
right of the U.S. to the Canal Zone and seeks greate
control over the operation of the canal. A new Cana
Treaty is ratified in 1977, setting a timetable for the retur
of the canal to the Republic. A period of increasin
Panamanian participation is to precede the final hand
over of the property on December 31, 1999. The Cana
Zone is transferred to Panama on October 1, 1979. U.S
troops invade Panama in December, 1989, deposing the
strongman, Gen. Manuel Noriega, wanted on drug:
charges.

Sightseeing

Trans-Panama Passage

The Panama Canal traverses a landscape of remarkable beauty. Throughout the eight-hour crossing the panorama is ever-changing, taking in the shimmering expanse of Lake Gatún and the jungle-clad hills of the Talamanca and San Blas ranges, the high, arched span of Americas Bridge and the intricate workings of the locks themselves. From the Atlantic, ships enter the canal via the port of Cristóbal, beginning a journey between two oceans.

Cristóbal and Colón

The Panama Railway line marks the boundary between the busy port of Cristóbal and neighbouring Colón, a major shopping centre and Panama's second-largest city

ith a population of around
0,000. Cristóbal and Colón
oth occupy Manzanillo Is-
nd at the Atlantic entrance
the canal.

Under the terms of the 1977
anal Treaty, **Cristóbal,** for-
erly within the Canal Zone,
as reverted to Panamanian
ontrol. Every year some
5,000 ships flying the flags
f approximately 60 different
ountries pass through here,
nd more than 200 million
ns of cargo are handled.

A few streets separate the
ustle of the port from **Colón**
roper. Front Street, lined
ith various duty-free shops,
as seen better days. But the
ree Zone to the east is a
ooming centre for the transhipment of bulk goods.
ndividuals however, can also
nake purchases here.

Apart from the cathedral,
he beach and a scattering of
nonuments, Colón has little
n the way of tourist sights.
his is rather a city of noctur-
al pleasures and rough bars,
atronized mainly by sailors.

hrough the Canal

From Cristóbal ships travel
bout 7 miles to **Gatún Locks,**
vhere they ascend a total of 85
eet to the level of Gatún
ake. Although there isn't
nuch room to spare—the twin

chambers in each lift measure 110 by 1,000 feet—ships pass neatly through the three sets of lifts. They're helped along by powerful mechanical "mules" mounted on special tracks.

The captain of a vessel in transit doesn't do the navigating here. Canal pilots familiar with the locks take complete control, easing the ship through. The operation is overseen by technicians in the control tower between the lifts. They open and close the gates to each lift and regulate the flow of water.

In contrast to the sophisticated workings of the locks is the virgin jungle all around. Lush, impenetrable, inviolate, the jungle with its crawling vines and exotic vegetation provides an extraordinary counterpoint to the concrete and steel of the canal itself.

Water for the locks (around 52 million gallons per transit) is supplied by **Gatún Lake,** an immense artificial reservoir of 168 square miles. When the lake was formed in 1914, animals in the area fled to the high ground of what has become Barro Colorado Island, now a nature preserve.

The trip across the lake brings vessels to **Gaillard Cut,** site of the continental divide.

This spectacular narrow passage between sheer cliffs is just wide enough for two-way traffic, except in the case of very large ships. It was opened by blasting, a seven-year-long operation supervised by David Gaillard of the U.S. Army Corps of Engineers. As a matter of fact, a good part of the some 60 million pounds of dynamite used in the canal's construction was detonated here. Off to one side lies Contractor's Hill, lowered about 80 feet in 1954 when landslides threatened.

Gaillard Cut continues for 8 miles to **Pedro Miguel Locks,** where one lift lowers ships 31 feet to Miraflores Lake. The final descent to sea level takes place in the two lifts of **Miraflores Locks.** The gates here are higher than those at the Atlantic end of the canal, owing to the greater variation in Pacific tides.

The final leg of the journey holds one last sight in store: **Puente de las Américas** (Americas Bridge), an impressive steel arch over 5,000 feet long. Set high above the narrow ribbon of the canal, the bridge spans the entrance to the Pacific and forms an important link in the Inter-American Highway. And so on to Balboa.

PANAMA CANAL

Balboa and Panama City

The Panama Canal Commission has its headquarters in the Pacific port of **Balboa,** which reverted to the Republic of Panama with the abolition of the Canal Zone in 1979. The Canal Treaty notwithstanding, Balboa remains a thoroughly American creation, with municipal buildings and tidy residential districts like those of any suburban town in the United States: there's something decidedly incongruous in the fact that Panama City lies less than 2 miles away.

A palm-lined avenue known as the Prado leads from the centre of Balboa to the Canal Administration Building in Balboa Heights. At the far end of the Prado stands a marble monument to George Washington Goethals, the American colonel who masterminded the building of the canal.

However fascinating the canal area, **Panama City** deserves a look. Begin with San Felipe, the old quarter, which dates from the refounding of the city in 1673. In the tranquil **Plaza de Francia** stands an obelisk in honour of the heroic but failed French attempt to build a canal. Not far away is **Paseo de las Bóvedas,** a promenade atop a section of the old city wall.

The nearby church of Santo Domingo has fallen to ruins but its brick and mortar **"flat arch",** constructed without internal supports, has withstood the test of time. As a matter of fact, the stability of the arch is said to have been the determining factor in the selection of Panama as the site for the canal, rather than earthquake-prone Costa Rica.

Other landmarks to look out for include the turn-of-the-century National Theatre, beautiful **La Presidencia** (President's Palace) and the **Church of San José,** also known as the "Church of the Golden Altar" for its magnificent Baroque altar.

Beyond San Felipe lie the business and residential districts of modern Panama City. Further still, about 4 miles outside the present city centre, are the ruins of the old city or **Panamá Viejo.** Founded on a vulnerable site in 1519, the city was burned to the ground by the pirate Henry Morgan in 1671. The remains of the cathedral, the original church of San José and various government buildings can still be seen, as well as King's Bridge, starting point for the Royal Road across the isthmus.

Eating Out

Panama's polyglot population brings all its diversity to the local culinary scene.

Sancocho, the national dish, combines chicken, yuca, sweet corn, plantain, potatoes, onions and coriander in a rich stew. *Ropa vieja,* another local speciality, contains beef, fried onions, garlic, tomatoes and green peppers.

Sopa de gloria—sponge cake soaked in a mixture of cream and rum—will satisfy just about any sweet tooth. Other popular desserts are *arroz con cacao,* chocolate-rice pudding, and *guanabana* (sweet soursop) ice-cream.

Beer and mineral water are readily obtainable and water from the tap is safe to drink in Cristóbal, Balboa and Panama City.

Shopping

Panama's renown as a shopping mecca has travelled the length and breadth of Latin America. A first priority for many is the wide range of low-duty or duty-free luxury goods. Popular, too, is the array of Oriental and Indian linens, clothing and other articles. But the most unusual items of all come from Panama itself: *bateas,* wooden trays; *chaquiras,* beadwork necklaces; Kantule perfume and *molas,* multi-coloured reverse appliqué cloth panels made by the Cuna Indians.

Practical Information

Currency. 1 *balboa* (symbolized B/) = 100 *centesimos.* Coins: 1, 5, 10, 25, 50 centesimos; 1, 5, 10, 20 balboas (used interchangeably with U.S. currency of the same denominations). Notes: 1, 5, 10, 20, 50, U.S. dollars (termed balboas locally).

Telephoning Home. To call the U.S. direct from Panama, dial 00 + 1 + U.S. area code + local number. To reach an AT&T Operator in the U.S., to place an AT&T Card or collect call, use the USADIRECT℠ service from specially marked telephones. To phone Panama from the U.S., dial 011 + 507 + local number.

SAN BLAS
ISLANDS

Panama

Introduction

The San Blas Islands, 366 small fragments of paradise strung out along the Caribbean coast of Panama, are no ordinary islands. Here you will have the rare opportunity to see the past at first hand. For the life of the islanders, the Cuna Indians, has changed so little over the centuries that it is almost like stepping into a time machine and emerging in another age.

It all started back in the days of the conquistadors. Vasco de Balboa, governor of the first permanent settlement in Panama, established good relations with the Indians, but his successor was less compromising. To escape slavery or death, the Cuna were obliged to flee to the high reaches of the Panamanian jungle and later to the San Blas Islands, where they lived in isolation, aloof from the white man's world.

Through the centuries the kept their culture free of foreign influence, responding with ferocity to any encroachment on their territory or independence. When they did eventually allow some visitors to land on the islands, they were never permitted to spend the night. Marriage with outsiders was taboo.

The Cuna Indians (some 20,000 strong) inhabit only 40 or so of the islets, since the other consist of little more than a stretch of sand and the occasional coconut palm. Yes, you will find some transistor radios now, men dressed in Western clothing and outboard motor on a few canoes. But the main threads of the Cuna civilization have not been broken. Their daily life continues in its age old rhythm, untouched by the 20th century.

A Brief History

16th century   Spanish explorer Rodrigo de Bastidas discovers Panama in 1501. The governor of the first permanent settlement in Panama, Vasco Nuñez de Balboa, makes friends with the Cuna Indians and marries the daughter of one of the chieftains. The Indians tell him about the great South Sea and accompany him on an expedition through the jungle that leads to his "discovery" of the Pacific Ocean in 1513. But instead of finding glory, Balboa is denounced by his enemies in Spain, charged with treason and executed. The new governor, "Pedrarias the Cruel", founds Panama City and opens the Camino Real (Royal Road) linking the Caribbean to the Pacific. He also enslaves and massacres thousands of Indians, forcing the Cuna to retreat into the jungle.

7th–18th centuries

As the principal route for transshipment of Spain's riches from the Pacific, Panama proves irresistible to enterprising pirates. In 1671, Henry Morgan besieges the city of Panama and burns it to the ground. The vulnerabilty of the route obliges Spain to switch to the longer but safer way round Cape Horn, depriving Panama of its main source of wealth. Meanwhile, many of the Cuna Indians migrate to the uninhabited San Blas Islands. Numerous attempts are made to "colonize" the islands, but after 1760 the Indians are left to themselves.

9th century

In 1821, Panama joins Colombia in declaring its independence from Spain. During the Gold Rush years, hordes of eager prospectors travel across Panama on their way to California. Revolution breaks out regularly in Panama for the rest of the century, as the Panamians try to sever their bonds with Colombia.

0th century

The United States supports Panama's bid for independence in 1903. In return, the Canal Zone—a strip of land extending 5 miles (8 km.) to either side of the canal—is granted to the U.S. in perpetuity. The Canal is completed in 1914, but it is not until 1978 that a new treaty is ratified, setting up a timetable for the return of the Canal to Panama. For the Cuna Indians, the 20th century marks the end of their long, self-imposed isolation. They begin to allow some outsiders on their islands. In 1951, the Panamian Republic establishes a departmental government for the Territory of San Blas—an initiative which meets with a good deal of resistance. Hostilities break out and there is a brief rebellion in 1925. In the end, the Cuna come to terms with Panama. Today, the islands are a semi-autonomous territory in which local government is handled by Cuna chiefs.

SAN BLAS

Sightseeing

Endowed with beautiful beaches, a plethora of palm trees, crystal-clear water, picturesque villages of bamboo huts and friendly people, the San Blas Islands can measure up to any island paradise. But for most visitors, it's the island-ers—not the islands—that ar the real attraction.

On arrival, you'll be greete by Cuna women selling handi crafts. Nothing particularly un usual in that—except for the way the women are dressed Their everyday garb is, in fact an elaborate outfit consisting o blouses with panels of intricat

embroidery (the famous *mola*), long wrap-around skirts and red and yellow headscarves. Their wrists and ankles are encircled with beads, and their noses are pierced by gold rings and painted with black beauty stripes. Special occasions warrant more jewellery—necklaces of gold and outsize earrings.

The Cuna society is basically matrilineal. The women control the economy: they are the artisans and the sales force and property rights pass through the female line. When a couple marries, the man goes to live with the family of the bride and works for her father. All property is owned communally, with the exception of coconut trees, for coconuts are used as currency. Today, money is becoming part of the economy, too, and you'll find the Cuna more than willing to accept either Panamanian *balboa* or dollars.

The daily rhythm of the Cuna hasn't changed much over the years. They rise before dawn; the men go off to work in their fields on the mainland, to fish or hunt game. Many of them speak Spanish as well as the Cuna dialect and some have adopted Western dress. The women also paddle over to the mainland in their *cayucos* (dugout canoes) to fill their calabashes with river water, to bathe and wash clothes. There is no fresh water on the islands.

Everyone comes home for the midday meal: rice or yucca, with plantain, fish, fresh fruit, coffee or a drink of mashed plantain and sugar cane juice. In the afternoon, there is a long siesta, after which the women

SAN BLAS

sit around sewing their exquisite *mola* embroidery and chatting; the children play; the men weave baskets, work on their boats, go off on errands or call at neighbouring islands. Inter-island visiting is a very important part of their social lives; everyone has relatives or childhood friends scattered around on other islands.

When a trading boat docks, it sparks off a flurry of activity—stocking up with provisions, selling coconuts, a good deal of bargaining and chatter. Most evenings involve a meeting in the council lodge, a large hut for communal use, where current problems and disputes are discussed and the day's events reviewed. The meeting is informal with people wandering in and out as they please.

When it comes to celebrations, the Cuna don't hold back. Among the most important ceremonies is the *Inna,* the coming of age of a young girl. The festivities last for three days, accompanied by much drinking of *chicha,* smoking, feasting and dancing. During this time, the young girl is enclosed in a roofless hut and regularly showered with cold water, a symbolic cleansing. At the end of the ceremony, her long hair is cut short to show that she is eligible for marriage.

Shopping for Molas

Most visitors to the San Blas Islands want to buy—or at least look over—some of the marvellous Cuna *molas.* In the Cuna dialect, *mola* means blouse, but the word is generally used nowadays to refer to the brilliantly coloured, exuberant panels of reverse applique made by the women of the islands. The panels come in pairs, with matching but not identical design, to be worn on the front and back of the blouse.

Molas, which first appeared about a hundred years ago, developed from the Cuna practice of body painting. The early *molas* were fairly simple and used the same motifs as the body painting—mostly plant life, animals and geometric designs. Later, as the art form became more elaborate, scenes of everyday life were depicted. In recent years, the outside world has provided much of the thematic inspiration. You'll see fanciful renditions of beer labels, space ships, political posters, Christian symbols and comic book characters. Though recognizable, they are hardly carbon copies; each motif is shaped by the artist's perceptions and modified to fit the formalities of the *mola* style.

Molas are made from several layers of fabric, each a different colour. The upper layers are cut and tucked under to reveal those below. The tucks are sewn down with almost invisible stitches and sometimes embroidery is added as an extra embellishment. Swatches of cloth may be sewn on top to introduce additional colours, but red, black and yellow predominate in most of the work.

To judge the quality of a *mola,* first examine the workmanship. The outline layers should be even, the corners fairly flat, the stitches tiny. The pattern should be evenly distributed with no empty patches. Many of the best *molas* show some fading. This is perfectly normal since the women usually keep their favourites for their own use, exposing them to the tropical sun and numerous washings. After checking the workmanship, step back a bit so you can see the *mola* as a whole and evaluate its pattern, colour scheme and overall conception.

SAN JUAN

Puerto Rico

Introduction

Most visitors to Puerto Rico get no further than San Juan —especially the glamorous strip of hotel-lined beach that stretches from Isla Verde, past Condado (the "action" centre) to Old San Juan. You can count on the sun and fun, but while you're here, savour, too, the island's Spanish heritage. Wander around Old San Juan, the city's beautifully restored colonial section. In-spect the formidable old forts, visit the late-Gothic churches, see the Spanish-style plazas, balconied houses, wrought-iron grilles and arcaded patios.

Old San Juan is no museum, though. The gracious build-ings are very much used—as homes, restaurants, shops and

The patio of the Dominican Convent shows the sumptuous style of the Spanish colonial epoch.

museums—and real life in the form of blaring transistor radios, the laughter of crisply uniformed schoolgirls or the click of dominoes in a shaded square will quickly break in on any illusion of another age. Shops in Old San Juan specialize in stylish resort clothes, handicrafts (like the naïve figurines called *santos*) and art by local painters and sculptors.

A better-known aspect of San Juan is its abundant and energetic nightlife. "The city that never closes" has it all: big-name nightclub acts, flamenco shows, theatre and concerts in historic settings, cosy piano bars, and enough discos and dancing clubs to keep you spinning for many a moon. There is gambling, too, in its government-regulated casinos, where the atmosphere is subdued and fairly sober.

En la isla—"out on the island"—is what the Puerto Ricans call everything beyond the sprawl of metropolitan San Juan. The change of pace from the bustling commercial centre is sudden and therapeutic. Nearby possibilities include a visit to a primitive rain forest teeming with exotic birds; a round of golf in beautiful Dorado (Golden) Beach; a drive through stately banana plantations—or just relaxing under a palm tree somewhere along the turquoise sea.

A Brief History

5th–16th centuries	The peaceful Taíno Indians welcome Christopher Columbus to their island of Borinquén on November 19, 1493. Columbus calls it San Juan after St. John the Baptist. In 1508, Ponce de León founds a Spanish settlement on the island, but its site proves to be unhealthy and indefensible. The colonists move to a beautiful bay, Puerto Rico ("Rich Port"). Somewhere along the way, though, the two names are exchanged: the island becomes Puerto Rico and the new town, San Juan.

The Spaniards soon exhaust the island's gold and put the Indians to work growing sugar cane. Slaves are imported to supplement the labour force. Then, to protect the growing colony from the fierce Carib Indians, French pirates and the ambitious English,

fortifications are erected. Sir Francis Drake puts San Juan's defence system to the test in 1595—and is forced to retreat, empty-handed. The English fare better a few years later when the Earl of Cumberland shrewdly outflanks and lays siege to the fortress of El Morro. The British actually take the fort but lose the island: they are routed by an epidemic of yellow fever and dysentery.

17th–18th centuries

Next come the Dutch. They sail boldly into the harbour, land and march into the deserted city. But El Morro refuses to surrender and the disgruntled Dutch finally sail off, after setting fire to San Juan. The British make one more attempt in 1797. This time they surround and blocade the city. Then suddenly, unexpectedly, the British withdraw—frightened, the legend goes, by a torchlight parade of praying women, which they mistake for Spanish reinforcements.

19th century

The repressive military rule of Spain is disturbed by a small insurrection in Puerto Rico in 1868. The insurgents are quickly suppressed but the weary Spanish decide to change their tactics and ease the tension. In 1872, slavery is abolished; in 1897, the island is granted autonomy. Dreams of an independent Puerto Rico do not last long, however. Eight months later, the United States, involved in the Spanish-American War, sends troops to take Puerto Rico.

20th century

Puerto Ricans are made U.S. citizens in 1917 and given more say in internal affairs. During the difficult years of the Depression and World War II, the leading figure in Puerto Rican politics is Luis Muñoz Marín, the founder of the Popular Democratic Party. Together with Governor Rexford Tugwell, he creates "Operation Bootstrap", a plan for economic expansion that will transform the island from an underdeveloped backwater to a pace-setting industrial society.

Since 1952, Puerto Rico has been a self-governing Commonwealth, freely associated with the United States. As to the future, opinion is divided: some Puerto Ricans want to maintain the status quo; others are working for statehood; while a third group believes that independence is the only way. The ever-present complication is that one-third of all Puerto Ricans live in the U.S.

SAN JUAN

Sightseeing

Old San Juan

You can take in the high spots of old San Juan in an intensive half-day tour. But don't try to see it all—there's too much to cover in a single round.

Start at **Plaza de Colón** (Columbus Square), where the buses arrive. The statue was erected here in 1893 on the 400th anniversary of Puerto Rico's discovery by Columbus.

Fort San Cristóbal, just up the hill, is a relatively modern element in San Juan's defence system. It was completed four years before the U.S. Declaration of Independence. Moats, ramps and tunnels link five separate units with the main part of the fort, which looms far above the Atlantic. The National Park Service conducts tours or you can wander around on your own.

Supplementing the bristling citadels of San Cristóbal and

El Morro, the **city wall** provided San Juan with almost total security. The wall is more sophisticated than it looks. The 17th-century Spanish engineers took advantage of the steep, rocky shoreline, then added twists and angles to increase visibility and overlap the field of fire.

Following the city wall all the way to the peninsula's tip, **El Morro** is San Juan's most impressive fort. You can look around at your leisure or take one of the tours run by the National Park Service.

Three flags fly above El Morro, summing up its history: four centuries under the red and white banner of imperial Spain, a few months of Puerto Rico's star and stripes and since 1899 the American flag. Within the seemingly impregnable stone bulwark of the fort, you will find gentle expanses of grass, even a golf course (though it's no longer in use).

Even if you're not a military buff, you'll marvel at the engineering work that went into this self-contained, six-storey city. Walk down the tunnels, stairways, ramps and parade grounds; visit the ammunition stores, cannons, dungeons and kitchens. No wonder so many foes failed to take this fortress. Often besieged, El Morro fell only once—to the British in 1598. But, on that occasion, the invaders had rolled in from the rear over an easy beachhead, where the Condado hotels rise today.

Plaza de San José looks like a provincial square in almost any outpost of the Spanish empire. The statue of Juan Ponce de León in his armour was cast from British cannons, captured after an unsuccessful attack on San Juan in 1797.

Ponce de León was buried in the church of **San José**—until 1908 when he was moved down the street to the cathedral. This all-white building, the second oldest church in the hemisphere, was begun in 1532. It's a fine sight, and, unusual for the tropics, a rare example of late-Gothic style brought to the New World. Don't miss the great vaulted ceilings from the 16th century.

Also on the Plaza de San José, music-lovers will find the **Pablo Casals Museum.** Here you will find memorabilia of the great Spanish cellist, who spent his last years in Puerto Rico. Exhibits include his cello and videotapes of Puerto to Rico's annual Festival Casals.

The big, beautiful **Dominican Convent** once gave refuge to women and children hiding out from the cannibalistic Carib Indians. More recently it was the headquarters of the U.S. Army's Antilles Command. Now the public can enjoy the tranquillity of its expansive, double-decker patio, a splendid example of Spanish colonial design. The meticulously restored building houses the Institute of Puerto Rican Culture, which sponsors the exhibition and sale of art and handicrafts here.

Puerto Rico's woodcarvers are best known for their *santos,* simple religious figurines. Some admirable historic *santos* may be seen in **La Casa de los Contrafuertes** (House of the Buttresses), a fortress-like mansion thought to be the oldest private residence in San Juan. Two other exhibits share the premises: a reconstructed old apothecary shop and a graphic arts show.

The U.S. Army again shows

its good taste in choosing headquarter sites in the **Casa Blanca** (White House), a sprawling, Spanish-style structure with delicious little gardens. The local commander was billeted here until 1966. Now filled with furniture and relics of the colonial days, the house looks as it might have done back in 1523 when Ponce de León's son-in-law moved in.

Heading downhill from Calle San Sebastián, the most pleasant route is the set of **step streets**—just for pedestrians. Tropical plants add to the charm.

A sweeping view of San Juan harbour awaits you at the **Plazuela de la Rogativa,** a small square that commemorates the lifting of the British siege in 1797. According to legend, a religious procession (*rogativa*) of torch-bearing women scared off the invaders. An inspired modern sculpture illustrates the story.

Down the hill, the **San Juan Gate** is the oldest portal in the solid city wall. Visiting dignitaries used to disembark at this spot to be escorted in procession up to the pink cathedral.

The **cathedral** of San Juan was thoroughly redone in the 19th century. Only the circular staircase and some adjoining rooms with Gothic ceilings remain from the 1540 structure. The marble tomb near the transept holds the remains of Ponce de León.

El Convento Hotel (off to the right as you leave the cathedral) was once a Carmelite convent. Today it welcomes guests to its handsome restored rooms and restaurant, originally the convent's chapel.

Now for another San Juan superlative: **La Fortaleza** is the oldest executive mansion still in use in the Western Hemisphere. La Fortaleza, meaning "The Fortress", was built in 1540 for defence against the primitive Carib Indians. But as more advanced enemies appeared, the old fort became a military white elephant, impressive to see but vulnerable. This was lucky for the governors of Puerto Rico, who have lived and worked in the 40-room mansion for over 400 years.

At the foot of Calle del Cristo you'll find a small **chapel** blocking the view of the harbour. It was erected, they say, in memory of a young horseman taking part in a fiesta horse race. Unfortunately, he failed to negotiate the turn and hurtled off the unprotected brink.

Parque de las Palomas, next to the chapel, is picturesque but overrun by the pigeons after which the park is named. Still, you can enjoy a fine bird's-eye view of the harbour from here.

The colonial mansions across the street from the park now house interesting exhibitions. The beautifully restored **La Casa del Libro,** (House of Books) contains an excellent collection of prints and rare books. **The Puerto Rican Fine Arts Museum** displays the works of island artists from the 18th century to the present.

The highlight of San Juan's **City Hall** *(Alcaldía)* is its vast assembly room upstairs with a checker-board marble floor, dignified chandeliers and a grand piano. It opens onto an arcaded balcony, tailor-made for an election night victory speech. The Tourism Information Centre is located on the ground floor.

Hundreds of years ago, citizen-soldiers drilled in the **Plaza de Armas** (Arms Square), the central square of Old San Juan. Later it became a favourite meeting place with band concerts. Restored in 1988, it now has a grandstand, pavilion, water fountain and snack bar.

Lively Calle Fortaleza leads to yet another installation of the busy Institute of Puerto Rican Culture—**La Casa del Callejón** (House of the Alley), an 18th-century mansion with two museums. On the ground floor you'll find colonial architecture and decoration; upstairs, the Museum of the Puerto Rican Family, depicting life in San Juan a hundred years ago. Furniture, toys, music-boxes and nostalgia are on view here.

The social centre of 19th-century San Juan, the **Tapia Theatre,** was restored in 1976 at about 300 times its original cost. The 1832 building had been financed by contributions plus a one-cent tax on every loaf of bread. The distinguished old theatre, again in use as an opera house and concert hall, is named after the Puerto Rican playwright Alejandro Tapia y Rivera (1826–82).

Metropolitan Area

The tourist track to and from Old San Juan normally passes through the area called Puerta de Tierra (Land Gateway). In transit have a look at Puerto Rico's El Capitolio, a neo-classic building resembling the U.S. Capitol in Washington. Another 20th-century landmark, the Caribe Hilton Hotel, was built by the government during Operation Bootstrap to launch the era of tourism. On the seafront alongside the hotel, the smallest of San Juan's 18th-century forts protected the eastern approach to the old city. **Fort San Jerónimo** now includes a Museum of Military History with old swords and flintlocks and a pre-1898 collection of Spanish uniforms.

Just to the east begins the **Condado** section, sometimes called the Miami Beach of Puerto Rico. This is where the action is. Here, big hotels on wide beaches generate a hectic pace of life, day and night.

Out on the Island

Seething San Juan is no more typical of Puerto Rico than New York City is of the U.S.A. Drive half an hour from the capital and you'll find yourself in utter wilderness. Two of the most popular outings from San Juan—**El Yunque Rain Forest** and Luquillo Beach—are usually combined in one tour.

As you'll soon discover, a tropical rain forest is just that: steaming hot, dripping wet, densely jungled. El Yunque (The Anvil), named after one of its prominent mountains, is 28,000 acres comprising a bird and wildlife sanctuary oper-

ated by the U.S. Forest Service. Even if you escape the average of five daily showers, you'll be impressed to learn that more than 100 billion gallons of water drench these tangled slopes every year.

About 240 species of trees grow here, all indigenous. Watch for the stout, gnarled Colorado trees. One well-known specimen is estimated to be 2,500 years old. You'll also see hundreds of intertwined woody liana vines reminiscent of Tarzan films, towering Sierra palms with white-blossomed fruit spikes and frond-topped tree ferns. Seek out tiny orchids and *asuséna,* a long white tuberose which exudes a glorious perfume— but only at night.

Luquillo Beach, with its attractive seaside coconut grove and colourful snack stalls, is the best known of the public beaches *(balnearios).*

For a first-hand experience of plantation days, visit the **Buena Vista Hacienda,** a restored coffee and vegetable plantation, just north of Ponce on the south coast.

Even if you aren't a spelunker you can take a walking tour through the **Caves of Camuy,** an impressive system of caverns on the north coast west of Arecibo.

Eating Out

Puerto Rico's remarkable array of food ranges all the way from exotic Caribbean through Continental to basic American—not to mention Chinese, Argentine and stateless vegetarian. But don't expect to find eating here inexpensive. Surprisingly little is grown locally and much of the food must be imported.

Island recipes, often old Indian dishes refined over the centuries, are proof that beans, rice and root vegetables need not be dull. Flavoured with two distinctly creole *(criollo)* seasonings—*sofrito* and *adobo*—Puerto Rican cooking tends to be mildly spicy with overtones of garlic, oregano and coriander.

First Courses

Puerto Rican black bean soup *(sopa de habichuelas negras)* can be superb. It's best garnished with chopped onion.

Tostones are fried plantain slices, something like potato chips. Plantain can also be boiled, baked, stuffed or pickled, but unlike its cousin the banana, plantain is never eaten raw. The leaves turn up wrapped around *pasteles,* the island's beloved meat patties.

Main Dishes

Nothing is more typically Puerto Rican than *asopao,* a rice stew with chicken, seafood or pigeon peas. Visitors do not always share the local enthusiasm for this soupy creation, but there are lots of other nice rice dishes to choose from, such as the Spanish standbys *paella* and *arroz con pollo* or "simple" rice and beans.

Pescado just means fresh fish. Try the red snapper *(chillo),* hake *(merluza)* or sea bass *(mero).*

Desserts

Pass over the staple Puerto Rican puddings and custard *(flan)* for the intriguing *dulce de lechosa con queso blanco,* papaya cubes cooked in sugar and cinnamon with white cheese, or *arroz con dulce,* boiled rice in coconut cream, sugar and cinnamon. Or enjoy some of the luscious fruit. Puerto Rico boasts that its pineapple *(piña)* is the world's sweetest. Coconut, papaya, mango, tamarind and breadfruit are among the other tropical treats worth trying.

Snacks

Though Puerto Rico has more than its share of hamburger, hot dog and fried chicken

stands, the most popular street snacks are strictly local creations. You'll find deep-fried codfish fritters (*bacalaitos fritos*), deep-fried meat and cheese turnovers (*pastelillos*) and banana croquettes stuffed with beef or pork (*alcapurrias*).

Drinks

To test the local wisdom that rum goes with anything, there are dozens of colourful concoctions to sample. Start off with the *piña colada,* a frothy blend of coconut cream, pineapple juice, rum and crushed ice. Local daiquiri flavours include banana and coconut. Rum punches abound. They're very refreshing, but don't forget that rum packs a punch—even in a seemingly innocuous, fruit-filled punch.

Shopping

Among the best buys in San Juan are the handicrafts. If this calls to mind crudely woven baskets and mass-produced trinkets, you'll be pleasantly surprised in Puerto Rico. Before buying compare quality and price.

Art. Painting, sculpture and graphics by island artists. Worth a look, even if you're not in the market.

Cigars. Puerto Rican tobacco is one of the ingredients in these hand-rolled cigars. The workers smoke them all day long, so they must be good.

Fabrics. Hand-screened textiles in novel designs are a growing industry on the island.

Guayaberas. The best-dressed Puerto Rican gentlemen wear these tailored, fancily embroidered shirts for almost any occasion.

Jewellery. From cheap mother-of-pearl pieces to chic 18-carat creations by skilled artisans.

Macramé. This variation on embroidery produces complicated, knotty inventions.

Papier-mâché fruit and vegetables that look almost good enough to eat.

Resort wear, especially for women, from this Caribbean fashion centre.

Rum. Puerto Rico's own—light, dark or aged—is perennially popular.

Santos. Eminently portable and uniquely Puerto Rican, these hand-carved wooden figures of saints originated in the 16th century.

Straw hats, like the *pava,* an upswept model worn by farmers *en la isla.* Available full-sized or in a miniature version.

Practical Information

Clothing: Away from the beach, it's fairly conservative, but shorts are acceptable in most public places. At night, people tend to dress up especially in the casinos and nightclubs, and jackets are often required for men in smart restaurants.

Currency: U.S. dollars are the official currency, though some establishments will accept Canadian money. Major credit cards are widely accepted.

Hours: Banks open from 8.30 or 9 a.m. to 2.30 p.m., Monday to Friday. Restaurants serve lunch from noon to 2.30 p.m. and dinner from 8 to 10 p.m. Most shops are open from 9 a.m. to 5 p.m., Monday to Saturday without a lunch or siesta break, but around the hotels the hours tend to be a bit later.

Language: Puerto Ricans consider Spanish their mother tongue. In San Juan, many people speak English as well.

Telephoning Home. San Juan (area code 809) is linked to the U.S. network. For U.K. visitors to ring home, dial 011 + 44 + area code + local number. To call San Juan from the U.K., dial 010 + 500 809 + local number.

ST. BARTHELEMY

Lesser Antilles

Introduction

This just might be the best piece of France anywhere. Known fondly as "St. Barts" —Columbus bestowed his brother's name, Bartholomew, on the island when he sailed past in 1493—it's a peaceful, beautiful little island of roller coaster hills, rocky coves and powdery beaches lining a limpid, emerald sea.

Twittering in the shrubbery of its 8 square miles (20 sq. km.) are countless thousands of yellow breasts, red throats and hummingbirds. They greatly outnumber the 3,000-odd inhabitants—mostly white, many the descendants of Huguenots from Brittany and Normandy.

These unusual Frenchmen and the relative handful of black families that have also lived here for generations strike visitors as extremely kind, open and simple. Among themselves they speak a nasal, old-fashioned French, accented in a way that reminds visiting Parisians of French-Canadian speech. Sprinkled through it are bits of English and Swedish. (For nearly a century, until 1878, St. Bart was the only possession Swe den ever held in the wester hemisphere.) The result is patois baffling to anyone no brought up on St. Barts.

Now that the island has modern international airport people are making their wa to St. Barts in ever-increasin numbers. Swelling the ranks o American vacationers are tren dy young Frenchmen from th *métropole*. They like the re laxed, low-key atmospher and Gallic flair of the place Some of the beautiful peopl wouldn't vacation anywher else, and that includes a fev Rockefellers and Rothschilds Everyone on the beach i wearing the latest version o the bikini or Cardin sports clothes.

The tourist influx has trig gered a building boom aroun the island and in the tiny cap ital of Gustavia, situated o a picture-postcard harbour Some new hotels have opened but so far, St. Barts has los none of its former charm.

Relaxation is the key-note You can head for one o the magnificent sand beaches linger over a cocktail on terrace bar overlooking th harbour, or just breathe i some French West Indian am bience.

A Brief History

5th–17th centuries	Columbus discovers St. Barthélemy in 1493, but Spain makes little effort to establish a foothold. The French, ambitious for conquests in the New World, stake a claim in 1648 and send over a boatload of Huguenot settlers in 1674 from Brittany and Normandy.
18th century	A short takeover of St. Barthélemy by the British during the Seven Years' War with France (1756–63) comes to an end with the Treaty of Paris: France elects to keep her West Indian possessions—extremely profitable because of the sugar trade—giving up Canada to Britain. The island's coves become popular hiding places for French privateers as they loot British merchant ships during the American War of Independence. In 1784, Louis XVI gives St. Barthélemy to Sweden in exchange for duty-free trading rights in Gothenburg.
19th century	France buys back St. Barthélemy from Sweden in 1878 for 320,000 gold francs. Sugar cane trading declines with the appearance of the cheaper sugar beet, but the island continues to thrive because of its free-port status.
20th century	The islands of the French West Indies suffer economic privation during World War II with the sharp decline in exports. In 1946, St. Barthélemy is made an administrative sub-prefecture of nearby Guadeloupe (which becomes a full *département* of France in the same year), a source of great pride to the islanders. A recent surge in tourism brings fresh prosperity to the economy.

Sightseeing

Gustavia

When you see it, you'll understand why Gustavia's rectangular harbour is a favourite with the Caribbean yachting set. From this ideal anchorage you can rent small excursion or fishing boats. *Caution:* Owing to the risk of *ciguatera* in the Caribbean, you'd be wise to check with local experts before eating any fish you catch in offshore waters.

In one morning you can get to know just about everybody in this unassuming island capital. The Swedes named it after King Gustav III and, in 1785, declared it the free port that it remains today: shopping is duty-free.

When sightseeing, you'll find the two thriving churches somewhat more interesting than the three ruined forts overlooking Gustavia. St.

Barts, of course, is completely undefended. But then this very particular island is hardly in danger of being invaded—except, of course, by tourism.

Scenic Drives

Sightseers have their choice of car hire or taxi, including the ubiquitous mini-moke and beach buggy ideal for local conditions. To spend more than four hours covering every paved and unpaved road, most of which terminate in sign-posted dead-ends, would be a difficult task. If you're stranded anywhere, hitch-hiking is accepted behaviour and you're sure to get a lift.

The seascapes and panoramas on this island are enough to tempt any driver to glance away from the serviceable but never-wide-enough roads. From the highest point on the **Vitet road,** you'll want to stop to take in the sweeping view over a bay called Grand Cul-de-Sac, which is favoured by wind-surfers, and out to Tortue islet in the Atlantic. Not far away is **Pointe Milou,** a wild, breathtaking headland from which on a clear day you can count nine isles or rocks in the sea. The strange cactus-like plants growing here in great profusion are called *Têtes à l'Anglais.* They have prom

Young musicians form a friendly group on a St. Barts beach.

...ent red protuberances and may have been named after the British redcoats.

The French West Indies may be matriarchal, but on St. Barts the father runs the family. Practically everyone goes to church, the Catholic majority either on Saturday evening or Sunday when mass is celebrated at different churches. It's worth going to church or visiting the fishing hamlet of Corossol just to see the ladies wearing the starched white bonnets called *quichenottes,* a St. Barts' trademark that dates back to the time of the original Huguenot settlers.

Beaches

The very best are difficult to get to, as is often the case with superior beaches in the Caribbean. Coconut trees and slop-ing cliffs ring the tranquil waters of **Colombier.** This northern beach of magnificent tan sand is most agreeably reached by boat. Otherwise, when the road gives out, you'll have to walk for about half an hour to this paradise bay which noted American banker David Rockefeller chose as the site of his Caribbean vacation home.

Very bumpy roads will take you almost as far as the second- and third-best beaches, **Gouverneur** and **Grande Saline,** in neighbouring coves on the south coast. Sea grapes and shrubs provide little shade here, but otherwise you should find no fault with either of these beaches. Legend has it that treasure lies buried somewhere hereabouts, hidden away by a renowned French buccaneer called Montbars the Exterminator.

There's no access problem to **Saint-Jean,** the best known and most-photographed of St. Barthélemy's 22 beaches. Swimming in this bay is perfect. The beach is actually two shimmering crescents of pale sand separated by a small rocky promontory.

At **Corossol, Anse des Cayes** and **Anse de Lorient,** you'll share the shore with fishermen, who set out to sea in gaily painted boats.

Currents can be surprisingly strong at the attractive **Flamands beach**—not recommended for children or poor swimmers. At many points around St. Barts and its small rocky offshore islets, there is fine reef snorkelling. Scuba divers and underwater photographers will never get bored.

Eating Out

Just as you'd expect, the French islands offer the best eating in the Caribbean. Surprising perhaps is that it's the piquant local dishes as much as the imported staples of French cuisine that make dining such a treat.

North American visitors are thrilled to find real *croissants,* non-plastic Camemberts, those incomparable crustly loaves of French white bread *(baguettes)* and château wines. Dining is often outdoors, never formal, though you might dress up a bit for the very best places.

First Course

Everywhere on St. Barthélemy you'll find excellent soups made of whatever fish and seafood the boats brought in that day. Or you might try *harengs fumés à la Créole*—smoked herring flamed in rum, served with a sauce of hot pepper, vinegar, oil and onion, accompanied by cucumbers or avocados.

Main Course

You'll see *langouste* (crawfish or spiny lobster) on many menus for a reasonable price. *Lambi* (conch) is tenderized, cut up and served boiled or

SAINT-BARTHELEMY

sautéed in oil with lemon, garlic and seasoning. Another popular dish is *matoutou* (or *matété) de crabes*—sautéed crab meat with onions, garlic, hot pepper, lemon juice, thyme and other seasonings.

Dessert

Hard to find, but worth looking out for, is a hot tart of grated coconut and delicate pastry. Coconut cake is another favourite, and there are creamy French-style *pâtisserie* products. Some of St. Barthélemy's restaurants feature marvellous chilled dessert soufflés.

Drinks

Ti punch, Creole for *petit punch,* is just that, a short snort of rum, sugar cane syrup and a dash of lime. Though most common as an apéritif, punch is the local early-morning pick-me-up, the late-night cordial and the most frequent drink with a meal.

More predictable for foreigners are the long rum punches: *planteurs* (with fruit juices), *au coco* (with coconut milk), *aux goyaves* (guava) and the daiquiri.

Shopping

For many items, St. Barthélemy has some of the lowest prices in the Caribbean. A few residents of the nearby "duty-free" U.S. Virgin Islands even do their Christmas shopping in Gustavia. Prices for French perfumes and fashions could be half of what Americans would pay at home. Some of the best buys: watches, liquor, cosmetics and perfumes, luggage, fashions (especially sportswear), fabrics, crystal, leather, figurines and children's clothes.

Items handcrafted on St Barthélemy include wicker baskets, straw beach-hats and mats, seashell jewellery, hand-printed cotton clothes and cloth hangings.

Practical Information

Banks: In Gustavia banks open from 8 a.m. to 3 p.m. in summer and from 8 a.m. to noon and 2.30 to 4 p.m. in winter, Monday to Friday.

Credit cards and traveller's cheques: Most hotels, restaurants and boutiques accept traveller's cheques. Many hotels and shops and some restaurants honour the major credit cards.

Currency: French franc (F) = 100 centimes (cts). The coins and banknotes in circulation on St. Barthélemy are exactly the same as those in France. Coins: 5, 10, 20, 50 cts; 1, 2, 5, 10 F. Notes: 20, 50, 100, 200, 500 F.

Restaurants: Lunch is served from 12.30 to 2.30 or 3 p.m., dinner 7.30 to 9 p.m. Dining is often outdoors.

Shops: In general, stores are open 8 a.m. to noon and 2 to 5 p.m., boutiques 9 a.m. to 1 p.m. and 3 to 6 p.m. Some establishments stay open after normal hours or on holidays when cruise ships are in port.

ST. KITTS / NEVIS

Lesser Antilles

274

Introduction

Smart St. Kitts and little Nevis are set like a pendant jewel in the blue of the Caribbean. When Columbus discovered the larger island in 1493, he was so taken with it that he named it after himself—and his favourite saint—Christopher. One hundred and thirty years later, down-to-earth Sir Thomas Warner took one look at St. Christopher and dubbed it a cosier, British "St. Kitts"—a name that stuck from that day to this.

Luscious vegetation in all its tropical brilliance, lacy coconut palms stretching along white or black sand beaches and mysterious, mist-shrouded volcanic mountain peaks make St. Kitts and Nevis one of the most desirable resort areas in the Caribbean. Adding to the allure of the islands are a year-round outdoor climate and dependable sunshine. Happily, the tropical squalls and brisk winds that send the islanders scurrying for shelter don't last long.

No wonder the British and French fought long and hard for control of the islands. Buccaneers, adventurers and pirates followed in their wake, looking for gold and loot. Dis-

regarding water sports ar sun-tanning opportunitie the different parties murdere each other with bloodthirs relish.

When the British final won the upper hand, a ne brand of explorer-exploite the sugar-planter, arrived c the scene. Soon a cracklir greeny-blue sea of sugar-car covered St. Kitts from end t end.

In the meantime Nevis wa making history of its own. young sea captain, in whirlwind romance while h ship was berthed off-shor courted one Fanny Nisbet, pretty and rich widow, marry ing her in Fig Tree villag church all of a Sunday morr ing. Little did she then kno that her husband was destine to become Britain's greates ever naval commander, Lor Horatio Nelson, Vice-Ac miral of the Fleet. And, as one famous name wasn enough for Nevis, the tin treasure island was also th birthplace, in 1757, of th American statesman an founding father, Alexande Hamilton.

Today the grim, black car non on St. Kitts' Brimston Hill are silent, and the 4,000 foot (1,100-metre) Moun Misery surveys the scene wit friendly eye. Newly-wed couples walk, hand in hand, barefoot along the surf-washed beaches and wish the moon would never go away. Tourist facilities have been increased and investments encouraged, but the islands remain largely unspoiled, thanks to a sensible policy of controlled development. The fishermen and sugar-cane cutters, as well as the other Kittitians and Nevigians, as they're called, are determined to keep it that way.

Brief History

16th–17th centuries	Columbus discovers St. Kitts (and sights Nevis) in 1493. Sir Thomas Warner lands on St. Kitts with his wife, son and a party of thirteen on January 28, 1623. A hurricane destroys the first tobacco crop in September of the same year. Sir Thomas and Pierre Belain d'Esnambuc of France conclude a treaty (1627) for division of the island, as well as a mutual defence pact against the Spaniards and Carib Indians. Warner starts a settlement on Nevis in 1628. Belain d'Esnambuc attacks the English in 1629 and regular skirmishes between the two occur over the course of the next seven years. Sir Thomas Warner dies in 1648. In 1680 Jamestown (Nevis) is destroyed by earthquake.
18th century	Britain gains St. Kitts under terms of the Treaty of Utrecht (1713); the French attack and capture Brimstone Hill Fort in 1782, but return it to the British the following year, as stipulated by the Treaty of Versailles.
19th century	Slaves are emancipated in 1834, but no equitable redistribution of land takes place. The islands of St. Kitts, Nevis and Anguilla are united in 1882.
20th century	St. Kitts-Nevis-Anguilla is established as an independent state in association with Great Britain in 1967. The same year Anguilla seeks independence from St. Kitts and is restored to colonial status in 1971. St. Kitts and Nevis gain full independence in 1983. The economy flourishes with the development of tourism and with the export of sugar, molasses, sea-island cotton, coconuts and citrus fruit.

Sightseeing

Sandy beaches, ruined forts, old colonial style mansions attract visitors to St. Kitts and Nevis. Other drawing cards include a selection of modern hotels, water sports and golf facilities.

St. Kitts' romantic place names will evoke a spirit of adventure even before you set out for a closer look: Mount Misery (or Liamuiga), Horseshoe Point, Golden Road, South Friar's Bay, Old Road Town, The Narrows. But, to start at the beginning, **Basseterre**—meaning "low land" in French—is the lively little capital town of around 15,000 population.

The bustling **port area** hums with activity as boats of every description come and go. Tenders serve those cruise ships and freighters that are too big to enter the newly constructed cruise ship dock, just a mile to the south of Basseterre. A colourful **market** is held in Basseterre, a mosaic of exotic sights, sounds and smells.

The Circus, with its ornate Victorian clock tower, is at the heart of Basseterre. Although the name and the staid 19th-century monument betray a nostalgia for England, the

lofty coconut palms swaying in the ocean breeze and the backdrop of volcanic hills put an end to prolonged reverie. The surrounding area, especially Fort Street and Independence Square, abounds in shops, cafés and old colonial buildings, many of which house administrative offices.

As you wander up the side streets, you'll come across tiny shops offering original, handmade jewellery—simple but decorative pieces made of shell or bone.

After seeing Basseterre most visitors head out of town for a round-the-island tour. Starting from Basseterre going north, the road leads straight into sugar-cane country; mile after mile of cane and cotton plantation speed by before you reach the first stop, **Brimstone Hill Fort.**

This massive construction, said to have taken 100 years to build, must surely be one of the wonders of the Caribbean world. It was from these majestic battlements, 700 feet (213 m.) high, that the English picked off the French galleons with pin-point accuracy during the 17th and 18th century battles for the island. But the English were not always invincible. In the Battle of Brimstone Hill in 1782, the French

on a gallant victory and, for while, the tricolour flew rom the warped and battle-scarred fortifications. Today ulls wheel lazily round the amparts, which command a pectacular **view** over the vast mpty ocean.

Continuing north you soon ome to **Old Road Town.** It as here that Sir Thomas Varner, "a man of extraordiary agility of body and good vitt" according to an ancient hronicler, landed in 1623. Vhatever the motives—some ay he had failed to find fresh ater on Barbados, others hat he planned to start a obacco plantation on St.

Kitts that he knew was neglected by the Spaniards—he stayed on, starting a settlement at nearby **Sandy Point.** He also died on St. Kitts and was buried in the churchyard of St. Thomas, Middle Island. With true pomp and regal chivalry, as befits a British Knight of the Realm, his epitaph remembers

"… one that bought
With loss of noble blud
Illustrious name,
Of a commander Greate in
Acts of Fame."

From Old Road Town the road curves north-west to **Dieppe Town Bay,** of interest mainly to vacationers looking for a quiet time. Good hotels and a nice beach make the resort popular for a relaxing swim and a snack before heading back through the cane fields to Basseterre.

South of Basseterre lies the airport (at Golden Rock) and the **Frigate Bay** tourist resort complex with its stylish shops and white sandy beach.

Nevis

When Columbus's men saw in 1493 they were transported "Las Nievas", they cried thinking of the snowy-cla mountains of their nativ Spain. In fact, the "snow" an almost permanent ring cloud that covers the island 3,600-foot (1,000-m.) volcan peak.

Today the crater is peace fully wooded with trees, fern and tropical plants, while th lower slopes are cultivate

Frigate Bay offers every facility in a magnificent setting.

ith sugar-cane, cotton, coconuts, oranges and limes. But, not far below Nevis' quiet surface, as the 18th-century settlers were first to find out, thermal waters bubble and boil.

Nevis lies two miles (3 km.) south of St. Kitts, across the strip of water known as The Narrows. The island has unbeatable beaches, fine accommodation and—history. The capital, Charlestown, with its old Bath House, was once one of the most fashionable spots in the world. Beribboned 18th-century belles took the waters, together with their menfolk—assorted dukes, lords, planters, investors and speculators.

About a century before their arrival, there was another arrival in Charlestown. He was Alexander Hamilton, born here on January 11th, 1755 (although he always claimed it was 1757). This outstanding American statesman was the son of Rahel Lavien of Nevis and a Scottish adventurer, James Hamilton. In 1765 Hamilton abandoned his family in St. Croix, leaving Rachel to fend for herself. When she died in 1768, Alexander was left entirely on his own. The rest is history: through dogged perseverance and sheer hard work the lad went on to become Secretary of the Treasury in George Washington's cabinet. He also helped to draft the Constitution of the United States. He died after a duel on July 11th, 1804. You can still see the remains of the **house** where he was born in Charlestown.

A generation later, Frances Herbet Nisbet, wife of the late Josiah Nisbet M.D., was joined in matrimony to Captain Horatio Nelson of *H.M.S. Boreas* under the blowing trees of **Montpelier plantation** on 11th March, 1787.

A plaque commemorates the spot, now in the grounds of the Montpelier Hotel. The register of **Fig Tree village church** contains the signatures of the happy couple. More memorabilia is on display at the **Nelson Museum.**

The rest of Nevis is **beaches**—including the beautiful Pinney's—,pretty plantation style accommodation, friendly islanders, good food and a roulette wheel or two thrown in for good measure. Water sports, riding, collecting shells or just plain sunning on the beach will provide you with all the ingredients for a perfect day.

Eating Out

Straightforward, fresh and delicious, food on St. Kitts and Nevis is a treat.

Seafood is tops, especially lobster, crab, sea urchin, turtle and other marine edibles, stewed, fried, baked or grilled and served with a variety of different—and often peppery—sauces.

Meat—beef and pork—and poultry is widely available. A favourite local dish is roast suckling pig; another is chicken served with rice, spices and vegetables.

The rich volcanic soil is good for growing vegetables manioc, cassava, yam squash and avocados. Tropical fruit is abundant: paw paw, breadfruit, banana, passion and citrus fruit, pineapple.

Round off dinner with coffee and Caribbean rum, the toast of the islands.

Shopping

Local **handicrafts** include shell jewellery, embroidery, ceramics, baskets, batik clothing and straw goods. **Imported goods** from England or Europe may tickle your fancy, too.

Practical Information

Currency. The East Caribbean dollar is the local monetary unit. Make sure when a price is quoted whether it's in EC dollars or US dollars.

Climate. Basically, balmy. Temperatures range from lows of 59° F (15° C) at higher altitudes to highs of 86° F (30° C), which means the average is a heavenly 73° F (23° C). Not too cold to swim yet not so hot that you broil.

Clothes. Casual wear, comfortable shoes and sun-glasses are the best outfit for day-time. Even in the evening, informal attire is acceptable everywhere. Beachwear in town, however, is definitely frowned upon.

Telephoning Home. St. Kitts and Nevis (area code 809) are linked to the U.S. network. For U.K. visitors to ring home, dial 011 + area code + local number. To ring St. Kitts or Nevis from the U.K., dial 010 + 1 + 500 809 + local number.

ST. LUCIA

Lesser Antilles

Introduction

This beautiful volcanic island midway between Martinique and St. Vincent boasts some of the best scenery in the Caribbean — rugged green jungles, undulating agricultural land, dazzling beaches and the volcanic, cone-shaped Pitons. There's even a dormant but still bubbling volcano called Soufrière that can be viewed from inside without danger.

Francophiles love St. Lucia for its French atmosphere. Many place-names are French — from the capital, Castries, to Vieux Fort on the southern tip of the island. English is the official language but most of the 140,000 inhabitants also speak French patois, a reminder of the French colonisation.

While St. Lucia (pronounced LOO-sha) remains agricultural, with bananas the most important crop, tourism is developing rapidly. There are provisions for all sorts of summer sports and you can enjoy good music every night and indulge in the excellent native cuisine, with its coconuts, bananas and tropical spices.

A Brief History

17th century	Early in the 17th century, a group of Englishmen from a ship called the *Olive Blossom* attempts to set up a permanent colony; most are killed by Carib Indians within a few weeks. Efforts by both the British and French to colonize the island prove abortive until the second half of the 17th century.
18th century	Beautiful and strategically placed, St. Lucia continues to tempt the British and French for over a century; the island changes hands between them more than a dozen times. In 1765, under the French, the first sugar plantation is started, small towns spring up and the island begins to prosper. But as the repercussions of the American and French revolutions spread to the West Indies, the battle between French and British for Caribbean supremacy intensifies. The Treaty of Amiens awards St. Lucia to France in 1802.
19th century	The last transfer of power at the end of the Napoleonic Wars leaves St. Lucia in British hands. The 19th century

is largely peaceful—an era of coconut, sugar cane, coffee and cotton plantations. The slaves are emancipated in 1836.

20th century St. Lucia heads gradually towards full self-government, finally granted by the West Indies Act of 1967. After a period of mild instability, caused by a tug-of-war between the leading political parties, the island has returned to its usual state of calm.

Sightseeing

Castries

The capital was named in 1785 after the Maréchal de Castries, then Minister of Marine responsible for the French colonies. However, few buildings remain from the 18th century, mainly due to two devastating fires which swept the town in 1948 and 1951. Today's city of about 45,000 inhabitants looks frankly jerry-built, though some quarters have a certain charm.

Take a look at the scenic **yacht basin** and the lively, ultra-modern Pointe Seraphine duty-free shopping complex at the harbour. Just across the way, the **market** for food and charcoal, which is used for cooking fuel, hums with activity in the morning. You'll see plenty of island produce for sale, the array varying with the season.

Along Bridge Street, you'll find the central post office and the largest shops. Spacious

Columbus Square, one of the capital's few picturesque corners, boasts tropical greenery, and a samman tree and a huge mahogany cast their shade. The 19th-century Catholic **cathedral** has interesting wooden columns, iron vaulting and frescoes painted by a pupil of the French artist Puvis de Chavannes. Opposite the cathedral stands the most handsome building in town, the **Central Library.** This red-and-white structure of stucco and stone, named officially after its benefactors, the Carnegies of America, looks older than it is (19th century).

Castries may lack charm, but the capital is backed up by its own mountain, Morne Fortuné, which signifies "Lucky Hill". A drive to the top up precipitous roads leads to 18th-century **Fort Charlotte,** an unremarkable military installation with good views. Both French and British conducted their squabbles from the ramparts.

In the middle of the 19th century, three military buildings were erected on Morne Fortuné. The buildings have been restored and now form part of the island's principal educational complex. But you can still see many reminders of the British and French forces who fought each other for St. Lucia. The **Inniskilling Monument** near by commemorates the British capture of Morne Fortuné in 1796.

The **Governor's Residence,** an attractive Victorian building, is on Morne Fortuné, as well as St. Lucia's small historical **museum.** From this hill you also have a sweeping view of Castries harbour, Vigie peninsula, Pigeon Island and the Pitons.

Towards the North

Many of the island's luxury hotels are situated to the north of Castries along a road as good as it is scenic. The hotels are friendly places and they admit non-residents for drinks, meals or a swim. In the area are sparkling crescent-shaped beaches, including VIGIE BEACH, CHOC BEACH and GROS ISLET.

A causeway links **Pigeon Island** to the mainland. The islet, remarkable for its high, green hill, finds favour with energetic climbers, and picnickers will enjoy views of Martinique to the north. The island was the main base of Admiral Rodney in the 18th century, and the name "pigeon" probably comes from Rodney's hobby of breeding the birds. Today the abandoned stone barracks once used by the British garrison looks like a haunted villa. The barracks, together with a museum, is situated within the national park that has been developed on Pigeon Point.

Exploring the South

Soufrière volcano and the Pitons are not to be missed on any visit to St. Lucia. You can reach these spectacular sights either by boat on a pleasant day's cruise, by organized tour or car. The circular coastal road that travels around the southern two-thirds of the island was established in the 18th century by the Maréchal de Laborie. It's wise to hire a driver familiar with all the hair-raising bends.

Just south of Castries, you pass CUL DE SAC, an aptly named sheltered harbour lined with banana plants—St. Lucia's biggest agricultural product. Next comes MARIGOT BAY, a secluded and still idyllic palm-fringed spot with several hotels and restaurants. Farther along are more attractive and isolated bays and beaches: ANSE LA RAYE, where local people make boats from gum trees and sails from flour bags; ANSE COCHON (French for pig) and the little fishing village of CANARIES.

By land or by sea, the sight of the cone-shaped **Pitons** will take your breath away. Postcards give no more than an idea of the majestic beauty of these volcanic mountains—the Gros Piton 799 metres (2,619 ft.) and the Petit Piton 750 metres (2,460 ft.).

Soufrière town, typically West Indian with brightly painted arcaded buildings, nestles just under the twin mountains. Unspoiled as it looks, the locals have seen all too many tour groups. Although official guides and the police formally discourage begging, you may be assailed by self-styled guides, palms extended for money, or little boys who forget school to dive naked for coins.

Follow the road leading to the renovated **sulphur baths,** situated just outside town. The baths were discovered by the French, and in 1784, Maréchal de Laborie, then in command of the island, sent samples of the water to Paris. They were

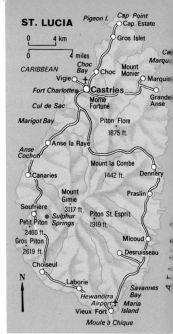

analyzed by Louis XVI's doctors, who pronounced the source to be beneficial.

A path leads through the tropical forest to the source. Don't plunge your hand into the water; it is boiling hot and can burn. If you walk farther along the path, beyond the hottest part of the source, you come to a lovely waterfall and pond. Do *not* wade or bathe here. This is a known breeding ground for the highly dangerous bilharzia parasite.

From the baths take the twisting road to **Soufrière,** advertised as the world's only drive-in volcano. And so it is. The road goes right up to the crater, steaming away like an inferno. Competent guides lead you quickly over the hot stones and through the noxious sulphur gases to an untouchable black pit. Efforts are being made to harness the steam energy for island use. Note that some rocks are coloured green by copper deposits, white by lime and chalk and yellow by sulphur.

In case you're apprehensive, remember that nobody worries about this dormant volcano erupting violently, since anything that lets off steam to such an extent probably won't blow up for a while. This line of reasoning may not be scientific, but it sounds convincing to anybody who has done some cooking.

Again take the road south and make for CHOISEUL and LABORIE, two ramshackle but picturesque little villages surrounded by splendid vegetation. You'll see men with machetes harvesting crops of bananas, cocoa, citrus fruit, coconuts, peanuts, sweet potatoes or cabbage.

The road levels out as it reaches VIEUX FORT and

the international Hewanorra Airport. The airport's name has its origin in a Carib word meaning "Land of the Iguana". Iguanas, large lizards that are harmless unless attacked, have dwindled in number on the island. You're unlikely to see one, unless you climb a mountain or stay at one of the hotels that keep a pet iguana in a cage.

A picturesque lighthouse stands on MOULE À CHIQUE cape. On a clear day the view from the cape is spectacular. If you look out to sea, you'll glimpse the island of St. Vincent. Look inland, across St. Lucia, and you'll see the Pitons. The seemingly endless Atlantic beach north of the cape is well whipped by winds and decorated with a glossy commercial hotel.

As you travel up the east coast, you'll find the circular road somewhat easier going, not that there isn't plenty to keep a driver alert—whether children on their way home from school or cows, donkeys and sheep wandering on the road. Headlands project into the ocean, and there are two little towns to explore, Micoud and Dennery. Inland rises Mt. Gimie, the highest point on the island at 950 metres (3,117 ft.).

Dennery earned renown as a den of iniquity, and until the 1950s a part of town called Oléon (or Aux Lyons) was closed to outsiders. Townspeople made a strong (and illegal) local brew known as *mal cochon*, and they were so belligerent in the defense of their privacy that even the police were reluctant to interfere.

Eating Out

St. Lucian cuisine features local produce, fresh seafood and spicy Creole dishes.

Soups and Starters
Accras, lightly fried herbed codfish balls in a piquant sauce, make a popular first course. The islanders have a gift for concocting delicious soups from local ingredients: breadfruit, pumpkin, groundnut.

Seafood
Lambi, chewy conch meat, can be found all over St. Lucia. *Langouste*, the Carribean lobster, is good whether grilled and served with melted butter or cold with herb-flavoured mayonnaise. Another good bet is just-caught *scampi*, deep-fried in batter.

Meat Specialities

Caribbean soups are so rich and filling that they hardly qualify as starters. Just one of several possibilities, pepperpot is a tasty mix of pork, beef and casareep, an aromatic blend of grated cassava, cinnamon and brown sugar.

Desserts

Fresh banana cake is a popular St. Lucian treat. Homemade ices and ice creams with a tropical taste include coconut, mango and pineapple.

Drinks

Surprisingly, St. Lucia brews its own reasonably priced Heineken beer—but you won't want to miss West Indian rum. Every bartender has a fabulous rum invention.

Shopping

A couple of shops in Castries sell very nice print and batik sportswear for women and there are boutiques for clothes and souvenirs in the better hotels. You can carry home the heady scent of tropical flowers in the form of locally blended perfume.

Dolls, pretty stamps and shell necklaces are sold everywhere, and you'll also see beaded jewellery, small carved wooden objects, and the usual local straw and sisal articles.

Practical Information

Banks and currency exchange: Open 8 a.m. to noon or 1 p.m. Monday to Thursday, Friday 8 a.m. to noon and 3 to 5 p.m.

Currency: Eastern Caribbean dollar (EC$), 100 cents = EC$1. Notes: EC$1, 5, 20 and 100. Coins: 1, 2, 5, 10, 25, 50 cents and EC$1.

Post Office: The General Post Office in Castries (Bridge Street) is open 8.15 a.m. to noon and 1 to 3.30 p.m. Monday to Friday, 8.15 a.m. to noon on Saturday.

Telephoning Home. St. Lucia (area code 809) is linked to the U.S. network. For U.K. visitors to ring home, dial 0 + 44 + area code + local number. To call St. Lucia from the U.K., dial 010 + 500 809 + local number.

ST. VINCENT

Lesser Antilles

Introduction

St. Vincent surges from the sea like a comet, capped by a simmering volcano and trailing a tail of islets in its wake. Constant and intense volcanic activity through the ages has endowed the island with a fringe of shiny black-sand beaches, notably on the Atlantic side. Yet the bleakly spectacular coast can melt into lush terraced hills a few miles inland, and in the south the beaches are golden coral. La Soufrière, the Caribbean's only active (well, semi-active) volcano, dominates the island's entire northern end.

Nature has been kind to St. Vincent's 113,000 inhabitants. Bananas, coconuts, cacao, eddoes and yams all flourish on the "Breadfruit Island", so called because was the first in the Caribbea to be planted with the bump skinned vegetable brough from the South Pacific by th legendary Captain Bligh. Th island has long been a grea producer of arrowroot, an grows sea island cotton, one o the softest fibres in the worle

There is something here fo everyone. The energetic wi enjoy the climb to the 4,048-f (1,233-m.) volcano summi Nightlife-lovers will appreci ate the Southern Caribbean only casino, boasting roulett blackjack and slot machines And for fishermen, snorke lers and yachtsmen, the strin of Grenadine islands i St. Vincent's domain (includ ing Princess Margaret's fa vourite Mustique) offers th ultimate Caribbean paradise

A Brief History

15th–17th centuries	Columbus discovers St. Vincent in 1498, but it remair one of the last of the Caribbean islands to be colonize because of fierce resistance from the native Cari Indians to British and French attempts. Escaped an shipwrecked African slaves begin intermarrying wit the natives towards the end of the 17th century, creatin a new race, the Black Caribs.
18th century	St. Vincent passes back and forth between the Britis and French, as the two European powers struggle fo Caribbean dominance. In 1795, the islanders side wit the French against the British colonizers in the Br

gands' War, but the British overcome the opposition and exile over 5,000 troublemakers (mostly Carib Indians) to Honduras. This time Britannia rules for nearly two centuries.

th–20th
nturies

Britain outlaws slave-trading throughout its colonies in 1807 and slavery itself in 1833. Indentured labourers are brought in a few years later from Portugal and India to work the cane fields, adding traces of their cultures to St. Vincent. In 1969, the island becomes a British Associated State, and achieves full independence ten years later.

Sightseeing

Kingstown

There are arcades to spare in t. Vincent's unassuming capital, many of them left over rom French colonial times. The **harbour,** in sight of Mount St. Andrew and Dorsetshire Hill, is always alive with schooners, fishing boats and the business of loading island produce. Kingstown's good **market** ranks among the best in the Caribbean, especially on weekend mornings.

Shops are situated near the seaport and market. In Grenville Street, towards the other end of town, you'll see a trio of churches: St. George's Anglican Cathedral, the Methodist Church and **St. Mary's Roman Catholic Church.** This last, a fanciful pot-pourri of Romanesque, Gothic and Renaissance styles, would delight any

storybook illustrator. There are towers, crosses and fretwork all over, and the courtyards are situated in odd places. Surprisingly, it's a recent construction, restored in the 1930s by Benedictine monks from Trinidad.

Learn all about Caribbean plant life at the **Botanic Gardens,** just below the Governor's Residence. The gardens, said to be the oldest in the western hemisphere, were founded in 1765.

Fort Charlotte, just west of Kingstown, merits a visit for the view, if nothing else. Take a panoramic look at the capital, harbour and nearby Grenadines through the handy telescope erected at the top of the fort's 636 feet (197 m.). The fort was built by the British as a defence against the French and named after the wife of King George III. Three of the original cannon are still in place, and the lookout point is used for monitoring ships.

The austere former barracks building now serves as a **museum** displaying colourful contemporary paintings by William Linze Prescott. The canvases depict some rather lurid scenes from St. Vincent's history.

The Women's Prison, a short distance downhill, looks out on one of the loveliest views in the world. For more stunning views of Kingstown and the harbour, climb east of the city up to **Dorsetshire Hill,** taking the twisting road from Sion Hill near E.T. Joshua airport.

Along the Caribbean Coast

From Kingstown, drive north-west via the Leeward Highway, the name for the narrow road that twists its way along the coast. As you travel northwards, you come upon one stunning sea view after another, and in between there are small towns like Questelles, a community of primitive houses and neat churches. Just before the small fishing village of Layou Bay, stop to admire **Indian petroglyphs,** stone carvings estimated to be at least 1,400 years old.

A further 3 miles (5 km) brings you to **Barrouallié,** or of the last whaling villages in this part of the world. Thes days a catch is rare, and you' not very likely to see a wha Some 30 miles (48 km.) from Kingstown, the road comes t an abrupt end near Richmon Beach, a deserted place idea for a picnic or swim.

Towards the Atlantic

Drive south-east along th coast past the Kingstown air port. You travel through th town's main residential an hotel district into suburb where English-style lawns su round large villas. You soo see **Young Island,** just 20 yards (182 m.) offshore. A though the island has bee developed as a luxury resor non-residents are able to cros over on the hotel boat to enjo a drink or a meal and explor the grounds. For a sma charge, you'll be permitted t use the pool or the sma beach. Fort Duvernette, o an adjacent islet reputed t have figured in battles with th Caribs, is now the scene o torch-lit barbecue suppers.

Head back to the mainlan and continue north past th yachting centre and a fe good beaches. You enter farm ing country, including lan

roken up into small plots
lanted with peanuts, yams,
otatoes, cassava and corn.

The road, now known as
ne Windward Highway, par-
lels the shimmering volcanic
lack-sand beaches of the At-
ntic coast. Stop at **Mount
leasant** for an impressive
ew of the pounding surf. But
eware: winds, rough water
nd sharp rocks make swim-
ing in the Atlantic danger-
us. Farther along, the green
rgyle district—a former
antation still planted with
rrowroot, coconuts and
ther crops—extends up to
eruvian Vale.

From here to the village
f Georgetown, you drive
rough more impressive At-
ntic scenery. From George-
wn, a poor road leads to
abacca Dry River, a region
arked by former volcanic
ctivity. You'll need a jeep to
ntinue on to Fancy, a vil-
ge situated at the northern
p of the island.

Alternatively, you can head
land to the **Mesopotamia**
istrict, otherwise known as
ne Marriaqua Valley, one of
ne island's most picturesque
egions. **Belvedere Point** looks
ut over this agricultural area.
reen and richly cultivated
elds climb neatly terraced
llsides interspersed with

pretty villages. Every inch is planted with peanuts, nutmeg, bananas and plantain.

La Soufrière

This full day's excursion for the very hardy is best attempted on an organized tour. Starting out early in the morning, you travel by car, switching to a land-rover which carries you over dirt roads to the vicinity of the 4,048-foot (1,233-m.) crater. The climb up takes 2 to 3 hours—through hot (and sometimes rainy) jungle territory, but with plenty of rewarding plant and bird life to be seen.

Soufrière's biggest explo-sion occured in May, 1902 when at least 2,000 inhabitants were killed. Later in the century, a scenic crater lake was formed, and in 1970 and 1971, minor explosions gave birth to an island in the centre of the crater. But all this scenery was destroyed by the gas-and-ash eruption of April 1979.

If you climb to the top of the crater today, you'll find steaming volcanic dome and pools of water, in place of the island and lake. Though walking is arduous, the excursion shouldn't be dangerous, as the volcano is constantly monitored.

Eating Out

Starters

Among a wide variety of first courses are *pastelles*, plantain or banana leaves stuffed with corn meal and savoury meat filling.

Soups

St. Vincent's soups are exotic enough for the most jaded palate: cream of breadfruit (hot or cold), avocado, cream of pumpkin or *christophene* (a local variety of squash). Highly spiced pigeon-pea soup is usually made with coconut milk and a little ham or salt-pork.

Fish and Seafood

Always ask for the catch of the day in the Caribbean. Sauces may be tangy, and many fish dishes are seasoned with curry spices.

Lambi, chewy conch meat, is chopped, stewed and served cold with lime. Conch is also used in pies and soups.

Meat

You'll find good steaks and other cuts of beef, as well as pork and lamb—prepared in all the usual ways with the chef's favourite sauce.

Chicken, duck, turkey and guinea fowl or *pintadeau* are served stuffed and roasted or spiced with sauces.

Vegetables

Imaginative cooking does justice to the exotic offerings of St. Vincent's gardens. Cucumbers are delicately sautéed, as is *christophene*. This vegetable can also be cooked *au gratin* in cream sauce. Breadfruit, which tastes like chestnuts, may be served boiled, sautéed or fried.

Water sports are tops on beaches such as this: Young Island, just 200 yards off the St. Vincent shore.

ST. VINCENT

Desserts

Sample the excellent fruit salads, which nearly always have a dash of liqueur or rum. *Crêpes flambées* may be filled with exotic fruits. Bananas are served flambéed, fried and in bread or cakes.

Drinks

While spirits and wine are available everywhere, prices can be high. Beer is usually reasonably priced and good. But the obvious drink is rum. You'll find it deliciously mixed into daiquiris, swizzles, screwdrivers, *piña coladas* (with coconut cream and pineapple juice) and rum punch.

Shopping

You'll find luxury goods suc as jewellery, china and cryst at reasonable prices in the be ter stores. Also look for bag baskets, hats and rugs, wove of straw or sisal.

The locally made women wear, such as airy sarong long caftans and sundresse is attractive. Some boutiqu sell sea-island-cotton cloth and printed fabric. Very hig quality batik can also b found.

Costumed dolls in ruffle dresses, coral necklaces, m hogany carvings and postag stamps are also popular.

Practical Information

Banks: St. Vincent's banks are open 8 a.m. to noon or 1 p.m., Monda to Thursday; 8 a.m. to noon or 1 p.m. and 2 or 3 p.m. to 5 p.m. on Frida

Credit cards and traveller's cheques: Most hotels, restaurants and sho accept traveller's cheques. Few establishments, on the other hand, w honour credit cards.

Currency: Eastern Caribbean dollar (EC$) = 100 cents.

Telephoning Home. St. Vincent (area code 809) is linked to the U.! network. For U.K. visitors to ring home, dial 011 + area code + loc number. To ring St. Vincent from the U.K., dial 010 + 1 + 500 809 + loc number.

SINT-MAARTEN
(ST. MARTIN)

Lesser Antilles

Introduction

This surprising little island embodies a dual personality—half French, half Dutch —each side trying to out-smile the other. And with such success that it has become a favourite Caribbean vacation spot. Its shores are scalloped with stunning white sand beaches, its interior dotted with blue ponds and green hills, the whole surrounded by water of crystal-line clarity. It has water sports, excellent duty-free shopping and some superb restaurants.

Whatever you call it, Saint-Martin, as the French do, or Sint Maarten with the Dutch, it is part of both the French West Indies and the Netherlands Antilles.

Certainly this island can qualify as having one of the world's longest-running governmental love affairs: since 1648 the French and the Dutch have shared sovereignty in almost total harmony. When the two nations divided it up, France got 20 square miles (52 sq. km.) and Holland agreed to take just 13,

but that included the important salt pond near the Dutch capital of Philipsburg. Legend has it that the division was accomplished by having a Frenchman and a Dutchman start back to back pacing off territory: some say the Frenchman got more because he had a longer stride—or that the Dutchman stopped too often for a snort of gin.

Another thing those early French and Dutch settlers agreed upon was that their island should be free of levies on any imported goods. That still means completely duty-free shopping today, and therefore—together with nearby St. Barthélemy—the Caribbean's lowest prices for many items.

Theoretically, there is a frontier, but there isn't a single customs official and it's been unguarded for over 300 years. On the main highway you'll know you've passed International Point by a stone monument commemorating the partition and signs reading *Bienvenue Partie Française* in one direction, "Welcome to Sint Maarten" in the other— that's all. So near, yet world apart, the two sides maintain their separate identities: the Dutch side, despite such holdouts as thin cigars, gin and ndonesian *rijsttafel,* has be-gun to resemble an American beachhead.

On the French side of the island—a sub-prefecture of Guadeloupe—every school-child learns the mother tongue. There is a Creole pa-ois, heavily influenced by im-migrants from Haiti, but it's essentially based on French. Here, on the northernmost of the French West Indies, you'll find such familiar trappings as *boulangeries,* restaurants fea-turing delicate wine sauces and gendarmes (if only a mere handful).

Lingering over a seaside dinner is the preferred after-dark activity on the French side, where most lights go out by 9 or 10 p.m. For livelier late-nights spots, head for the Dutch side with its revues and well-publicized hotel casinos.

A Brief History

15th–17th centuries	Columbus discovers St. Maarten in 1493. The island is first settled in the 1630s by France and Holland. In a struggle with Spain over the island's Dutch settlements, Governor Peter Stuyvesant (later Governor of New York during its period as a Dutch colony) loses a leg. Spain finally gives up its claim, and in 1648 France and the Netherlands sign a treaty agreeing to share sovereignty of St. Maarten.
18th–19th centuries	The British become interested in France's Caribbean possessions during the first half of the 18th century and manage three short seizures of St. Maarten. The treaty ending the Seven Years' War between Britain and France leaves French Saint-Martin definitively in Gallic hands. Ownership of the island is eventually shared between the Netherlands and France in 1816.
20th century	The French part of the island is made a sub-prefecture of Guadeloupe in the 1940s. Harmonious relations between the two sides of St. Maarten continue. Some 8,000 people currently live on the French half, about 11,600 on the Dutch.

Sightseeing

Philipsburg, the bustling capital of Dutch St. Maarten, is usually crowded with taxis, islanders and tourists. Cruise ships tie up at Little Pier, on the town's eastern edge. Nearby Front Street is the busiest shopping avenue. At the north-west corner of the town's main square, across Front Street, take a look at the old **Courthouse,** which dates from 1793.

A short stroll through Philipsburg will soon get you oriented. But walking enthusiasts will probably prefer visiting the quieter, easier-to-explore towns of Marigot, Grand-Case and Quartier d'Orleans, all on the French half of the island.

Whereas Dutch St. Maarten is one of the more upbeat places in the Caribbean, much of the French side's charm is that it seems content to slumber languidly in the sun. Marigot, the modest capital on its wide bay, is so quiet that large fish venture in surprisingly close to shore.

When Marigot does liven up—early in the day at the quayside—you'll want to be there. Like their Guadeloupean and Martiniquais counterparts, St. Maarten's fisher-men invariably chug hom with their catches to a clamor ous welcome. Nearby, ladie with broad smiles—an beams—sit on little stool selling breadfruit and cinna mon. Things become almos chaotic, by Marigot stan dards, when an inter-islan cargo scow arrives with hap hazardly tethered livestoc and straw-hatted voyagers.

The Dutch have a fort, s the French have a fort. For th view over Marigot Bay, it' worth the four-minute clim up to deserted old **Fort Sain Louis.** This 17th-century bas tion looks its age and the some. Sheep graze alongside rusty, disused cannon—stan dard armament of Frenc West Indian forts.

A few minutes up and ove the hill by car is **Grand-Case,** delightful village strung un pretentiously along a long curving beach. Much smalle than Marigot and even lowe keyed, it has several restau rants and places to stay. A salt flats nearby is tiny Espé rance airport, a one-strip, one shed affair used for flights t and from Guadeloupe an St. Barthélemy.

Probably the most excitin things to see on the island ar other islands. Outside Philips burg from a roadside lookou

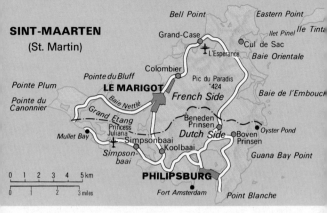

point you'll make out four islands rising out of the sea in the distance: Nevis, St. Kitts, Sint Eustatius and Saba. More dramatically, from the high, serpentine road to Oyster Pond from Philipsburg, you'll be stunned by the beauty of St. Barthélemy across a royal blue swath of the Atlantic.

The Beaches and the Sea

Counting little coves you can only reach by boat, St. Maarten has 36 beaches of fine, dazzling white sand with hotels located on some of the best. Following the avant-garde lead of big sister Guadeloupe, St. Maarten has introduced a nudist beach.

Surfy or serene, deep blue or aquamarine, the water is clear and clean. Snorkelling and skin diving are particu-

larly rewarding at a number of isolated inlets and nearby islets, and boats to take you there are available. The 180 wreck of a British warship on a reef three miles (5 km.) offshore is a diver's dream; for the non-scuba set there's a glass-bottomed boat for viewing big groupers and perhaps sea turtles swimming around the sunken ship's cannons.

Sailboats of various sizes are offered for hire around the island. Beginners appreciate the calm waters of Simson Bay, the largest lagoon in the West Indies. There's a choice of one-day group excursions by motor launch or sailboat to the smaller Dutch islands of Sint Eustatius or Saba. Hotels will be able to arrange for deep-sea fishing and water-skiing.

Eating Out

You'll find outstanding French cuisine on the island, plus spicy Creole variations. Either way, 4,000 odd miles from Paris, you'll notice that touch of flair characteristic of a nation that cherishes good food above almost all else. A few restaurants on the Dutch side offer the bountiful *rijsttafel* (rice table), a buffet of Indonesian dishes around a mountain of rice.

Appetizers and Soups

French classics include *escargots* (snails), stuffed crabs and seafood crêpes. Don't miss the *soupe du pêcheur*, featuring the day's catch of fish and shellfish. *Potage à la crème de coco* is cream of coconut soup, served hot, perhaps in the husk itself. You'll also come across refreshing cucumber soup and *soupe au fruit à pain* —breadfruit soup with onion and celery.

Main Dishes

Menus offer French specialities (tournedos, steak *au poivre*, bouillabaisse, frogs' legs) but don't rule out these intriguing Creole dishes: *matoutou de crabes* (sometimes *matété*)—sautéed crab meat with onions, garlic, hot pepper, lemon juice, thyme and other seasonings; *blaff*— stewed or "soused" fish (very fresh) with lemon or lime, garlic, hot red pepper and spices; *court-bouillon à la Créole* —fish slices marinated in lemon, crushed garlic, hot pepper and salt, simmered with chives, tomatoes, more garlic and lemon and *fines herbes*. *Langouste* (crawfish or spiny lobster) is always outstanding, whether served hot with butter or spicy Creole sauce or cold in a salad with mayonnaise and lemon.

Desserts

You may be lucky enough to be offered sherbet of fresh coconut, guava or pineapple, perhaps topped with whipped cream, or a delicious tropical fruit mousse. Since French cheese travels well, even into the tropics, you'll find a surprising variety from the provinces of the mother country.

Drinks

The greatest pride of the West Indians must be their rum. It comes in all manner of cocktails, long drinks and punches.

St. Maarten also has a wide choice of French wines and a selection of Dutch beers.

Shopping

Experienced Caribbean tourists have known about the incredible shopping on duty-free St. Maarten for some time. Every store on the island sells at the same taxless prices, among the lowest in the West Indies. You'll find great buys in Philipsburg, Marigot, even Grand-Case.

In Marigot, capital of the French side, look for bargains in perfumes, cosmetics, fashion accessories, sportswear, lingerie, porcelain, houseware and French crystal.

On the Dutch side, at the busy Front Street shops in Philipsburg, the "lowest tobacco prices in the Caribbean" include a selection of Cuban cigars. Other best buys here: watches, radios, binoculars, tape recorders, some cameras, Delft blue china, jewels, Thai silks, linens, Peruvian mirrors, old silver and liquor.

Not everything is automatically a bargain: American tourists may find that certain calculators and cameras, for example, are just as inexpensive at discount stores back home. However, on St. Maarten you'll be saving the city or state sales tax that may be levied at home.

Practical Information

Banks: St. Maarten's banks open from 8.30 a.m. to 1 p.m. Monday to Thursday, 8.30 a.m. to 1 p.m. and 4 to 5 p.m. on Friday.

Credit cards and traveller's cheques: Major credit cards are honoured by most hotels, better restaurants and shops. Traveller's cheques are accepted almost everywhere.

Currency: On Dutch St. Maarten, the Netherlands Antilles florin or guilder (NAf) = 100 cents (cts.); on the French side the French franc (Ff) = 100 centimes (cts). Shops will also accept U.S. dollars, and a few offer discounts for U.S. cash.

Restaurants: Lunch is served from 12.30 to 2.30 or 3 p.m., dinner 7.30 to 9 p.m. Restaurants on the French side usually include a 10 per cent service charge; this practice is variable on the Dutch side so don't hesitate to ask.

TOBAGO

Lesser Antilles

Introduction

Tobago takes its name from the tobacco plant, or from the Spanish word for the natives' pipes. It has been christened "Robinson Crusoe's Island" for no good reason, except that it looks like the sort of place where Defoe's hero might have been stranded. Nearly all of Tobago's 42 by 11 kilometres (26 by 7 miles) provides perfect scenery and relaxation.

The Tobagonians could not be more different from the people of nearby Trinidad. Most citizens are descendants of black slaves, and there is nothing like the heterogeneous mix of the larger island. Tobago was one of England's great sugar-producing colonies, giving rise to the local expression "rich as a Tobago planter".

When emancipation took place in 1834, slave labour became paid labour, after a fashion. Sugar, rum and cotton production boomed, and rich little Tobago was made a Crown Colony in 1877. But prosperity came to an abrupt end when the sugar market collapsed in 1884. As a result of the economic disaster, Tobago was made a ward of Trinidad five years later. Today the two islands form the independent republic of Trinidad-Tobago.

People on Tobago are basically kind and helpful, although they complain constantly about the government in Trinidad, the laziness of their fellow Tobagonians, and so on.

Although construction and development has brought change to the island, Tobago has kept a great deal of its primitive aspect and charm.

A Brief History

Early History	Groups of Amerindians make their way from South America to Tobago. By A.D. 300 tribes of Arawaks—peaceful farmers and fishermen—are in residence.
14th century	A war-like tribe called the Caribs sweeps up from South America, killing off the Arawaks and probably eating their flesh—if not for food, then for ritualistic purposes.

5th and 17th centuries	Although Spain colonizes neighbouring Trinidad, Tobago is left to itself. Early in the 17th century the English attempt to settle the island, but disease and Carib raids decimate the inhabitants. The island changes hands between the Dutch, French and English dozens of times. The Dutch invade in 1658, then English privateers take over (1666), followed the next year by the French, and so on. Between battles, slaves are imported and plantations started.
8th century	The island is declared neutral territory in 1748, but English-French rivalry intensifies. Around 1770, when the first slave uprising occurs, there are 3,000 African inhabitants and only 200 whites. From 1781 the French hold sway, but the British regain control in 1793.
9th and 20th centuries	Tobago is returned to France by the Treaty of Amiens in 1802. However, a year later the British are back to stay. Tobago slaves are emancipated in 1834. In spite of a severe hurricane in 1847, sugar, cotton and rum production continue to flourish. Tobago becomes a Crown Colony in 1877, but prosperity ends abruptly in 1884 with the collapse of the sugar market. Five years later Tobago is joined to Trinidad. The two islands gain independence in 1962. In 1976 Trinidad-Tobago becomes a republic.

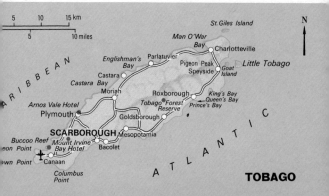

Sightseeing

Scarborough, Tobago's capital, is a sleepy little town of some 10,000. Scarborough looks like a shantytown when public works are underway, as is often the case, but it's a friendly place.

Fort King George (completed 1779), the principal sight, stands high above the town. From here you can see neighbouring Bacolet and beyond, across the Atlantic, to Trinidad. Tobago's hospital and former prison are situated downhill from the fort. The once formidable prison was the scene of a revolt in 180 that ended in the sentencing t death of 39 prisoners. Accord ing to legend, the governc was loath to carry out so man executions, but to save face, h ordered that one body b strung up over and over again

The fort bears witness t French-English rivalry for th island, and a plaque comme morates every change of for tune: France 1781, Great Bri ain 1793, etc. A bronze car non from the George III pe riod remains in place, an there are plenty of exoti plants to admire, especiall in the peaceful garden of ruined church on the site.

South-west of Scarborough

Heading south-west in the direction of the airport, you pass excellent sandy beaches, often with hardly anyone in sight. This is an inviting place to snorkel and go swimming in the surf.

For a nominal admission, you can enjoy the spectacular stretch of fine sand at **Pigeon Point,** near the swampy Bon Accord Lagoon. There are changing rooms, cabanas and a simple bar-restaurant.

Buccoo Reef, an extensive coral reef that is one of Tobago's main attractions, lies about a mile offshore from Pigeon Point and Bon Accord Lagoon. Glass-bottom boats reveal the wonders of the warm tropical sea, and you'll marvel at the Queen trigger-fish, blue tang, yellowtail, snapper and other beauties of the deep. For a clear view underwater, be sure to make the trip on a fair day at low tide. Swimmers can use the boat's snorkel equipment, and there are rubber-soled sandals for protection against coral cuts and sea urchins.

You may want to make use of the beach facilities at the **Mount Irvine Bay Hotel,** a luxury installation just north, for its 18-hole golf course, one of the best in the Caribbean.

Towards the Caribbean

A scenic road leads north-west of Scarborough, passing **Fort William,** a well-maintained red-brick building that serves as the official residence of the Trinidad-Tobago President. Farther along you'll see a plantation Great House called The Whim. Not long afterwards you arrive at the town of Plymouth on the coast. A tombstone in Plymouth was inscribed in 1793 with a puzzling epitaph in memory of Betty Stivens: "She was a mother without knowing it, and a wife, without letting her husband know, except by her kind indulgences to him". Islanders translate this as a classic love story between a master and his black mistress. She was the mother of the man's children, and was honoured by marriage to him only after her death, when the master also recognized the children.

The **Great Courland Bay Monument,** situated on a point, commands a striking view of the sea, and there is good swimming from the beach below. The monument was erected in memory of "the enterprising and industrious Courlanders from faraway Batavia on the Baltic shores, who lived in this area…" The cannon nearby mark the site of Fort James, built in 1768.

Continue north-east along the coast to the **Arnos Vale Hotel,** a former sugar plantation. A disused sugar mill fitted out with a formidable crushing wheel made in Glasgow in 1857 stands on the grounds. Some of the guest rooms are situated in the gracious plantation house, and an 18th-century clavichord lends its elegance to the sitting room.

The event of the day at Arnos Vale is **bird-watching** at tea-time. This pleasant activity will never tire you, for while you sit and sip your tea, the birds flock to you: the yellow-breasted bananaqui Tobago blue tanager, ruby to paz hummingbird and hand some, orange-breasted king o the woods or mot-mot. In jus one afternoon, you can be come an amateur ornitholo gist.

Not far away at Grafto Estate, you can also watch th birds. For either place, g around 4 p.m., the best time t see and feed the birds.

From Arnos Vale poo roads travel north-east t Charlotteville, a fishing towr but a good local driver wi have no trouble negotiating th turns. Scenic highlights includ precipitous views of headland and the sea, alternating wit picturesque huts on stilts ser ving as bars, stores or pos offices. There are good swim ming beaches at Castara Bay Englishman's Bay and Parla tuvier, a fishing village wit pastel houses. You can make detour inland, where the **To bago Forest Reserve** trails in vite long hikes.

Atlantic Sights

A scenic road travels east from Scarborough along the wild Atlantic coast. Tiny village like Mesopotamia, Golds borough and Roxborough lin the way. You may want t stop for a swim at one of th ays just before Roxborough: rince's, Queen's or King's.

Continue to Speyside, a olourful beach settlement. rom here you can see tiny Goat Island and **Little To-ago,** a 450-acre bird sanctury, also called Bird-of-Parase Island. In addition to the ative birds that congregate ere, there are dozens of other pecies, including gilt-plumed irds-of-paradise.

Eating Out

You can sample Caribbean ooking at its best on Tobago. Black-bean soup is popular, nd you can hardly go wrong ith fish broth or cream of rab, an aristocrat among oups. You'll find good steaks nd other cuts of beef as well s pork and lamb—prepared n all the usual ways with the hef's favourite sauce. Chick-n, duck, turkey and guinea owl or *pintadeau* are served requently too. The usual ac-ompaniment to both meat nd fish is *coo-coo,* a moulded ish of cornmeal or semolina nd okra.

But there is one outstanding eat dish served in various orms all over the island. This peciality, known as pepper-ot, reputedly originated with the South American Indians. It's a succulent stew of pork and beef, perhaps even chick-en, though the key ingredient is casareep, a spicy mixture of grated cassava, cinnamon and brown sugar.

As for fish and shellfish, always ask for the catch of the day—red snapper, scallops, swordfish or kingfish, per-haps. Shrimp is wonderful, whether deep-fried in batter, in a cream sauce, grilled barbe-cue-style or served cold as a salad. Spiny lobster can mis-leadingly be referred to as lobster. It's also called craw-fish. But whatever the name, this tasty (but expensive) crus-tacean is delicious, whether grilled and served with melted butter or cold with herb-fla-voured mayonnaise.

The wealth of fresh fruit provides a host of refreshing desserts. Mangoes, passion-fruit, grapefruit, bananas, pawpaws and pineapple are just a few of the possibilities. Fruit salads can be excellent, especially with a dash of li-queur or rum. *Crêpes flambées* may be filled with exotic fruits. Bananas are served fresh, flambéed, fried and in bread or cakes.

Coconut is used liberally in cakes, puddings, cream-filled pies and tarts. And the English preference for trifle is well catered for, since the rich dessert calls for a liberal dose of rum.

Drinks

Non-alcoholic island favourites include fruit punch and coconut water from a freshly opened shell.

While spirits and wine are available everywhere, the prices vary widely. Many hotel restaurants serve table wines by the glass, but they're often expensive. Beer is usually reasonably priced and good—but the obvious drink is rum.

Each bartender has his own recipe for rum punch. *Piña colada,* the perennial Caribbean treat, combines rum, coconut cream and pineapple juice, in a drink so rich it seems more like a sweet. Rum is added to daiquiris, swizzles and screwdrivers, too.

Shopping

Tobago is not really a place to shop, though you can find a few interesting local souvenirs like shells and dolls, as well as a small selection of luxury goods and sportswear in the larger hotels.

Practical Information

Banks: Banking hours are from 9.00 a.m. to 2.00 p.m. Monday to Thursday, and from 9.00 a.m. to 1.00 p.m. and 3.00 to 5.00 p.m. on Friday.

Currency: Trinidad-Tobago dollar (TT$). 100 cents = TT$1. Coins: 1, 5, 10, 25 and 50 cents. Banknotes: 1, 5, 10, 20 and 100 dollars.

Shops: Most establishments open from 8.00 a.m. to 4.00 or 4.30 p.m. Monday to Thursday, until 6.00 p.m. on Friday, Saturday until noon.

Telephoning Home. Tobago (area code 809) is linked to the U.S. network. For U.K. visitors to ring home, dial 011 + area code + local number. To ring Tobago from the U.K., dial 010 + 1 + 500 809 + local number.

PORT-OF-SPAIN

Trinidad

Introduction

Take an island with rich natural resources and lush scenery, people it with a vast selection of races and faiths, add plenty of steel-band music—and you have a thumbnail sketch of Trinidad.

The island covers a large area of 4,828 square kilometres (1,864 square miles) or about 80 by 56 kilometres (50 by 35 miles). It probably broke away from Venezuela in a distant geological age, a theory given credence by the striking similarities in rock formation, flora and fauna between Trinidad and Venezuela which lies some 11 kilometres (7 mi.) to the south.

Columbus himself named Trinidad in 1498—both for the Holy Trinity and the triple mountain peaks he could see from his ship. Spain founded a rather half-hearted colony on the island in 1532, but Trinidad remained poor and

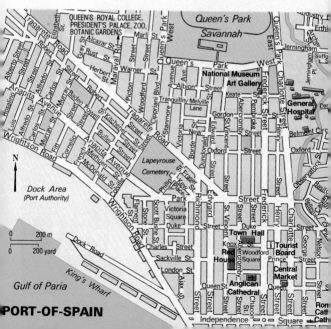

PORT-OF-SPAIN

argely undeveloped. Sir Walter Raleigh chanced by in 1595 and burned down most of the newly founded Spanish town of San José.

During the next hundred years, the number of Spanish colonizers dwindled to about 30. Then new settlers arrived, bringing with them black African slaves to work extensive coffee, sugar cane, cacao and cotton plantations. New blood and energy flowed into the island in response to a 1783 Spanish royal proclamation calling upon Roman Catholics of all nationalities to settle and work on Trinidad. This encouraged the ethnic diversity that still characterizes the island.

Spanish Trinidad was captured by the British in 1797. Thus the island became a British colony, loyal to the crown.

The collapse of the sugar market in 1884 bankrupted neighbouring Tobago, and the island was joined to Trinidad in 1889. Nowadays Trinidad and Tobago form the independent republic of Trinidad-Tobago.

Compared with sleepy Tobago, Trinidad buzzes with activity and excitement. It is the birthplace of the calypso and the steel band, the home of gaiety and good humour.

A Brief History

Early history	Groups of Amerindians make their way from South America to Trinidad. By A.D. 300, tribes of Arawaks —peaceful farmers and fishermen—are in residence.
4th century	The Caribs, a warlike tribe, sweep up from South America, killing off the Arawaks and probably eating their flesh—if not for food, for ritualistic purposes.
15th and 16th centuries	Columbus sights Trinidad on his third voyage in 1498. Spain founds a colony on the island in 1532 but uses it mainly as a base from which to search for the gold of El Dorado. Trinidad remains poor and largely undeveloped. In 1595 Sir Walter Raleigh burns down the newly founded Spanish town of San José and discovers Pitch Lake.
17th and 18th centuries	African slaves are introduced to work the coffee, sugar cane, cacao and cotton plantations. In 1783, a Spanish royal proclamation calls upon Catholics of all national-

ities to settle on the island. The British capture Trinidad in 1797, although Spain does not concede ownership until 1802.

19th century   Slavery is abolished in 1833 and the former slaves move inland to set up small farms. Thousands of indentured labourers—Hindus, Muslims and Parsis from India and the Far East—are recruited to replace the slave work force. Trinidad and Tobago are joined in 1889.

20th century   Oil is discovered on Trinidad early in the century. The island remains largely unaffected by World War I, but during World War II the United States builds bases on Trinidad to protect the Caribbean. Trinidad-Tobago wins independence on August 31, 1962. The islands are declared a republic in 1976 but continue as a parliamentary democracy.

Sightseeing

Lush green hills surround **Port-of-Spain,** the capital of Trinidad-Tobago, and the multi-racial population lives in everything from shacks to imposing colonial palaces. The architecture embraces a variety of styles from neo-Gothic to glossy contemporary, and the restaurants vary from French or Indian to fast food. Port-of-Spain is dotted with parks of all shapes and sizes, which Trinidadians like to compare to London's. However, the similarity between England and Trinidad ends with cricket, and you'll never doubt for a moment that you're in the tropics.

Begin your tour with **Fre-**derick Street, a main artery lined with shops that runs from north to south between Queen's Park Savannah and the port. Frederick Street is closed to traffic at the harbour end; souvenir sellers congregate here, urging passersby to part with their money. The colourful scene extends to **Independence Square,** laid out by the Spanish as a military parade ground. This wide, double thoroughfare serves as an assembly point for participants in carnival parades—*the* event of the Trinidad year. The Catholic church in the square is a simple stone structure of 1832, with two bell towers and a vaulted interior.

Heading north you come to

Woodford Square, a large green space in the centre of the town, site of the stately Parliament building, **Red House,** and the neo-Gothic Anglican **cathedral** with its beautifully carved mahogany altar and choir stalls.

Queen's Park Savannah, a vast expanse of greenery, boasts a racecourse, playing fields and plenty of food stands. On the south side stands the **National Museum and Art Gallery,** interesting for its displays of Amerindian relics and carnival costumes.

North along Maraval Road lies an amazing collection of **old mansions** known as the "Magnificent Seven". Here lived the cream of Trinidad society. Roodal's House, called the "Gingerbread House", is decorated in a frothy Creole style that belies its description of "French Second Empire". Whitehall, a Moorish-style structure, serves as the Prime Minister's Office. Stollmyer Castle, a white elephant of a house, once belonged to a German family. This turreted stone affair has been bought and re-

A footpath meanders through Trinidad's tropical rain forest

stored by the government and is now an art gallery.

The **Emperor Valley Zoo** on the northern side of the Savannah contains chimpanzees and colourful birds, as well as misleadingly benign-looking Cayman alligators and restless ocelots. But the **Botanic Gardens** next door is one of the town's major attractions. You'll see everything from frangipani and sausage trees to the raw beef tree, which seems to bleed when you cut into the bark. Adjoining the garden is the President's Palace, formerly the Governor General's residence, a Caribbean version of the neo-Renaissance.

You'll want to admire the view of town from **Fort George,** on the outskirts. The small house at the top of the fort overlooks the whole of Paria Bay. On a clear day you can see all the way to Venezuela from this 334-metre (1,100-ft.) vantage point.

The **Caroni Bird Sanctuary** is about 11 kilometres (7 mi.) south of Port-of-Spain. Magnificent blue and white herons and other exotic birds nest in the sanctuary, but the climax of the tour is at sunset when hundreds of scarlet ibis fill the sky with their flame-coloured plumage.

Island Sights

Well worth a visit is **Lopinot,** a cacao estate in the mountains near ARIMA. Established by a French nobleman fleeing the Revolution, it gives a fascinating glimpse into the life of an 18th-century planter. A river tumbles through the groves and the views are idyllic.

A trip to one of the most popular swimming areas on the island, **Maracas Beach,** makes another pleasant outing. You travel there on the panoramic North Coast Road or Skyline Drive. Swimming is easy at Maracas Beach, though life guards are on duty in case of trouble. There are changing rooms, and snacks and drinks are available.

You could also visit the little town of **Chaguanas,** about forty-five miles south-east of Port-of-Spain, in the morning when the food market is in full swing.

One of Trinidad's prime attractions, the **Asa Wright Nature Centre,** lies about an hour's drive east of Port-of-Spain. A state-sponsored scientific foundation has been established here. Tourists are welcome to join the birdwatchers, entomologists and botanists with special scholarly interests who assemble here to study the flora and auna of Trinidad. Many people come just to see the rare oilbird or guacharo that nhabits the caves in the grounds.

Eating Out

The cuisine of Trinidad is the result of a happy marriage of fresh products and time-honoured recipes evolved from the culinary traditions of Spain, England, Africa and India.

First relax with an aperitif and crisp plantain chips deep-fried in coconut oil. For a first course try *accras,* lightly fried herbed codfish balls served with "floats"—puffy, fried yeast biscuits. Or sample typical Trinidadian *bol-jol,* salt-cod served with pickled cucumber and lime. Callaloo is an exotic soup concocted from local products: dasheen leaves (similar to spinach), okra, onions, garlic, chicken stock, salt pork or beef, coconut milk, crab meat and hot pepper seasoning to taste.

Fish and shellfish (ask for the catch of the day), are all fresh and quite delicious. Be sure to try crab backs, crab shells stuffed with spicey crab-meat filling—an island speci-

ality. The shrimp are good whether deep-fried in batter, in a cream sauce or grilled. You may be offered spiny lobster, or crayfish, grilled and served with melted butter, or cold with herb-flavoured mayonnaise.

The outstanding meat dish, known as pepperpot, originated with the South American Indians. This succulent stew combines pork and beef spiced with casareep, a mixture of grated cassava, cinnamon and brown sugar. The Muslims introduced *pelau* (or *pilau*), a rice-based dish that contains fish or chicken, tomatoes, garlic, onions and plenty of coconut milk, raisins and *garam masala* (curry spices). Warm plantain balls *(pound plantain)* and okra and corn meal or semolina cooked in a mould *(coo-coo)* accompany many dishes.

Take your choice from the wealth of fresh fruit—mangoes, passion fruit, grapefruit, bananas, pawpaws and pineapples, to name just a few. Fruit salads can be excellent, especially with a dash of liqueur or rum. Trinidadians with a sweet tooth like guava cheese, made by boiling the fruit down with sugar till it reaches a jellied consistency when cooled.

Street stands sell snacks such as apples (wash them before eating), plus Indian specialities like deep-fried *kachouris* (chick-pea fritters), *poulouris* (balls of split-pea meal) and *sahinas* (fritters of ground split peas with saffron). Use the accompanying sauces with caution... they can be extremely potent.

The locally brewed beer *(Carib)*, tastes good and is reasonably priced. Imported spirits and wine are readily available but expensive. The obvious drink is rum: every bartender has his own recipe for rum punch. *Piña colada* combines rum, coconut cream and pineapple juice. Rum is added to daiquiris, swizzles and screwdrivers, too.

Shopping

Port-of-Spain's best shops are in Frederick Street, Independence Square, and in or near the luxury hotels. Look for duty-free (in-bond) goods, including cameras, binoculars, watches, perfumes and spirits. Larger shops stock china, crystal, glass and silver.

Indian silks, cotton shirts and caftans could be good buys, and typical loose shirts can be picked up in the street for a song.

Other popular items include silver and gold filigree Indian-style jewellery. There are many local handicrafts for sale, such as carved Indian- or African-style wooden or ivory statues and figurines.

Practical Information

Banks: Banking hours are from 9.00 a.m. to 2.00 p.m. Monday to Thursday, and from 9.00 a.m. to 1.00 p.m. and 3.00 to 5.00 p.m. on Friday.

Currency: Trinidad-Tobago dollar (TT$). 100 cents = TT$1. Coins: 1, 5, 10, 25 and 50 cents. Banknotes: 1, 5, 10, 20 and 100 dollars.

Telephoning Home. Port-of-Spain (area code 809) is linked to the U.S. network. For U.K. visitors to ring home, dial 011 + area code + local number. To ring Port-of-Spain from the U.K., dial 010 + 1 + 500 809 + local number.

LA GUAIRA/
CARACAS

Venezuela

Introduction

Caracas is a city in a hurry. A city with growing pains—and problems. The traffic jams inspire nightmares. Pollution sometimes obscures the view of nearby Mt. Avila. Almost half the city's people live in slums. And the noise, well, noise comes with urban expansion.

There are compensations, though. Caracas has one of the best climates in the world, a perennial spring. Exciting architecture, stunning shopping centres and first-class restaurants attest to the city's wealth. And, when you want to get away from it all, there's the sea and a mountain right at the doorstep.

Meanwhile, Caracas hums with energy. It is still "a-building". No doubt about it: this is a boom town. But the Caraqueños seem to take it all in their stride.

A Brief History

5th–16th centuries	Columbus sights Venezuela in 1498 and claims it for Spain. The following year, Amerigo Vespucci names it "Venezuela" or "Little Venice" in Spanish, because the houses built on stilts along the water remind him of home. German and English expeditions venture into the hinterlands in search of gold and the legendary El Dorado. They find neither. Caracas is founded in 1567.
7th–18th centuries	Settlements grow up along the coast. They export cacao, tobacco and cotton cloth and get slaves in return. Smuggling (i.e., trade not carried on with Spain) is very important to the local economy and involves mostly the Caribbean islands. Caracas becomes the capital of the newly created Captaincy-general of Venezuela in 1739. Uprisings against the Spanish take place in 1749 and 1797. The French and American revolutions make a profound impression on local patriots.
9th century	A creole (native-born Venezuelan) by the name of Francisco de Miranda heads a group in Caracas that deposes the Spanish governor in 1810. But the early success is followed by setbacks; Miranda is imprisoned and Simón Bolívar takes over leadership of the movement. By 1823, the Liberator has freed not only Venezuela but also Colombia, Panama, Equador, Peru and Bolivia. Hopes for a union of South American states fade quickly. Venezuela breaks off from a federation with Colombia and Equador in 1830, but the new Republic of Venezuela does not last long either. The rest of the century sees a succession of dictators amid instability and violence. Numerous slave rebellions occur.
0th century	The luck of the country finally changes for the better in 1917, when a huge deposit of oil is discovered at Lake Maracaibo. Today, Venezuela is one of the world's leading oil exporters and the richest country in South America. Though declining oil production in recent years and a sizeable foreign debt have caused some concern, the outlook is generally very optimistic. Political stability has been harder to achieve: dictatorships have alternated with democratic régimes but since 1958 popularly elected governments have ruled the land.

324

Sightseeing

La Guaira, Caracas' busy port, still has a few vestiges of its Colonial days. There's the old **Customs House,** dating from the 17th century, and behind it the Casa Boulton. The tall, beamed house, now a **museum,** presents the story of the port—in maps, old documents and paintings—since its founding in 1589.

A short ride on the superhighway and you're in Caracas, the country's dynamic capital. Caracas has a small Colonial section, too, **La Pastora,** but it's shrinking fast. The competition from eager developers has just been too much for the old houses.

Plaza Bolívar—named, of course, after Venezuela's national hero—is the historic heart of the city. And because most of the older monuments are close by, it's a good place to start a tour of Caracas. A larger-than-life equestrian statue of Simón Bolívar dominates the handsome square. Looking around, you will find the Casa Amarilla, now the home of the foreign ministry, the Consejo Municipal (Town Hall), numerous other government buildings and the **Cathedral.** The original, built in 1595, was destroyed in an earthquake and what you se now is a 19th-century recon struction. A rather sober exte rior contrasts with the marble filled interior, adorned with paintings by Rubens, Murill and Venezuelan Arturo Mi chelena. It's easy to pick ou the **Capitol** because of its shin gold cupola. Built in 1873 un der President Guzmán Blanco —in an incredible 114 days— this is where the Nationa Congress meets. Paintings o the great moments and men o the nation's history cover the walls and ceilings. Look fo the series by Caracas artis Martín Tovar y Tovar on the decisive Battle of Carabobo the turning point in the War o Independence. The Capitol' lovely tropical gardens pro vide a welcome respite from the city's hustle and bustle.

Visiting Caracas is like re tracing the life of Simón Bolí var, so many of the city' monuments are related to the great man in some way. Hi birthplace, **Casa Natal,** rank as a national shrine. This fine looking colonial home is also a modern reconstruction (Again, the original was de

Old and new stand side by side and merge comfortably in Caracas

molished by an earthquake.) Paintings show key scenes in the Liberator's life. You can see the font where he was baptized and the bed where he slept. Next door the Bolívar Museum has lots more relics and war memorabilia.

Bolívar's body lies in honour in the **National Pantheon,** an impressive edifice set by itself on a hillside. Military cadets stand guard. Among the tombs of the nation's other heroes, you will notice one that has been left open, still awaiting the body of Francisco de Miranda, who died in prison in Spain. They call him the Precursor, the one who preceded Bolívar.

Bolívar received the title of the Liberator in the **Church of San Francisco** in 1813. This is one of the few buildings in Caracas remaining from the early Colonial days. Note the beautiful woodwork and golden altar.

You should visit the **Colonial Art Museum** both for the house itself, an excellent example of Colonial architecture, and for the fine furnishings on display. This was the residence of the Marqués del Toro, a Spaniard who embraced the Venezuelan cause and a good friend of Simón Bolívar's.

Finally, to bring Bolívar t modern times, there's the **Centro Simón Bolívar,** a muc photographed city landmark The twin towers of this commercial centre soar 32 storey into the sky.

Caracas is not a city t stand still and you'll find som handsome modern shoppin centres, such as the high-clas **Concresa** which houses ar galleries as well, and the Pase **Las Mercedes** with fountain and gardens. **Sabana Grand** is now closed to car traffic an has been converted into business and shopping mall. A **museum complex** in the Par que Central includes an excel lent Museum of Contempo rary Art and a Children' Museum.

A more modern architectu ral extravaganza is **University City,** a somewhat futuristic campus of flowing concret structures and harmonizin sculptures that blend into th landscape. Only 30 years ag this was a sugar plantation

Round off your tour of Caracas with a good overall view The *teleférico,* a Swiss-buil cable car, will take you to th top of Mt. Ávila in a thrillin 10 minutes—when it's run ning. At the summit 7,000 fee above Caracas, the panoram is simply stunning.

Eating Out

The first thing to say about the food in Caracas is that it's expensive. The second, that it's generally excellent. The selection ranges from classy French and Italian to lusty Spanish but don't overlook the native cuisine, *cocina criolla*.

Some Venezuelan specialities you might try: *arepas:* hot corn cakes; *cazón:* ground shark meat; *empanadas:* meat turnovers; *guasacaca:* relish of chopped tomato, avocado, onion served with grilled meats; *hallacas:* the traditional Christmas treat eaten all year long, made of banana leaves filled with meat, cornmeal, olives, onions and peppers (ingredients vary with chef); *lomito con queso:* steak with cheese; *natilla:* cheese from Coro served with *arepas; cabellón:* shredded beef served with fried plantain, black beans and rice; *parrilla criolla:* marinated beef cooked over hot coals (often sold on the street); *sancocho:* thick vegetable soup; *tequeños:* hors d'œuvre consisting of cheese wrapped in dough and deep fried; *tostadas:* sandwiches made with *arepas.* Finally, the high-quality meat of Venezuela makes a simple steak dinner a real treat.

Shopping

Even if you're not planning to buy anything, you should take a look at one of the *centros comerciales* (shopping centres) in Caracas. They're a far cry from your everyday suburban mall. The architecture of these multi-layer complexes is often innovative, featuring retractable roofs, mirrored columns and hanging gardens. The shopping is sophisticated and, on the whole, expensive. Try the Centro Comercial Chacaito, which has a lot of restaurants, or the Ciudad Comercial Tamanaco, the most up-to-date.

Those in search of Venezuelan souvenirs might take into consideration:

Cacique coins. Symbolic gold pieces bearing likenesses of the Indian chieftains who fought the Conquistadors.

Cotizas. Sandals worn by Guajira Indian women, topped off by enormous pom-poms.

Jewellery. Especially filigree, in *oro cochana* (18K and 20K gold).

Pearls. From the Island of Margarita, mostly of the baroque type.

Rugs. Gaily coloured wool throw rugs. Nice for hanging on the wall.

Practical Information

Banks: 8.30 to 11 a.m., 2.30 to 4.30 p.m. Monday through Friday.

Clothing: On the formal side in Caracas: for men, jackets and ties most restaurants, jackets in some museums and national monument Better to be overdressed than embarrassed.

Currency: The monetary unit of Venezuela is the *bolívar* (Bs.), whic comes in coins of 1, 2, and 5 Bs. and notes of 5, 10, 20, 100 and 500 B There are 100 *céntimos* to the *bolívar*.

Shops: Open from 8.30 a.m. to noon and 2 to 6 p.m. Monday Saturday, inclusive.

Tipping: 10% service charge usually added to restaurant bills but i customary to leave a small tip as well. Taxi drivers are not general tipped unless they carry luggage.

Telephoning Home. To call the U.S. from La Guaira, dial 00 + 1 + are code + local number. To call La Guaira from the U.S., dial 011 + 58 31 + local number. To call the U.K. from La Guaira, dial 00 + 44 area code + local number. To call La Guaira from the U.K., dial 010 58 + 31 + local number.

SLA DE MARGARITA

Venezuela

Introduction

Baptized the "Pearl of Venezuela", more as a compliment to its authentic charm than an idiomatic reference to its ancient pearl fisheries, Margarita Island moves to the langorous rhythm of the Caribbean at its southernmost end.

If in centuries past it proved a haven for pirates along the Spanish Main, today the island is besieged by hordes of sun-and-sea lovers from the Venezuelan mainland, while its well preserved forts stand as benign and silent witnesses to its tumultuous past. Its 167 km. (105 mi.) coastline skirts round long, white beaches and mysterious mangrove lagoons.

Together with the islands of Coche and Cubagua, Isla Margarita constitutes the State of Nueva Esparta. Lying 38 km. (23 mi.) north from the Araya Peninsula, directly opposite Cumana on Venezuela's eastern coast, Margarita is in fact two islands joined by a narrow isthmus, 18 km. (11 mi.) long: to the east lies Margarita, and to the west, Macanao, little inhabited and dotted with isolated villages. Here it is wilder, drier and more mountainous (yet with secluded and photogenic beaches towards the weste end near Boca de Pozo), wh Margarita holds the more in portant townships.

Shortage of natural wate limited to a few springs, f long hampered Margarita growth and development. T problem was finally resolve by the inauguration of 38 km. (24 mi.)-long underse aqueduct and water is no piped in from the Carinicua River in the State of Sucr

Not least of the island charms is its diversity. Scene and flora range from palm fringed beaches backed by flo wering trees and shrubs, t arid stretches of scrub an sentinel cacti. Lush valley planted with bananas, pa payas, pineapples, sugarcan corn and oranges contra with semi-arid mountains vary ing from 1,500 m. (4,650 ft to 3,000 m. (9,300 ft.). In fac two of these "hills" were fo long an identification mar for navigators and mariner

Margarita is blessed with temperate climate. Mean tem peratures never exceed 28 Celsius, and there are almos continuous cooling breeze blowing in off the ocean Rainfall is sparse, other tha in the wet season which start around late November through to January. And a plus" much appreciated by avellers and inhabitants ike: there are no mosquitoes r insects—apart from an odd y!

ightseeing

he state capital, **La Asunción,** a small town of barely 2,000 inhabitants inland in he Sta. Lucia Valley, with ome of the earliest examples f Venezuelan colonial archicture. On its outskirts lies **acarigua,** famous for its raftsmen, who make the mall and exquisite *cuatros,* a our-stringed guitar.

Porlamar, founded in 1536 y a Franciscan priest, metaorphosed from a quiet fishg port into a thriving comercial and trade centre. Poramar boasts a long, white each which stretches along he mangrove-lined El Morro ay.

Pampatan is a picturesque illage which has managed to etain its origins as a fishing ort, while becoming a duty ree port. It has kept its charm nd its share of colonial archiecture, ranging from the retored **San Carlos Borromeo Castle** to the Yellow House now painted pink), La Ca-

ranta Fort and **El Morro del Vigia** which dominates the whole of the south coast.

A hamlet of 4,000 inhabitants, **Santa Ana** is dotted with small squares and groves, also popularly called the Garden of Margarita. Its core is the parish church; an unadorned exterior belies its interior treasures, including a bell renowned for its size and purity. A splendid panoramic view of Juan Griego and the Macanao peninsula is to be had from **España Fort,** a fortification on a hill overlooking the city. Nearby lies El Cercado, that reputedly produces the finest ceramics on Margarita Island.

A very colourful fishing village and ferry terminal, **Punto de Piedras** has quaint houses with deepset doors and bay windows and boasts a magnificent **cathedral.**

Fishing boats lie at anchor in the wide bay of clean and fresh waters at Juan Griego. The town is set on a curved beach climbing up to the **Galera Fort,** a romantic building if ever there was one.

La Restinga is the narrow 19 km. (12 mi.) lagoon, enclosed to the north by a long, narrow isthmus formed principally of seashells, and crisscrossed by whimsical channels. It simply swarms with seabirds, and is a noted sanctuary for the scarlet ibis. For bathing, there's a fantastic white sand beach between the lagoon and the ocean—just the place to work up an appetite for the small, delicious oysters that abound in the area.

Shopping

Traditional handicrafts and folklore are closely linked to fishing and seafaring. The islanders earn their living by pearling, fishing and fibrework. Indigenous handicrafts vary from **basket weaving,** knitting **fishing nets** to *alpargatas* (cloth sandals), straw hats, ceramics and earthenware figures inspired by marine life. **Hammocks** are a speciality, the *chinchorros* being highly sought after. Handmade, using woven mariche palm leaves and embellished by coloured yarn, they are very decorative—and practical too. Comfortable to lie in, they have the added advantage of not absorbing moisture when used on the beach and are excellent for camping. Look out too for *manares* and *sebucous,* used for straining juice from yucca and sieving to make the big, round, flat loaves of yucca bread.

Local **pearls** are much sought after. They come in all shades—black, white, pink and blue. Some are rounded and fairly perfect, while others are baroque (i.e. with bumps and marks). However, the oysterbeds have diminished considerably over the years, thereby greatly reducing the quantity produced. Another local occupation is the harvesting of **sea-salt,** as all Venezuelan salt comes from Margarita, Araya and Coche.

As Margarita is a free-port, tantalising goods and merchandise abound, but it's wise nevertheless to compare prices with discount sales in your own country.

TORTOLA

British Virgin Islands

Introduction

Few people can tell you for sure how many British Virgins there are—it all depends on the tide. The official figure is "more than 40", of which 16 are inhabited.

These tiny and almost forgotten islands, the BVI as they are known locally, are a sleepy relic of an empire. Yet British rule rests lightly on the 12,000 inhabitants whose dignity and independent outlook stem from a long tradition of land ownership. They will greet you with overwhelming charm —even if their local dialect of English baffles you at first.

Despite a benign British rule, American influence from the much larger and more heavily populated U.S. Virgins to the west is unavoidable. And the currency is dollars. Yet the British Virgins have a separate appeal, one which is jealously guarded.

These islands are unspoilt—a refuge for sailors big-game fishermen and divers. The few dozen hotels are lowslung and scattered. On those islands which have roads—mostly narrow, paved single lanes—goats and cows compete with the cars.

The best known and largest islands are Tortola, where nearly 80 per cent of the population lives, and Virgin Gorda. Others with few or no inhabitants include Anegada, Jost van Dyke, Salt, Peter, Norman, Dead Chest and Great Dog—names surviving from the buccaneering days of violence and plunder.

Sweeping past most of the islands is the magnificent Sir Francis Drake Channel where yachts have now replaced the pirate ships. The yachtsmen, like the pirates once did, regard these sheltered waters as some of the finest blue-water cruising grounds in the Caribbean— but for more peaceful reasons.

A Brief History

Pre-Columbian	The first known settlers of the islands are the Ciboney Indians from the South American mainland. They are followed by the Arawak Indians who in turn succumb to the warlike Caribs.
15th and 16th centuries	Columbus meets a hostile reception in 1493 when he tries to land on the islands during his second voyage. He names them Las Once Mil Vírgenes in honour of St. Ursula's 11,000 martyred virgins and claims them for

Spain. Spanish slave-hunters and pirates wipe out the Indians by the end of the 16th century.

7th century	Dutch buccaneers build a settlement and a fort on Tortola in 1648. The British seize Tortola and annex the islands in 1672. Settlers establish cotton, sugar and indigo plantations on Tortola and Virgin Gorda.
8th century	The first half of the century sees increasing prosperity and the arrival of missionaries—notably Quakers. The seat of government is transferred from Virgin Gorda to Tortola in 1741, and in 1774 the first elected assembly meets. The American War of Independence marks the start of economic decline. By the end of the century, law and order are reported to have broken down.
9th century	The Napoleonic Wars bring British warships to Road Harbour which becomes a free port, but the economic decline is accelerated by drought and a disastrous hurricane. The islands become part of the Leeward Island Federation in 1816. In 1834 the islands' 5,133 slaves are freed. A revolt breaks out in 1853, and cholera sweeps the islands. Plantations are abandoned and the islands revert to bush.
20th century	The colonial government makes an attempt to revive agriculture, but two hurricanes in 1916 and 1924 spell economic setback.
	The British Virgin Islands become a separate colony in 1956. A new constitution in 1967 gives the islands a ministerial system of government and they are now largely self-governing. Since then, tourism and offshore banking have emerged as major industries. In 1989 Hurricane Hugo causes some damage—but no lives are lost and recovery is swift.

Sightseeing

Tortola

Tortola is the principal island of the British Virgins. It is also Spanish for turtle dove, a bird which makes about as much noise as you're likely to hear,

except at a few weekend discotheques.

Road Town has no pretentions—a main street winds through town and a waterfront drive connects the old town to the newly developed **Wickhams Cay.** Formerly a burial ground for slaves, many banks and other financial institutions are now located there. There is also a Government House and Legislative Assembly building as befits a colonial capital.

The motto here is: "The best thing you can do is to do nothing", but if you can spare a few minutes, look in at the tiny **Folk Museum,** with photographs of local history and architecture, and artifacts from the shipwrecks that strew the islands.

Before, during and after any sightseeing on Tortola, you'll want to throw yourself off a beach into the refreshing, turquoise water. The best bathing spots are on the north coast. You'll probably choose **Cane Garden Bay,** where the beach slopes from leaning palm trees into the sea. Behind the beach you can see one local industry that hasn't changed much in 300 years — distilling rum. There's the Grand Copper Boiling Vat, a huge copper still made by slaves some 200 years ago.

On your way to the beaches you will pass the overgown ruins of the big sugar estates that used to be the mainstay of the island's economy early last century. In better condition are the ruins of three forts

called Recovery, Shirley an Charlotte and a dungeon a Havers, all on the south shor

Scenery is the high point a tour of Tortola. The top Joe's Hill, on the western si of Road Town, gives you bird's-eye view of Road Ha bour. **Soldier's Hill** affords th spectacular view of Brewer Bay, where forested hills er close a superb snorkelling an bathing beach.

The energetic might want t walk or ride to the top 1,780-foot (542-m.) **Mou Sage** to see what the islan must have looked like be fore machete-wielding slave cleared it for cane. A nationa park preserves the remains the Virgins' virgin rainfores

From Mount Sage, try t make out a "fat virgin" reclin ing in the sea. That's what C lumbus thought he saw, an so he named the island Virgi Gorda. It's the BVI's third largest yet most developed is land, and to its south-wes stretches a string of cays, no tably **Norman Island,** said t be Robert Louis Stevenson Treasure Island. You'll enjo snorkelling and exploring th sea caves at Treasure Poin Close by is the rock Dea Chest celebrated in the "yo ho-ho and a bottle of rum song.

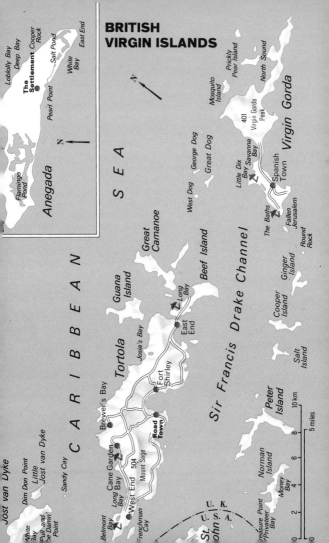

Beyond Dead Chest lies **Salt Island,** which used to provide the English monarch with an annual sack of salt from its salt ponds. Divers go there to see **the wreck of the Rhone**—a trans-atlantic Royal Mail steamer smashed against a reef by a hurricane in 1867.

Excursion to Virgin Gorda

During the half-hour journey you'll have a spectacular view of parts of Tortola inaccessible by road, as well as of the islands west of Virgin Gorda.

Caribbean pleasures: blue-water cruising and tropical fruit.

Fewer than 1,500 people li on Virgin Gorda and it is ha to believe that it was once thriving commercial centre.

The capital is Spani Town, a quaint settleme with shops, restaurants at tiny hotels. But this island best known for **The Bat** about a mile down Milli aire's Road from the town. I as if a giant hand has flu house-sized boulders acro the white sand of a cove. T sea rushes in to form a lab rinth of crystal-clear channe and pools, which shimmer the reflected light. It is one the island's 20 beaches at offers superb snorkelling.

Eating Out

It's extraordinary what can be done with the coconut. Apart from cracking it open, drinking the milk and eating the meat, you can ask an islander to turn it into: coconut soup, coconut and avocado salad, frozen coconut chips, coconut bread, coconut dumplings, coconut-cheese tart, coconut ice-cream or a coconut daiquiri.

Another staple on the top of the menu could be conch fritters—they say the conch is an aphrodisiac—or a selection of tropical fruits including a papaya garnished with lime juice. On Tortola, the papaya is made into a memorable soup, and fish soups and stews are what the islanders take for granted.

The local speciality is *kallaloo*, a spicy soup made of pigs' tails and diced beef. Also, try marinated strips of local fish, deep fried and served with sauce, or chicken stuffed with flakes of white crab-meat.

Many of the islands will have their own seasoning to add spice to the meat, fish, soups and stews. One of the tangiest comes from Salt Island. It's called Caribbean seasoning and is made of Salt Island salt, thyme, *chibble* (chives), black peppercorns,

whole cloves, hot yellow peppers, fresh celery, nutmeg, mace and garlic—all pounded in a mortar.

Drinks

The rum that kept Britain's Royal Navy fighting for 300 years—Pusser's Rum—has its origins in the British Virgins. Today it forms the basis of a choice of colourful flips, fizzes, punches, daiquiris, sours and *piña coladas*.

And the popular cure for a hangover is tea, not the classic British favourite, but "bush tea" which is said to have a flavour midway between a banana and a pineapple.

TORTOLA

Shopping

Island craftsmen have managed to retain traditions dating from the Virgins' turbulent history of slavery and piracy.

Dolls. Island mothers have traditionally made rope dolls for their children. A *mocko jumbie* doll, with magic overtones, comes dressed as a clown.

Jewellery. The slaves were forbidden to wear jewellery, so it has more than casual symbolism here. Necklaces, bracelets and pendants can be made of seeds, shells, precious corals or even pottery.

Macramé, a sailor's art, dating from the days of sail, still flourishes here. You will find elaborately knotted belts, wall hangings and plant holders

Seashells. Diving for living shells is discouraged, but you can find any number on the beach or buy them. Most popular are the big conch shells which was used as a trumpet and the geometric sand dollar

Scrimshaw, another seaman's hobby, is still practised in the form of intricate engravings on bone or seashells.

Other interesting items include BVI postage **stamps,** native **jams, basketwork, antique bottles** and local **batik.**

Practical Information

Banks: Open from 9 a.m. to 2 p.m. from Monday to Thursday, and Friday from 9 a.m. to 2 p.m. and from 4 p.m. to 5.30 p.m.

Currency: The official currency of the BVI is the U.S. dollar. The major credit cards and traveller's cheques are increasingly accepted. There are no restrictions on the amounts of currency brought in and you are allowed to take out up to the sum imported and declared.

Prices: Hotels and restaurants are as expensive as on the U.S. Virgin Islands. The cost of international telephone calls is prohibitive.

Shops: Usually open from 9 a.m. to 5 p.m., Monday to Saturday.

Telephoning Home. Tortola (area code 809) is linked to the U.S. network. For U.K. visitors to ring home, dial 011 + 44 + area code + local number. To call Tortola from the U.K., dial 010 + 500 809 + local number.

ST. CROIX

U.S. Virgin Islands

Introduction

Long, leisurely and lovely, St. Croix lies totally surrounded by the Caribbean some 40 miles (64 km.) south of the other Virgin Islands. It's pronounced *Saint Croy* and means "Holy Cross".

Soon after landing, you'll appreciate that this is a very special tropical island. The unhurried islanders, known as Crucians, number about 50,000 and live on St. Croix's 82 square miles (212 sq. km.) of rolling countryside and satellite isles. That makes it by far the largest of the Virgins, but boasting's not the style.

The pace of island life is languorous, the scenery glorious, the thought of a skyscraper or a revolution ridiculous. Unwinding is dictated behaviour. Cocktail hour seems to stretch well past the spectacular sunsets, even if you don't succumb to the omnipresent island rum.

In these tranquil surroundings it is easy to forget that the island has had a chequered, often violent, history. Originally inhabited by Carib Indians, it was discovered by the Spaniards, settled by the English and Dutch, conquered by the French, bequeathed to the Knights of Malta, sold to the Danes and eventually bought by the United States, to form a trio of U.S.-owned Virgin Islands along with St. John and St. Thomas.

Traces of the past survive in the old forts, ruined plantation houses, and the shady Danish arcades of the two old towns of Frederiksted and Christiansted.

But if your taste runs more to sport, you will find excellent golf and an array of other attractions, from fishing and water-skiing to tennis and riding (including moonlight expeditions). Or, best of all, take a trip to the fabulous underwater nature trail along the coral reefs of nearby Buck Island.

A Brief History

15th–16th centuries	Columbus discovers St. Croix, naming it after the Holy Cross (Santa Cruz), on his second voyage to the New World in 1493, and calls the whole group of isles the Virgins, after St. Ursula's 11,000 martyred Christian maidens. The Spanish set up no permanent colonies on

St. Croix, but round up the native Carib Indians for slave labour in the gold mines of Hispaniola, Cuba, Puerto Rico and Jamaica.

17th–18th centuries

In 1625, English and Dutch settlers establish rival outposts on the island. After 20 years of bloody struggle, the English prevail, but are expelled by Spanish forces in 1650, who themselves surrender to the French in the same year. St. Croix is bequeathed in 1653 to the Knights of Malta, who sell out to the French West India Company 12 years later. Thousands of African slaves are brought in to work the sugar cane fields and the island prospers. France sells St. Croix to the Danish West India Company in 1733.

19th century

The Danish government bans trade in slaves in its colonies in 1803 but, under heavy pressure from cane planters, hesitates to free them. Some 8,000 rebellious slaves gather at Fort Frederik in Frederiksted in 1848, forcing Governor-General Peter von Scholten to declare emancipation on his own authority to avert an all-out slave revolt. Severely hit by hurricanes, drought and fire in the second half of the century, St. Croix's economy declines.

20th century

In 1917, the United States, attracted by the excellent harbour at Charlotte Amalie on St. Thomas, buys St. Croix, St. Thomas and St. John, plus a sprinkling of smaller islands in the Virgins, from Denmark for $25 million. Islanders are granted voting rights in 1936, and further political independence in 1954 and 1970. Tourism and the rebirth of the rum industry bring new economic well-being.

Sightseeing

Frederiksted

Here stalk echos of West Indian yesterdays. Fronting on the tranquil west-coast sea, Frederiksted wears a sleepy look, and its few modern buildings don't begin to disturb the old-fashioned, world-passed-by atmosphere.

Its vital feature is a long and venerable **pier** protruding out to navigably deep water. It attracts swarms of nocturnal scuba divers as marine life teems around the encrusted supports.

Fort Frederik, now restored, stands near the pier; it was built in the mid-18th century, primarily to discourage smuggling which flourished from the west end of St. Croix. As unlikely as insurrection seems here now, it was at this fort that harried Governor von Scholten declared, in an explosive situation in 1848: "All unfree in the Danish West Indies are from today free".

Strolling Frederiksted's esplanade and handful of downtown streets, you'll notice an odd architectural mélange. It's nicknamed "Victorian gingerbread". When local leaders went on a flaming rampage in the 1878 labour riots, the upper levels of the buildings were destroyed in the blaze, but the Danish stone bases survived.

The mid-18th-century outdoor produce market is open some mornings, but an even better show is the seaside **fish market** which also began life when Frederiksted did.

Around the Island

Leaving Frederiksted, a pleasant little coastal road runs north, meandering through the dense foliage of St. Croix's small **rainforest** and on to the Virgin Islands' most celebrated golf course. Part of the

Carambola Beach Resort, it's richly green, hilly and windy 18-hole course, famous bot for its beauty and its chal lenges. It features nine wate holes where local kids ofte dive to recover lost balls.

A main highway, Centrelin Road, crosses the island, t link the two towns of Fre deriksted and Christiansted Near its western end is S Croix's proudest landboun attraction, **Whim Greathouse** You'll want to spend at lea an hour on this elegant estat with its great house built b an eccentric Danish planter i 1794. Past the old cookhous a fascinating 1832 apothe cary shop has been recreated complete with proprietor' rocking chair beneath myste rious bottles. A huge ston windmill and mule mill, bot used to grind sugar, have als been fully restored.

Christiansted

Everything in this surprisin harbour town is within fi minutes' stroll of everythin else. On perhaps the mo charming **waterfront** in th West Indies, the swayin masts are mesmerizing, th boardwalk's beams meande ing.

They say the French burie non-Catholics on the little i

land in the harbour and therefore named it **Protestant Cay.** Out beyond, swells break on the formidable reef which runs protectively along much of St. Croix's north shore. To the everlasting advantage of Christiansted, the tricky channel through the coral and shallow harbour waters keep large ships away.

In from the wharf, past the curious but inviting maze of small hotels, cafés and open-doored shops you'll find thick-walled buildings with shaded arcades. Here, in relaxed surroundings, shopping is very close to duty-free, as it is everywhere on the U.S. Virgins.

A small wedge of Christiansted, beginning at King's Wharf, was the heart of the Danish capital. It's preserved as a historic site by the U.S. National Park Service and contains just enough sights to convey the original flavour without tiring the visitor.

It's hard to take too seriously a fort which was never fired on. But **Fort Christiansvaern,** overlooking the harbour, at least manages to appear somewhat formidable. On the parapet, the guns are shinily unused, and the view is superb over Gallows Bay (named after what they used

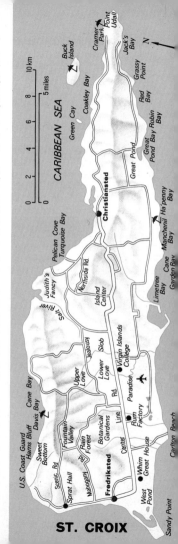

ST. CROIX

to do to the pirates). Dating back to 1734, the neat red fort is the oldest structure on the island, though greatly restored.

Leaving the fort through the sally port, you'll spy a steeple straight ahead at the edge of town. Thereunder lies a tale. The **Steeple Building** existed by the 1750s as the island's first Danish Lutheran church. Military, medical, municipal and educational functions followed over the years. Today, beneath the steeple which dates to 1795, the edifice is an instant museum of the Danish West Indies. Apart from displays of the history of

sugar and rum, recently discovered aboriginal Indian artefacts show how the Caribs and Arawaks cooked, fished and hunted.

Nostalgia fans may want to climb St. Croix's most imposing steps into **Government House** on King Street to inspect the narrow ballroom where the Danish elite drank and danced away the long colonial evenings. Not only governors but wealthy planter-merchants lived at times in this admired residence, part of which stood as early as 1747. The red wooden sentry box dates back to the Danish period.

Across King Street no trace remains of the hardware store where the future American statesman, Alexander Hamilton, clerked as a young man, but the present commercial building and its alleyway are named after him anyway.

Buck Island

This could be your best experience in the Caribbean. Any morning at the Christiansted wharf, take your choice of sloop, schooner, catamaran or even glass-bottomed boat for the 5½-mile (9-km.) trip to Buck Island close off St. Croix's north-eastern shore. Wear a bathing suit.

With its fabulous **underwater trail** through an encircling coral reef, the island was proclaimed a U.S. National Monument by President John F. Kennedy in 1961. Boat skippers provide masks and fins, and if you can float, they'll have you peering down into the under-wonderworld within minutes. Otherwise, there are various raft-glass viewing devices so that no one need miss the fish.

You'll be guided along the natural trail, which has sunken arrows and signs identifying coral species perfectly visible in water no more than 12 feet (4 m.) deep.

Eating Out

Local chefs seem to have taken the most inspired elements of West Indian cooking and applied them to island produce.

Starters

Try *gundy,* a pâté of salt cod or lobster mashed with olives and onions. Pumpkin soup is popular, as are avocado purées. And almost every restaurant features fresh fish and seafood soups.

Fish and Seafood

Conch is served with lemon and butter, lime sauce or spicier Creole sauces. Lobsters usually come grilled, though Puerto Rico-influenced chefs also chop them up into a soupy rice stew called *asopao.*

You'll lose count of the delicious fresh fish to choose from. Complementing your fish course will be either hush puppies, a fried corn-meal concoction, or Johnny Cake, an oven-baked dumpling.

Main Course

Kallaloo or pepperpot is a filling soupy stew of pork, fresh fish, crab or conch, spinach, okra, garlic and hot pepper. Stewed goat and rack of lamb are other island specialities.

Try deep-fried chicken drumsticks seasoned with garlic.

Drinks

St. Croix has long been famous for its rum. Try "Cruzan champagne"—chilled white rum without adornment. If you prefer your rum in a cocktail, daiquiris come in coconut, banana, soursop, peach and strawberry flavours.

Two local "Christmas wines", of guavaberry and sorrel, are worth asking for at any season.

Shopping

Merchants have to pay a tax on imported goods, but there are no punitive luxury taxes.

Visitors from the U.S. can carry home exempt from duty double the amount of goods allowed to travellers arriving from foreign countries.

Local handicrafts. Baskets, *mocko jumbie* dolls, resortwear, jams, coral jewellery, macramé, scrimshaw and seashells.

International goods include: Brazilian gems, Danish porcelain, English pottery and scarves, Finnish earthenware and knitwear, French crystal and perfumes, Haitian fashions and carvings, Indonesian fashions, Japanese cameras and watches, Norwegian cutlery and linens, Portuguese embroidery, Scottish cashmere sweaters, Swedish crystal and rugs, Swiss watches and knives, and Thai fabrics.

Practical Information

Banks: St. Croix's banks are open 9 a.m. to 2.30 p.m., Monday to Thursday; Friday 9 a.m. to 2 p.m. and 3.30 p.m. to 5 p.m.

Currency: The currency is the U.S. dollar divided into 100 cents.

Telephoning Home. St. Croix (area code 809) is linked to the U.S. network. For U.K. visitors to ring home, dial 011 + area code + local number. To ring St. Croix from the U.K., dial 010 + 1 + 500 809 + local number.

ST. THOMAS
ST. JOHN

U.S. Virgin Islands

Introduction

This cluster of islands, islets and shrub-swathed rocks has been collectively called the Virgins since Columbus sailed through; because they were so beautiful and numerous, he named them after St. Ursula's 11,000 martyred maidens of Christian belief.

Rising out of a crystal-blue sea, they're surprisingly green and hilly. Just as unexpectedly, there are a great many of these Virgin Islands—more than 100, owned either by the United States or Britain. Most are tiny and inhabited only by lucky birds, and most are verdant and volcanic. All form part of the extended arc of islands known as the Lesser Antilles which haphazardly define where the Atlantic ends and the Caribbean begins.

Relic from the age of marauders: Blackbeard's Tower, St. Thomas.

Thanks to the steadily soothing trade winds, the Virgins boast fairly of the best weather in the West Indies; lower humidity than elsewhere and an average annual temperature of 78° F. Rare is the day without predominantly blue sky and sunshine, and swimming is perfectly comfortable all year round.

Most Virgin Islanders are descendants of African slaves who laboured for European plantation owners until emancipation in the mid-19th century. More and more of the population, however, is not native-born: "down islanders" from elsewhere in the Caribbean, Puerto Ricans and mainland Americans have been moving in to these still sparsely inhabited islands, particularly St. Thomas and St. Croix. The ethnic and cultural blend is intriguing—and unusually harmonious.

ST. THOMAS

A Brief History

15th and 16th centuries	Columbus discovers the Virgin Islands on his second voyage in 1493. He calls them las Vírgenes and claims them for Spain, but they are not colonized. The Indian inhabitants are captured and forced into slavery and the islands eventually become the haunt of pirates.
17th century	In 1657 Dutch settlers establish a colony on St. Thomas but soon abandon the island. They are followed by Danes and Englishmen, but the latter also give up. A contingent of Danes and Norwegians found the settlement of Charlotte Amalie in 1672 and St. Thomas soon grows into a major trading centre and slave market.
18th century	Edward Teach, the legendary buccaneer Blackbeard, sets up headquarters in Blackbeard's Tower, overlooking Saint Thomas harbour. Danish settlers from St. Thomas cross to St. John in 1717, establishing plantations of cotton and tobacco. St. Thomas is declared a free port in 1724. A slave uprising on St. John in 1733, during which Danish planters and British relief forces are slaughtered, gives the slaves a free community for six months. New forces brought in quell the rebellion and all the slaves die, many committing suicide at Mary's Point. Denmark names St. Thomas a crown colony in 1734.
19th century	St. Thomas and St. John change hands several times while the English and the Danes struggle to establish supremacy. The economy of St. Thomas declines in the 1820's with a slump in cane sugar prices and the advent of the steamship. Governor von Scholten frees the slaves of the Danish islands in 1848. Cholera epidemics sweep the Virgins between 1853 and 1868. Riots break out as the economy worsens and sugar production all but ceases.
20th century	During World War I, the United States buys St. Thomas and St. John, together with St. Croix and some 50 islets and outcrops for $25 million, in order to deprive Germany of a strategic position in the Caribbean. Islanders are granted voting rights in 1936. They gain greater independence in 1954 with the creation of a three-branch central government, headed since 1970 by an elected governor.

Sightseeing

Busiest and best-known of the Virgin Islands, St. Thomas has a reputation as a shoppers' paradise. But that is only one of the many pleasures which it has to offer. Exploring the island, with its dramatic wooded hills, intimate beaches, historic houses and inspiring seascapes, is another.

Charlotte Amalie

The capital and only city of St. Thomas is Charlotte Amalie, named for the consort of Denmark's 17th-century King Christian V. Most of the island's population lives in the town, which rises steeply and beautifully from the port district.

The Virgin Islands **Legislature,** a 15-member Senate, occupies the stately lime-green building just beyond the Coast Guard headquarters at King's Wharf. It was built over a century ago to house Danish police, and is where the Danish flag was lowered for the last time when the U.S. formally took possession of the Virgin Islands in 1917.

Across the road, a solid chunk of history is embodied in an aloof fortress with the date 1671 on its façade. Actually, the date of its construction is uncertain. Today **Fort Christian** serves as the local museum. Exhibits of old navigational charts, African ornaments, stone-age Indian tools found on the island and a collection of rare Caribbean seashells are set up in the former cells.

Between the fort and the post office, **Emancipation Park** commemorates Governor von Scholten's pace-setting proclamation freeing the slaves in 1848. The big bell on the southwest corner of the park is a replica of Philadelphia's Liberty Bell.

For 133 years the former **Grand Hotel,** facing the north side of the square, was a leading hostelry. Notice the huge columns and the grand old West Indian architecture. Now, the ground floor is occupied by shops and a hospitality lounge which offers tourists free information, rest rooms, telephones, drinking water and a package-checking service. Upstairs the glamour and grace of a 19th-century ballroom have been turned into office spaces. The floor above that was blown away by a hurricane.

Two nearby churches of interest: **Frederick Lutheran**

Charlotte Amalie, headquarters of U.S. Virgin Islands Legislature.

Church, thought to be the island's oldest, was built in 1826 to replace an 18th-century church destroyed in a fire. A wide staircase leads to an imposing entrance. Further east along the same street (Norre Gade), the **Moravian Memorial Church** with its fine wooden cupola dates from 1882.

Government House, a gracious, three-story brick edifice, with long balconies in wrought iron, was built by the Danish rulers in 1867, as the red sentry box at the bottom of the ceremonial stairs reminds us. It's now the official office of the elected governor of the Virgin Islands and the place where he receives visitors.

The higher you climb in St. Thomas the more thrilling the views. This is why the well-to-do 18th-century colonists built their houses on hilltops overlooking the harbour. The hills were too steep for roads, so stone staircases were built as step-streets. The most famous is called the **99 Steps,** at the top of which is a stone tower with a superb view. This is the legendary haunt of the celebrated pirate Blackbeard (born Edward Teach). Aside from his fierce buccaneering, Blackbeard is renowned for his feats with women. He's said to have accumulated 14 wives, though it's uncertain whether they were wed consecutively or rather deployed concurrently on various islands. The scandalous career of this giant among scoundrels ended in a shootout with the British navy in 1718. Blackbeard's tower achieved sudden respectability in 1831 when it was converted to an astronomical observatory. Today it has a new incarnation as a hotel and restaurant.

Near the top of the 99 Steps is Crown House, the former residence of the island's governors, now privately owned.

A historical highlight of St. Thomas is the **synagogue**, rebuilt in 1833 on the site of several previous Jewish temples. A French architect laid out this traditional design, with three sides of benches facing inward. The sand on the floor is thought to commemorate the exodus of the Jews from Egypt. In St. Thomas, Jews have made history since the 17th century, when Gabriel Milan was installed as governor. He was later called home to Copenhagen, charged with assorted crimes and hanged.

Downhill from the synagogue, the shopping district of Charlotte Amalie is concentrated on or near Main Street (still officially known by its Danish name, **Dronningens Gade).** By any standard, this is a shopper's dream come true. Few streets in the world sell so many luxurious goods so temptingly displayed.

Amidst the carefully remodeled Danish warehouses filled with duty-free delights, the building at **14 Dronningen Gade** provides an artistic footnote: this was the birthplace of Camille Pissarro (1830–1903), sometimes called the Father of French Impressionism. Though he lived most of his life in France, Pissarro was a Thomian and always maintained his Danish citizenship.

Main Street becomes less glamorous—but no less fascinating—at **Market Square** where islanders buy and sell local fruits and vegetables.

The Charlotte Amalie **waterfront** is always a drama. If it's not a faded little tramp steamer loading cargo for St. Lucia it's a sleek catama an picking up tourists for St. John. The glass-bottom boats and other excursion craft leave from here.

Around the Island

Following are more sights to see around St. Thomas, beginning at the harbourfront and continuing clockwise around the island.

Hassel Island used to be separated from the "mainland" by a narrow, shallow isthmus. When the United States bought the Virgins, the navy quickly dredged a major channel to separate the mile-long island from St. Thomas, thus providing the American fleet an alternate escape route in case the harbour should be attacked. Among Hassel Island's landmarks is a mountaintop fort built in the 19th century as a signal tower.

The area called **Frenchtown,** to which Hassel Island is almost attached, got its name from the French-speaking settlers who came from the French Caribbean colony of St. Barthélemy in the mid-19th century. They've retained their ancient Norman dialect... and fishing skills.

During World War II, lucky navy frogmen trained in the limpid waters of **Water**

Island, nearly two miles long. Now it's a private resort.

Another pretty spot is Brewer's Bay Beach, a charming white-sand beach owned by the **University of the Virgin Islands** but open to the public. The college occupies 175 acres of attractively landscaped hillsides.

St. Peter Mountain, nearly 1,500 feet high, affords a magnificent view down onto Magens Bay and out to an array of U.S. off-islands and the British Virgins. The parking lot vendors sell banana daiquiris here. A hotel which once stood on the mountaintop, history tells us, was the inventor of the tasty drink.

A vantage point with breathtaking views is **Drake's Seat.** Legend says that Sir Francis Drake sat here in 1595, while he surveyed the fleet he had assembled to attack Puerto Rico. By that time in his round-the-world career, the most famous of Elizabethan admirals had captured many Spanish bastions. But the tactics he devised on this hill failed to match the firepower of El Morro fortress, defending San Juan. Embittered and feverish, the navigator died soon after this defeat and was buried at sea off Panama.

Magens Bay is the island's biggest and most flawless beach. The palm-backed mile of sand, amazingly unspoiled due to government conservation efforts, really is, as claimed, one of the most beautiful beaches in the world. Arthur S. Fairchild, an American publishing tycoon, gave the property to the people of the Virgin Islands in 1946.

More of the best beaches are just downhill from the Smith Bay road heading to the east end of the island. At Coki Beach, **Coral World,** an underwater observation tower right on the seabed, gives insights into the habitat and inhabitants of the marine world—exotic fish, coral formations, deep-water flowers and so on. Coki is also rated the best local beach for snorkelling. Luxury hotels and condominium projects snuggle on secluded coves with names as romantic as Pineapple Beach, Pelican Bay and Sapphire Beach.

Heading back toward Charlotte Amalie on the south coast, the road goes along a mangrove lagoon, then climbs through the Frenchman Bay area. The island's biggest hotel, on a promontory above Frenchman's Reef, enjoys a grandiose panorama.

A final sight to see, inland, as nautical overtones. **Bluebeard's Castle** is a round stone tower of brick and rubble masonry, built by the Danish government in 1678 as a coast defense installation. Its 11 cannon were manned until 1735. According to the local legend, Bluebeard used this tower as a lookout, lair and love-nest. One version says the 19th-century pirate slew his bride there before sailing away forever. In fact, no official record of Bluebeard's tenancy exists. But it adds a piquant touch to what's now the honeymoon suite of a luxury hotel.

St. John

A short boat ride from Red Hook on St. Thomas will bring you to an even quieter place. On **St. John,** the smallest and most beautiful of the three major American islands, nature reigns. The intrusion of humans is minimal, and the result is the envy of the Caribbean.

There are forty coves enclosing a hundred hues of blue and green and semi-circular beaches of powdery white coral sand. Behind them coconut groves and then tangled forests with ruins of old Danish plantations. Flowers, ferns and butterflies abound.

This island of only 20 square miles boasts 110 types of trees—far more, they say, than in all of Western Europe. Nesting in them are about the same number of bird species.

St. John owes its unspoiled tranquility to the fact that 60 per cent of its rugged landscape and most of its offshore waters are preserved as the **Virgin Islands National Park.** This park has existed since 1956 on acreage donated by Laurance Rockefeller. There are more than 20 hiking trails throughout the park, along with guided tours and historic programmes. Be sure to stop by the Visitor's Center—on the north side of the harbour.

The sleepy capital of St. John, **Cruz Bay,** is so tiny that no-one has even bothered to name its streets. The harbour, also called Cruz Bay, is used by yachts and the ferries from St. Thomas. Modern life has made some inroads—even here there are now shopping malls: Mongoose Junction and the Wharf at seaside.

Once out of Cruz Bay, from high on **Centerline Road** which climbs up around the tallest peak, Bordeaux Mountain

(1,277 feet), there are truly breathtaking views of the Atlantic, Caribbean and nearby islands. You'll see down to remote **Mary's Point** on the north shore where St. John's 1733 slave rebellion ended tragically. It's also known as Suicide Point.

From another lookout you can see St. Croix on a clear day across the 40 miles of water.

From **Coral Bay Overlook** eleven of the neighbouring British Virgin Islands lining the channel named for Sir Francis Drake make a photograph to remember. Here you gaze down on St. John's **Hurricane Hole,** a protected bay where sailors have fled storms over the centuries. This panorama has been called the best in the Caribbean.

An unruffled sea full of islands, viewed from heights of St. John

Towering above the picturesque north shore ruins of the Annaberg sugar and rum factory is a 150-year old **windmill,** one of the largest in the Virgin Islands.

Those Beaches

No picture book can prepare you for the glorious beaches strung one after another along St. John's reef-fringed northwestern shore. Swimmers and snorkellers may never want to leave bays named Trunk, Francis, Cinnamon, Caneel, Hawksnest and Maho.

Trunk Bay, endlessly praised and photographed, may well be the most perfect of the perfect beaches. In the emerald water, the 200-yard-long **snorkelling trail** is ideal for novices. Its sunken symbols and signs are clearly seen at a maximum depth of 12 feet.

When Greta Garbo wanted to be alone, she checked in to **Caneel Bay,** a resort founded by Laurance Rockefeller. Celebrities, politicans and industrialists appreciate its gentle beaches and unobtrusive luxury. The resort itself is one of St. John's tourist sights. Ordinary mortals may stroll the grounds, examine the beaches with sand as fine as powdered sugar and buy a drink or lunch.

Eating Out

The names are exotic, the tastes delicious. In the Virgin Islands' version of West Indian cooking, you'll find an imaginative variety of dishes totally tropical.

Appetizers

Conch fritters could well be on the menu. Or chilled papaya with fresh lime juice. Or a *gundy,* a spread featuring salt cod or lobster mashed with onions, olives and peppers. Deep-fried banana or plantain chips and fritters are a concept imported by the sizeable Puerto Rican community, as is *escabeche,* pickled fish served cold.

Soups

While you might decide against bullfoot soup, don't miss papaya soup. When you can find it, *tannia* (sometimes *tannier*) soup, based on a Caribbean root vegetable and including cheese, potatoes, carrots and bacon, is well worth trying. Cucumber soup is more common. And there's a happy surfeit of fresh fish and seafood soups.

Fish and Seafood

Widely admired for its magnificent shell, the conch (pronounced conk), appears not only in salad courses but also as a main dish. A French touch is conch strips sauteed in garlicky oil with herbs. Conch also goes into a tart-like dish with ground beef, chicken and peppers.

Among the most favoured island fish are red snapper, kingfish, bonita, tuna and the fish known here as dolphin (not the porpoise). Dried salt fish, often imported, is usually available.

Properly with fish you should be served Johnny Cake, absolutely delicious when straight out of the oven, uninspiring when cold. This is a sort of dumpling. The original name was Journey Cake: wives used to make a batch for their husbands going out for a long day's work in the fields.

Meat

No main dish is more typically West Indian than *kallaloo*. This fragrant, soupy stew normally includes at least: seasoned pork, salt meat, fresh fish, crab or conch, okra, spinach or other greens, onions and garlic.

Complementing local stews are pieces of *fungi* (pronounced FOON-jee), cornmeal boiled with okra. *Goat water* is a spicily liquid concoction of goat meat boiled with brown flour, onions, cloves, thyme, garlic and celery. It's not to be confused with *"stew goat"* which is much drier. For the adventurous another favourite is *sous* —boiled pig's head or feet with onion, celery, hot peppers and lime juice.

Side Dishes

Your vegetables might be white sweet potato, breadfruit, okra, squash, christophene, cassava root or *taro*. Deepfried fruit fritters are considered special, seasoned rice ordinary. Accra are deep fried, mashed black-eyed peas. Chutney or pickle made of fresh mango may accompany your meal or sea moss, pickled papaya, lime jelly, stewed guava. One, two or three drops of liquid pepper sauce (red or yellow) is enough. Sweet potato stuffing is eaten at any time.

Fruit

You'll no doubt want to sample papaya and genip, tamarind, sea grapes, mango and soursop and, of course, coconut. Refreshing drinks are made of many of these fruits.

Other Drinks

Rum—the national "poison" —is the main ingredient of many punches, daiquiris, flips, sours and fizzes. An especially popular drink, originating in Puerto Rico, the *piña colada,* consists of rum, coconut cream, crushed pineapple (or juice) and crushed ice. After-dinner rum may be served with chocolate liqueur, or mixed with anisette, crème de cacao and lemon. "Cruzan champagne" is a class of chilled white rum.

Beer connoisseurs can enjoy some of Europe's—as well as America's—best brews at reasonable prices, thanks to the duty-free advantage. Islanders of all ages like *maubi,* a cooling drink made of tree bark, ginger, rosemary, sweet marjoram, sugar and pineapple skin. Though non-alcoholic, it's said to pack a punch when aged. Papaya Creole combines papaya pulp, chopped bananas, guavas, lime and cherry juices.

"Bush tea", many things to many people in the West Indies, might be made of soursop. This has a flavour midway between an banana and a pineapple, according to one description. It's also claimed to be the only certain cure in the world for a hangover.

And, some go into an array of tantalizing pies, tarts and cakes which island bakers turn out.

Wine

The French and Italian wines served in the Virgins are not of top quality, and are expensive, but two local "Christmas wines", of guavaberry and sorrel, are worth asking for at any season. They're unusually satisfying, though powerful.

ST. THOMAS

Shopping

The entire territory of the U.S. Virgin Islands is duty-free which means that prices in all duty-free shops are more or ·less identical. The most varied and luxurious goods are found on or near Main Street in St. Thomas.

Because the Virgin Islands rate a special dispensation, U.S. residents are allowed a duty-free quota of $800 (provided not more than $400 of this was acquired in other countries). In addition, U.S. residents over 21 can take home up to one U.S. gallon of spirits duty free, as long as no more than one quart comes from outside these islands. They may also mail home to friends and relatives an unlimited number of gifts (perfume, spirits and tobacco excepted), provided each is worth no more than $100.

All Virgin Islands store-owners have up-to-date information on the intricacies of the customs situation and will advise you if there are any doubts.

Virgin Islands Products

Basketry. Two traditions survive in the Virgin Islands: the African art of basketweaving and the French tradition maintained in Frenchtown, St. Thomas, for the production of hats.

Candles. Hand-made candles come in unusual scents: hibiscus, jasmine, lemon, mango and sandalwood. You can see the wax being poured into moulds at the workshops.

Ceramics. Pottery and earthenware plates, mugs and figures, either naïve or sophisticated.

Dolls. Since slave days, island mothers have made rope dolls for their children—a skillfully knotted piece of rope, clad in bits of colourful cloth. A *moko jumbi* doll, from the heart of native folklore, comes dressed as a clown.

Fashions. Locally designed fabrics with cheerful tropical motifs made into men's and women's resort clothes; fine for poolside here, sensational elsewhere.

Food products. Homemade jams and jellies in exotic flavours—tamarind, papaya pickle, seagrape, genip, hibiscus. West Indian spices and seasonings packed in miniature baskets. Bush tea—the kind of tea leaves the natives use for a brisk, possibly therapeutic infusion. Hardcandy rum-balls.

Jewellery. The slaves were forbidden any personal adornment, so jewellery has more than casual symbolism here. Necklaces are made of dried *tan-tan* seeds. One amateur archeologist makes pendants out of shards of fine old Danish pottery excavated from plantation ruins. Or you can buy a solid gold pendant in the shape of a sugarmill.

Macramé. An old sailor's art; look for knotted belts, purses, wall-hangings and plant-holders.

Paintings. Most buyers pick recognizable local scenes. Oils, watercolours or prints of Virgin Island seascapes.

Perfumes. The scent of tropical spices and flowers distinguishes locally manufactured perfumes, cologne, suntan oil.

Staggering variety of cheap alcohol is duty-free bonus in U.S. Virgins.

ST. THOMAS

Seashells, such as the geometric Sand Dollar, are made into jewellery as well as collages in the form of floral arrangements and other fantasies.

Scrimshaw, an 18th-century fishermen's hobby, is still alive in the Virgin Islands. Pendants and buckles hand-engraved with nautical scenes.

Sculpture. Whimsical bird statues made of metal salvaged from wrecked cars. Sculpture in many forms suggested by the grain of local wood—mahogany, saman and thibet.

Practical Information

Banks: Open 9 a.m. to 2.30 p.m. Monday to Thursday, Friday 9 a.m. to 2 p.m. and 3.30 p.m. to 5 p.m. Although several internationally known banks are represented in the Virgin Islands, few are geared to handle foreign currency transactions.

Credit cards and traveller's cheques: Major U.S. credit cards and traveller's cheques may be used in most places. Foreign visitors are advised to carry U.S. dollars in cash or traveller's cheques since European credit or banker's cards are not recognized.

Currency: Since the Virgin Islands is a territory of the United States, the currency is the U.S. dollar; the bills and coins in circulation are the same as on the U.S. mainland.

Post Offices: Open 8 a.m. to 4.30 p.m. Monday to Friday, 8 a.m. to noon Saturday. Commercial stamp-vending machines may be found where postcards are sold, but they charge much more than the face value of the stamps.

Shops: Usually open 9 a.m. to 5 p.m. Monday to Saturday. On Friday nights Havensight Mall is open to 9 p.m.

Telephoning Home. The U.S. Virgin Islands (area code 809) are linked to the U.S. network. For U.K. visitors to ring home, dial 011 + 44 + area code + local number. To call The U.S. Virgin Islands from the U.K., dial 010 + 500 809 + local number.

Index

An asterisk (*) next to a page number indicates a map reference. Where there is more than one set of page references, the one in bold type refers to the main entry.

Abaco, Bahamas *50*
Andros, Bahamas *10*, 50*
Antigua *7, 9, 11*,* **21–8**
Aruba *7–8, 11*,* **29–36**

Bahamas *8, 10*,* **37–52**
Balboa, Panama *16, 237*,* **239,** *240*
Barbados *8–9, 11*,* **53–60,** *55**
Barbuda *9, 11*,* **61–8**
Basse-Terre, Guadeloupe *154,* **159**
Basseterre, St. Kitts *41,* **276**
Bermuda *9–10,* **69–76**
Berry Islands, Bahamas *50*
Bimini, Bahamas *50*
Bonaire *10, 11*,* **77–84**
Bridgetown, Barbados *9, 11*, 53, 54, 55*,* **56–7,** *60*
British Virgin Islands, see Virgin Islands (U.K.)

Cancún, Mexico *10*, 16, 221, 222,* **226–7,** *228*
Cap Haïtien, Haiti *10*, 14, 161,* **163–4,** *165**
Caracas, Venezuela *11*, 19, 321, 322, 323,* **324–6,** *327, 328*
Carmen, Playa del, Mexico *16, 221,* **226**
Cartagena, Colombia *11,* **85–92,** *89**
Castries, St. Lucia *11*, 18,* **283–4,** *285**
Cat Island, Bahamas *50*

Cayman Islands, see Grand Cayman
Charlestown, Nevis *279*
Charlotte Amalie, St. Thomas *11*, 20,* **352–5,** *355**
Chichén Itzá, Mexico *16, 217, 218,* **219–20**
Christiansted, St. Croix *342,* **344–7,** *345**
Colombia (Cartagena, San Andrés Island) *11,* **85–96**
Colón, Panama *17,* **236–7,** *237**
Cozumel, Mexico *10*, 16, 221, 222, 223,* **224–6,** *227, 228*
Cristóbal, Panama *17, 236,* **237,** *237*, 240*
Cuisines
~ Antigua *27*
~ Aruba *34–5*
~ Bahamas *43,* **51–2**
~ Barbados *59–60*
~ Barbuda *67–8*
~ Bermuda *75*
~ Bonaire *84*
~ Cayman Islands *135*
~ Colombia *91, 96*
~ Curaçao *103*
~ Dominica *111–2*
~ Dominican Republic *118–9, 127*
~ Grenada *143–4*
~ Grenadines, the *151–2*
~ Guadeloupe *159–60*
~ Haiti *166–8, 175–6*

Cuisines (cont.)
~ Iles des Saintes *183-4*
~ Jamaica *190-1, 198-9, 207-8*
~ Martinique *215*
~ Mexico *227*
~ Montserrat *232*
~ Panama *240*
~ Puerto Rico *262-3*
~ St. Barthélemy *271-2*
~ St. Kitts-Nevis *280*
~ St. Lucia *287-8*
~ St. Vincent *295-6*
~ Sint-Maarten *303*
~ Tobago *311-2*
~ Trinidad *319-20*
~ Venezuela *327*
~ Virgin Islands (U.K.) *339*
~ Virgin Islands (U.S.) *347-8, 359-61*
Curaçao *11*, 12*, **97-104**

Dominica *11*, 12*, **105-12**
Dominican Republic (Puerto Plata, Santo Domingo) *10*-1*, 12-3*, **113-28**

Eleuthera, Bahamas *10*, 50*
English Harbour, Antigua *24-6*
Exumas, Bahamas *10*, 50*

Family Islands, Bahamas *50*
Food, see Cuisines
Fort-de-France, Martinique *11*, 16, 209*, **212-3**, *216*
Frederiksted, St. Croix *11*, 342*, **343-4**, *345**
Freeport, Grand Bahama *8, 10*, 37*, **39-40**
French West Indies, see Guadeloupe/Martinique/ St. Barthélemy/Sint-Maarten (St. Martin)

George Town, Grand Cayman *10*, 13*, **132**, *133**
Grand Bahama *8, 10*,* **38-44,** *50*
Grand Cayman *10*, 13,* **129-36**, *133**
Grenada *11*, 13,* **137-44,** *142**
Grenadines, the *11*, 13-4,* **145-52**, *293**
Guadeloupe *11*, 14,* **153-60**
Guaira, La, see La Guaira
Gustavia, St. Barthélemy *267-8, 271**

Haiti (Cap Haïtien, Port-au-Prince) *10*-1*, 14,* **161-8,** *165**
Hamilton, Bermuda *9, 69,* **71-2**
Harrington Sound, Bermuda *74*

Iles des Saintes *11*, 15,* **177-84**
Isla de Margarita, Venezuela *11*, 19,* **329-32**

Jamaica (Montego Bay, Ocho Rios, Port Antonio) *10*, 15,* **185-208**, *186*-7**

Kingstown, St. Vincent *11*, 18,* **291-2**, *293**
Kralendijk, Bonaire *10, 11*, 77, 78, 79,* **80**

La Guaira, Venezuela *19, 321,* **324**
Little Tobago *307*, 311*
Long Island, Bahamas *50*
Lucaya, Grand Bahama *40*

Martinique *11*, 15-6,* **209-16**
Mexico (Cancún, Chichén Itzá, Cozumel, Tulúm) *10*, 16,* **217-28**

Montego Bay, Jamaica   10*, 15, **185-92**, 186*

Montserrat   11*, 16, **229-32**

Nassau, New Providence   8, 10*, 45, 46, **47-9**, 48*-9*

Nelson's Dockyard, Antigua   25, 25*

Netherlands Antilles, see Bonaire/Curaçao

Ocho Rios, Jamaica   10*, 15, 187*, **193-200**

Oranjestad, Aruba   8, 11*, 29, **31-2**, 35

Panama (Panama Canal, San Blas Islands)   16-7, **233-48**

Panama Canal   17, 233, **234-8**, 237*, 239

Panama City   16, 237*, **239**, 240

Paradise Island, Bahamas   48*-9*

Pétionville, Haiti   165*, 175

Philipsburg, Sint-Maarten   11*, 18, **300**, 302*, 304

Playa del Carmen, see Carmen, Playa del

Plymouth, Montserrat   11*, **231**, 232

Pointe-à-Pitre, Guadeloupe   11*, 14, 153, 154, **156**, 160

Port Antonio, Jamaica   10*, 15, 187*, **201-8**

Port-au-Prince, Haiti   10*, 14, 165*, 169, 170, **171-4**

Port-of-Spain, Trinidad   11*, 19, 313, 314*, **316-8**

Puerto Plata, Dominican Republic   11*, 12, 113, 115, 115*, **116-8**

Puerto Rico   11*, 17, **249-64**

Road Town, Tortola   20, **335-6**, 337*

Roseau, Dominica   11*, 12, **108**

St. Barthélemy   11*, 17, **265-72**, 271*

St. Croix   11*, 20, **341-8**, 345*

St. George's, Grenada   11*, 13, 138, **140**, 142*

St. John   11*, 20, **357-9**

St. John's, Antigua   23-4, 25*

St. Kitts   11*, 17, 273, 274-5, **276-8**, 280

St. Kitts-Nevis   11*, 17, **273-80**

St. Lucia   11*, 18, **281-8**, 285*

St. Martin, see Sint-Maarten

St. Thomas   11*, 20, **349-64**, 355*

St. Vincent   11*, 18, **289-96**, 293*

San Andrés Island, Colombia   11, **93-6**

San Blas Islands, Panama   17, **241-8**

San Juan, Puerto Rico   11*, 17, 249, 250-1, 252*, 253, **254-60**, 264

San Salvador, Bahamas   50

Santo Domingo, Dominican Republic   11*, 12, 115*, 121-8, 125*

Scarborough, Tobago   11*, 19, 307*, **308**

Shopping
~ Antigua   28
~ Aruba   35
~ Bahamas   44, 52
~ Barbados   60
~ Barbuda   68
~ Bermuda   75-6
~ Bonaire   84
~ Cayman Islands   135-6
~ Colombia   92, 96

Shopping (cont.)
~ Curaçao 104
~ Dominica 112
~ Dominican Republic
   120, 128
~ Grenada· 144
~ Grenadines, the 152
~ Guadeloupe 160
~ Haiti 168, 176
~ Iles des Saintes 184
~ Jamaica 192, 199-200, 208
~ Martinique 216
~ Mexico 227-8
~ Montserrat 232
~ Panama 240, 247-8
~ Puerto Rico 263-4
~ St. Barthélemy 272
~ St. Kitts-Nevis 280
~ St. Lucia 288
~ St. Vincent 296
~ Sint-Maarten 304
~ Tobago 312
~ Trinidad 320
~ Venezuela 327, 332
~ Virgin Islands (U.K.) 340
~ Virgin Islands (U.S.) 348,
   362-4

Sint-Maarten/St. Martin 11*,
   18, 297-304, 302*

Tobago 11*, 19, 305-12, 307*
Tortola 11*, 20, 333-6, 337*,
   339
Trinidad 11*, 19, 313-20
Tulúm, Mexico 16, 217, 218,
   220

U.S. Virgin Islands, see Virgin
   Islands (U.S.)

Venezuela (Caracas, La Guaira,
   Isla de Margarita) 11*, 19,
   321-32
Virgin Gorda 20, 334, 336,
   337*, 338
Virgin Islands (U.K.—Tortola,
   Virgin Gorda) 11*, 20,
   333-40, 337*
Virgin Islands (U.S.—St. Croix,
   St. John, St. Thomas) 11*,
   20, 341-64

Willemstad, Curaçao 11*, 12,
   97-104